Revaluing Modern Architecture

Architecture

Changing Conservation Culture

'revalue – to calculate the value of something again, especially to give it a higher value than before'

The Cambridge Business English Dictionary

Revaluing Modern Architecture

Changing Conservation Culture

RIBA ⾧ **Publishing**

JOHN ALLAN

© John Allan, 2022

Published by RIBA Publishing, 66 Portland Place, London, W1B 1AD

ISBN 9781914124235

The right of John Allan to be identified as the Author of this Work has been asserted in accordance with the Copyright, Designs and Patents Act 1988 sections 77 and 78.

British Library Cataloguing-in-Publication Data
A catalogue record for this book is available from the British Library.

Commissioning Editor: Ginny Mills
Assistant Editor: Scarlet Furness
Production: Jane Rogers
Designed and typeset by Mercer Design, London
Printed and bound by Short Run Press, Exeter
Cover image: Detail from the restored Isokon Apartments, Lawn Road, London NW3
Photo: Nicholas Kane

The opinions expressed in this publication are those of the author. They do not purport to reflect the opinions or views of the RIBA or its members. While every effort has been made to check the accuracy and quality of the information given in this publication, neither the Author nor the Publisher accept any responsibility for the subsequent use of this information, for any errors or omissions that it may contain, or for any misunderstandings arising from it.

Design Note: Our colour palette for this book is inspired by Le Corbusier's colours.

www.ribapublishing.com

CONTENTS

ABOUT THE AUTHOR

JOHN ALLAN MA (Edin), BA Hons, Dip Arch, MA, Hon Litt D (Sheffield), CAABC, ARB, Architect

A Director of Avanti Architects from 1983 to 2011, John Allan led all Avanti's Modern Movement conservation work, including projects and studies on listed buildings by: Berthold Lubetkin; Sir Denys Lasdun; Ernö Goldfinger; Patrick Gwynne; Topham Forrest; Oliver Hill; Connell, Ward and Lucas; Burnet, Tait and Lorne; Owen Williams; David Roberts; Peter Moro; Maguire and Murray; Chamberlin, Powell and Bon; Charles Holden; Wells Coates; Gollins Melvin Ward; Maxwell Fry, and Gillespie, Kidd and Coia.

Conservation advisory work included authoring listed building management guidelines for the Barbican and Golden Lane estates for the City of London and English Heritage; also listed building management guidelines for the University of Leeds, and the Arts Tower and Library, University of Sheffield; also conservation management plans and assessments for Ernö Goldfinger's Brownfield Estate, east London, Wembley Arena, northwest London, and St Peter's Seminary, Cardross, Scotland (for the Archdiocese of Glasgow and Historic Environment Scotland). Schemes for adaptation or reuse have included Plymouth Civic Centre, Hastings seafront and the 12 listed Tecton buildings at Dudley Zoo.

New build work has included Bethnal Green Health Centre; the Ilford Town Centre Health Clinic; Millwall Park Club for the LDDC; the ACAD Centre, Central Middlesex Hospital; schools in Southwark, Hammersmith, Hackney, Lewisham and Peterborough; housing in the Royal Borough of Kensington and Chelsea; and bespoke private houses in Oxfordshire and Sussex. Conversion and rehabilitation projects have included work at Liverpool Street Station, the GWR Goodshed, Bristol, and regeneration projects at Priory Green, King's Cross and Norton Folgate, Shoreditch. Previous employment included the Greater London Council Department of Architecture and Civic Design (1971–73) and Shepheard Epstein and Hunter (1973–82).

John Allan has served on several English Heritage/Historic England committees, including the London Advisory Committee, Designation Review Panel and Post-War Listing Advisory Committee. He was an elected councillor in ARCUK, 1976–86, and a Project Enabler at CABE, 1999–2007. He was founding Chairman of Docomomo-UK, 1989–91, and for 12 years served on the Editorial Board of *The Journal of Architecture*. He is author of the award-winning biography *Berthold Lubetkin – Architecture and the Tradition of Progress*, first published in 1992 and now in its second edition. In 2008 he was awarded an honorary doctorate by the University of Sheffield and he has served as a Visiting Professor there in the Architecture Graduate School Conservation Course. He is a member of the Finsbury Health Centre Preservation Trust and more recently led the team creating the new Isokon Gallery at Lawn Road Flats, Camden, which opened in 2014, and where he is Chairman of the Isokon Gallery Trust.

ACKNOWLEDGEMENTS

I owe debts of gratitude to the many people who have supported me in this project, whether through wise advice, constructive criticism, assistance with images and information, guidance through the publication process or simply essential encouragement. The alphabetical roll call that follows will appear as a long undifferentiated list, but I hope that each will recognise their particular and vital contribution.

Adrian Forty, Alan Powers, Alec Forshaw, Alexey Ginzburg, Amir Ramezani, Ana Tostões, Avanti Architects, Barnabas Calder, Christiane Anders, David Fixler, David Heath, Diana Boelhouwer, Edward Smith, Elain Harwood, Fiona Lamb, Geraldine O'Riordan, Ginny Mills, Graham Morrison, Hannah Lewi, Helen Castle, Hubert-Jan Henket, James Connell, James Dunnett, Jane Rogers, Julian Honer, Justin Desyllas, Katherine Prater, Kathryn Glendenning, Kelvin Dickinson, Magnus Englund, Margaret Smithglass, Morley von Sternberg, Natalia Ginzburg, Paola Corsini, Peter Clegg, Peter Cook, Peter Reilly, Ptolemy Dean, Ray Main, Richard Battye, Roland Jeffery, Sally Rendel, Scarlet Furness, Sheridan Burke, Susan Macdonald, Tom de Gay, Wendy Hawke.

This is also an opportunity to pay tribute to all the clients, consultants, contractors and colleagues with whom I and Avanti Architects have collaborated on many of the projects featured in this book. I have been privileged to work on some of the finest Modern architecture in the UK, but am acutely aware that in all matters of building, as in the writing of books, it is always a team effort.

Finally, I want to acknowledge the support of my family, and most importantly my wife Julie, who remains my most steadfast, candid and loving critic.

JOHN ALLAN
September 2021

FOREWORD

THE EXISTING THAT FORMS THE NEW

At this tipping point in history, the revaluation of the existing is one of the key strategies to shape a sustainable future for all. The reuse of the vast building stock we have already makes perfect sense in combating climate change, simply due to the embedded energy stored in its construction. Equally important are the ambitions of our predecessors, which the buildings and urban environments of the past show us. They contain the wisdom and accumulated experiences – both good and bad – of previous generations. They offer us a sense of communal identity and belonging which gives strength, particularly in confusing times. In short, the revaluation of the past offers lessons that help us to comprehend and give meaning to the new.

The above applies to buildings of any age, but revaluing the architecture of the Modern Movement is of particular concern due to its proximity, extent and way of thinking. Its aim – to create a better future for all – concentrates on inclusiveness, emancipation, an egalitarian society and the rational use of resources. Yes, large-scale mistakes have been made in the name of invention, experiment or progress. Yet many beautiful and inspiring icons of architecture, as well as a host of interesting everyday buildings, have resulted worldwide, giving service, radiating optimism and hope. Some of the fascinating results that can be achieved by conserving and reusing such buildings may be witnessed by viewing the winners of Docomomo's inaugural Rehabilitation Award (DRAW).[1] John Allan's firm, Avanti Architects, is one of the winners of this award, for the Isokon project in London.

As authoritative practitioner, researcher and author, John Allan guides us through the complexities of modern conservation. Critically yet wittily he unravels overcomplicated systems and overdesigned instruments, all derived from good intentions but often resulting in confusion or underperformance. In a subtle way, he urges the voluntary organisations dedicated to the protection of Modern heritage to leave their ivory towers and focus their collective energy on informing the outside world – building owners, politicians and the public at large. Moreover, he broadens the scope of conservation beyond the icons to include reusing the potential of the vast reservoir of ordinary Modern buildings instead of constantly building anew.

I sincerely hope this important publication will find its way beyond the borders of the British Isles. What counts now is widening awareness and understanding. So hopefully it will not only reach conservationists, architects and students worldwide, but all those involved in the urgently needed improvement of the built environment and the future of our planet.

When I arrived in London in 1971 as a recently qualified architect (having studied at the TU Delft in the Netherlands), I had the good fortune to become the first director of the Housing Renewal Unit – a small multidisciplinary research unit advising local authorities and local residents about cellular renovation and renewal of their neighbourhoods. The early 1970s saw the first wave of housing renovation in Britain, and several years later this caught on in the rest of Europe as well. However, it took a lot of effort to convince particularly politicians and architects that conservation and the reuse of buildings was not beneath their dignity after all. Gradually this situation changed in the first decade of this century. The interest in conserving Modern Movement buildings and their ideas started little by little in the 1980s. In 1988 we formed a niche organisation, Docomomo, at the faculty of architecture of the TU Eindhoven in the Netherlands, where I held a chair. The cause has grown exponentially, and now Docomomo International consists of 79 national working parties worldwide.

I am happy to note that today even leading politicians are convinced of the importance of renovation and the revaluation of the ideas of the Modern Movement. It might be of interest, also to British politicians, to read what the President of the European Commission – Ursula von der Leyen – had to say in her State of the Union address 2020 to the European Parliament.

I want Next Generation EU to kickstart a European renovation wave and make our Union a leader in the circular economy. But this is not just an environmental or economic project: it needs to be a new cultural project for Europe… This is why we will set up a New European Bauhaus, a co-creation space where architects, artists, students, engineers and designers work together to make that happen… The future will be what we make it… let's go to work and build the world we want to live in.[2]

These stimulating words lead me to an optimistic conclusion. Celebrate this supportive message, it deserves adoption internationally. Be ambitious, stop talking and get started now! This book is a very welcome step towards the world we want to live in.

HUBERT-JAN HENKET ARCHITECT
Emeritus Professor TU Delft, Honorary President Docomomo International

6 September 2021

INTRODUCTION

'It's really very simple…'

This introduction sets out the intentions and structure of the book, suggesting some of the limitations of 'conservation' as conventionally defined and the widening context of environmental crisis in which the subject – specifically as applied to Modern architecture – will surely have to find its place.

I REMEMBER A CONVERSATION WITH THE EMINENT professor of architecture Peter Blundell Jones some years ago when we were talking about conservation, and he said, 'Conservation is really very simple – you just change as little as possible.'[1] This piquant *aperçu* surely resonates with the philosophy of conservative repair espoused by the Society for the Protection of Ancient Buildings (SPAB, founded in 1877), where discussions on conservation (modern or otherwise) often begin. The society's website indeed declares, 'To us the skill lies in mending [buildings which are old and interesting] with the minimum loss of fabric and so of romance and authenticity. Old buildings cannot be preserved by making them new.'[2] Peter may indeed have been subconsciously reciting the well-worn mantra of the ICOMOS (International Council on Monuments and Sites) Burra Charter, which enjoins its followers to adopt 'a cautious approach of changing as much as necessary but as little as possible'.[3]

There's something very appealing about Blundell Jones's definition: it makes it all sound so easy. But, as with many such precepts, things soon become more complicated when subjected to detailed critical scrutiny – or when you step into the real world of practice. It could, of course, be suggested that just by invoking the term 'conservation', the concept of change becomes contradictory. Much of this book seeks to investigate and clarify this supposed contradiction, specifically in the still evolving field of *Modern* architectural conservation.

When do buildings become 'old'? Who decides which buildings are 'interesting' – why are they so, and for whose benefit? Are the propositions of a pre-Raphaelite brotherhood from over 140 years ago in an age of craft building still relevant to the industrialised construction of today? To what extent are those who claim 'cultural ownership' of 'interesting' buildings to be given precedence over those who actually do own them? Taken further, could zealous 'conservationism' really be regarded as a variant of the concept of 'moral hazard', whereby those advocating a preferred course of action are insulated from the economic consequences of pursuing it? What about building owners who may be obliged to protect other kinds of value apart from 'interest' and 'oldness'? What about building users who might be better served if their buildings were less authentic, but more comfortable? Does 'change' invariably result in the dreaded loss of authenticity? What if 'old and interesting' buildings have been changed already? They almost invariably have. And so on, and so forth.

Let me continue to complicate matters. Another mantra that I used to intone in student lectures (and also when I was a principal in my practice) was 'conservation is not a sector – conservation is a strategy'. What I meant by this is that classifying conservation alongside, say, 'health care', 'schools', 'housing', 'community buildings', etc. is to commit what the celebrated philosopher Gilbert Ryle would have called a 'category mistake'. His famous example is of the visitor to Oxford who, having been shown the colleges, the library, the playing fields, the laboratories and the administrative offices, then asks if he can see the university. His error is to have assumed that 'the university' is another institution in the foregoing series, rather than understanding that it is the way in which they are all organised.[4] By analogy, conservation, howsoever defined, is not a building typology, but an index of culture – a reflex, a predisposition, a philosophy – that might (or might not) apply to any kind or age of building and with varying degrees of relevance.

Avanti Architects, my former practice, works across a wide range of building sectors and types – but 'conservation' is not one of them. Or to put it another way, conservation might be a part of any of them. I could choose – more or less at random – a period when we were working on (among other things) a terrace of 18th-century houses in Shoreditch, a 19th-century hospital in Bristol, an interwar zoo in Dudley, a post-war comprehensive school in London, and a derelict 1960s Roman Catholic seminary near Glasgow, all of which were 'designated heritage assets' – to use the official vocabulary – and all of which involved various kinds of conservation. Yet this response was just one aspect in the respective agendas of these projects, alongside a whole diversity of other motives and strategies – and not necessarily even the main one.

In the case of the school, for example, which was listed Grade II, our client's brief ranged over any number of imperatives – only a few of which could be said to be driven directly by heritage considerations. Some years earlier, when we restored and adapted the north façade of the Great Eastern Hotel as a member of the British Rail Architects team, this assignment was merely a footnote to the primary task of regenerating Liverpool Street Station to become a major 21st-century transport interchange. I could cite innumerable other examples from my years in practice.

My point is simply this: that 'conservation' cannot necessarily expect to enjoy a pre-eminent or privileged position in the definition of projects involving 'interesting old buildings' (in the SPAB terminology), still less interesting new ones. Myriad other requirements and pressures also have to be addressed. Yet to acknowledge this is not to say that conservation does not still have an important – and sometimes crucial – part to play. It is this weighing and balancing of differing, and sometimes conflicting, objectives that in my experience constitutes the reality (and fascination) of modern conservation work and which I would like to explore in this book. My interest is in challenging the oft-assumed simplicity of categorising architectural assignments as either conservation projects or not, and instead considering the ways in which in the real world the demands of both conservation and change must usually be served simultaneously.

As to the book itself – which has been germinating for years and might have been written any time in the last decade during my putative 'retirement' – in the event this only came to fruition as a result of the lugubrious lockdowns of 2020/21. It nearly, if not quite, belongs to that literary genre that 'may be read in any order', being partly a critique of selected recurrent themes and recent episodes in the developing philosophy and politics of modern conservation (predominantly as experienced in England), partly a selective anthology of my own lessons learned in practice, partly a compilation of questions and answers most frequently encountered in discussion with students and others, and partly an attempt to envision the future of a progressive discipline that even over the period of my own involvement has been steadily merging with that still greater challenge of Conservation (with a capital C) which preoccupies anyone concerned with the fate of our embattled planet.

These various themes have informed the dual structure of the study, the first part – Retrospect – seeking to track the evolution of the field since its inception some 50 years ago, the second – Prospect – treating the said field as a work in progress, with suggestions for its further development, ideally assisted by selected experiences to date serving as tools for the future. I hope thereby that it may engage a range of different audiences, including students embarking on the subject, professionals already immersed in it, owners (public or private) of significant Modern buildings, and also a less easily defined category of others from a wider and more 'secular' *Gesellschaft* that belong to no singular occupational group yet share an interest in, and concern for, the vast inheritance of 20th-century architecture that in one way or another continues to impact us all.

To get our eye in, it may help to briefly reprise the key developments in modern conservation in Britain over recent years. This 'story so far', inevitably selective, could doubtless be told with differing emphases depending on the narrator, but there can be little dispute that over, say, the last half-century it has become a distinct historical phenomenon that has established the context – cultural, procedural and professional – for the revaluing of Modern architecture.

PART ONE: RETROSPECT

1
The story so far

This chapter offers a concise narrative of the development of the modern conservation initiative, from its origins in the early designations of Modern Movement buildings in the 1970s up to the present day. Its aim is to provide new students with a general overview from a predominantly UK perspective of how the subject has become established, referencing key milestones in the form of official recognition, professional discourse, popular campaigns and selected high-profile conservation projects over this 50-year period.

THE STORY OF REVALUING MODERN ARCHITECTURE is roughly five decades old and still in full flux. It may be considered both as a cultural phenomenon in charting changing public attitudes and also as a survey of modern conservation's practical manifestations in the emergence of new regulatory instruments and organisations, as well as in its technical exposition in fieldwork and professional discourse. The several spheres, of course, cannot be separated, as it is clear that a growing awareness of the significance of Modern architecture as 'heritage' itself acts as a stimulant to the development of new theoretical propositions, procedures and practices. The survey suggests that while significant progress can be measured over the period under review in terms of consciousness raising, governance, pedagogy and practical achievement, the recognition and appropriate stewardship of 'Modern heritage' in the UK is far from secure but remains a work in progress, still affected by a mixture of controversy, passion, ignorance and neglect.

IN THE BEGINNING… WAS THE END

Implicit in the very idea of 'revaluing Modern architecture' is the assumption that Modernism, or more specifically the Modern Movement itself, had reached some sort of terminus. Innumerable attempts have been made to nominate a definitive date for the moment that the Modernist hegemony came to an end. Of course, as the critic Robert Hughes has authoritatively stated:

Histories do not break off clean like a glass rod; they fray, stretch and come undone, like rope; and some strands never part. There was no specific year the Renaissance ended, but it did end, although culture is still permeated with the remnants of Renaissance thought. So it is with modernism, only more so, because we are that much closer to it… The modernist achievement will continue to affect culture for decades to come, because it was so large, so imposing and so irrefutably convincing.[1]

Referring to a cultural phenomenon so diverse as 'Modernism' in such singular terms is self-evidently problematic (as Charles Jencks has elaborately demonstrated[2]). Nevertheless, history is usefully made more navigable by adopting individual events as signifiers of a larger turning point. The deaths of Modernism's founding fathers Le Corbusier (in 1965), Walter Gropius and Mies van der Rohe (in 1969) and Alvar Aalto a little later in 1976 were surely key milestones, likewise for the UK the partial collapse of Ronan Point, in 1968, in Newham, London (Figure 1.1).

The demolition of Pruitt-Igoe housing estate in St Louis, Missouri (from 1972 onwards) is conventionally cited as the moment of Modern architecture's international demise. By this time, Jane Jacob's radical critique of modern city planning, *The Death and Life of Great American Cities* (first published in 1961), and Robert Venturi's *Complexity and Contradiction in Architecture* (1966) had become established as the alternative new wisdom in leading architectural schools, public authorities and professional discourse. Whichever way you look at it, something traumatic occurred between, say, 1965 and 1970 that would forever alter the way in which Modernism was perceived. As Hughes sagely went on to observe, 'Our relation to its hopes has become nostalgic.'[3] From being an active movement borne upon an almost worldwide consensus, its social ambitions, theoretical underpinnings and operational methods had become the subject of increasing doubt and disparagement or, in the words of Lionel

Figure 1.1
The partial collapse of Ronan Point in 1968, just two months after it opened, symbolised the demise of Modern architecture in the UK.

Esher, 'a broken wave'.[4] It cannot be a complete coincidence that around this very same time the Civic Amenities Act (1967) in the UK introduced the concept of conservation areas, or specifically that proposals for listing important Modern Movement buildings were first mooted by England's Historic Buildings Council.[5] Just as the Victorian Society had been founded in 1958 at perhaps the high point of popular dislike of Victorian and Edwardian architecture, so, with hindsight, it appears as if at the very moment when Modernism's present became its past, the process of its revaluation began.

A useful starting point in introducing the British picture is thus to chart the progress of designation – that is the statutory protection of Modern buildings on account of their architectural or historic interest. While historians may disagree as to the moment an architectural movement gains popular recognition as heritage, the official designation of particular buildings at least establishes an objective public record of places, names and dates. In the UK, the concept of enforceable statutory protection per se was established a little over a century ago with the Ancient Monuments Consolidation and Amendment Act of 1913, which repealed several earlier unwieldy pieces of legislation and acknowledged for the first time that there are physical remains of the nation's history which are so special and so significant that the state has a duty to ensure their continued survival. Thus began the systematic compilation of a public roster of important ancient monuments. (Paradoxically, in view of the pioneering work of William Morris, the Act included the 'ecclesiastical exemption' whereby churches and other religious buildings in use were excluded from its protection.)

However, more than half a century would elapse before such recognition would extend to explicitly Modern buildings. As far as Modern architecture in the UK is concerned, the beginnings of its appreciation as cultural heritage on an official basis may be traced to Nikolaus Pevsner's proposal in 1966 to prepare a select list of significant Modern buildings worthy of statutory designation. The template for designation of important buildings had been established through the wartime practice of 'listing', whereby 'salvage lists' were compiled by the Royal Institute of British Architects identifying buildings surviving bomb damage that were deemed capable and deserving of retention. This protection system had acquired statutory force in the Town and Country Planning Act of 1947 (albeit limiting formal designation to buildings constructed before 1840) and now operates in England and Wales under the Planning (Listed Buildings and Conservation Areas) Act 1990.[6] The Historic Buildings Council Listing Subcommittee (of which Pevsner was a key member) was persuaded to support his proposal for consideration of significant buildings from the 25-year period 1914–1939 and the resulting so-called 'Pevsner List' identified a range of key works, including many cutting-edge Modern Movement buildings by such leading architects as Berthold Lubetkin, Amyas Connell, Wells Coates, Ernö Goldfinger, Maxwell Fry and others, who had played a pioneering role in the introduction of Modern architecture to the UK in the 1930s (Figures 1.2 and 1.3).

However, the list was not wholly partisan and also included several of the 'transitional Modern' type – for example Charles Holden's 55 Broadway, near St James's Park, London (1929) and George Grey Wornum's RIBA building in Portland Place, Marylebone, London (1934). Although the eventual formal listing ensued over several years, depending on their local authority location,

Figure 1.2
The Penguin Pool, London Zoo, by Lubetkin and Tecton, 1934. The pool was in the first group of MoMo (Modern Movement) buildings to be listed.

Figure 1.3
High and Over, Amersham, by Amyas Connell, 1931. The house was in the first group of Modern listings.

Figure 1.4
The Penguin Pool, Dudley Zoo, by Tecton, 1937. The pool was demolished in c. 1979.

this was an important milestone in conferring heritage status on the more significant buildings of the 'heroic' period (generally recognised to be the interwar years, especially the 1930s), and also helped to situate the period historically. It would take a good deal longer to develop a 'culture' of modern conservation in terms of theory and practice.

Through the 1960s and 1970s, most interventions in (and demolition of) Modern buildings, occasionally even listed ones, continued to be undertaken as a pragmatic response to operational and technical demands, with little attempt to objectivise the architectural criteria or ethical protocols that might be applicable for good conservation practice as such. Tecton's Penguin Pool at Dudley Zoo (Figure 1.4), one of a unique ensemble of 13 listed structures dating from 1937, was unceremoniously demolished in c. 1979.

Another conspicuous example of Modern heritage insouciance involved a high-profile house in London's Chelsea district (Figure 1.5). This rare work, listed Grade II in 1970, was one of the very few English buildings by Walter Gropius during his short tenure in England in the 1930s. It was pragmatically overclad in the 1970s in artificial slate shingles as a practical means of overcoming weathering problems rather than attempting to remediate the concrete envelope itself in such a way as to preserve its architectural character.

It is inconceivable that such an approach would be proposed, still less permitted, today. Bizarrely, however, extensions to the immediate neighbour of this 'white MoMo' house, the Grade II* listed Cohen House by Mendelsohn and Chermayeff, have been added as recently as 2020, albeit in the latter case on the basis of a personal consent valid only while the existing occupant is in residence – evidence of the continuing uncertainty of Modernism's protection, even when listed.

Nonetheless, with increasing recognition of Modern buildings of the 1930s, it would be only a matter of time before listing reached architecture of the post-war period. The original 1840 cut-off date, already revised to 1939, was superseded by a DoE (Department of the Environment) Circular 8/87 in 1987 with the adoption of a '30-year rule' – a dramatic revision with far-reaching consequences, as instead of the relatively simple test of eligibility, namely age, the more elusive criterion of 'significance' became paramount.[7] The new dispensation brought post-war buildings within the ambit of designation, the first case being the *Financial Times* building, Bracken House (Figure 1.6), in the City of London, designed by Sir Albert Richardson – a Neoclassical office block in refined brickwork with bronze trimmings that might better be described as 'sui generis' than Modern, but which had been built barely 30 years previously, in 1959. This new status, however, did not prevent its partial demolition and a substantial new insertion by Michael Hopkins that ensued in 1988–91, just a year after the listing (see Figure 6.2).

However, the principle of post-war listing was now established and the protection of more recent buildings has progressed ever since – though still controversially in many cases and with uneven results. This may be attributed to the relatively late arrival of Modern architecture in the UK (as compared with Europe) and its widespread unpopularity – mostly in regard to state-funded housing of the 1960s and 1970s and specifically works in the Brutalist manner. With the 30-year rule now bringing the construction date of potential candidates for listing well within living memory, it was less easy to assume popular 'heritage recognition' – a product of respect through age.[8] Accordingly, under the reduced age provision, the promotion of statutory protection has increasingly tended to be led by historians or 'experts', currently seen by some as a discredited species, thereby imparting an elitist aspect to the process that only compounds the difficulty of cultivating wider support. It may thus be suggested that for Historic England (see below), post-war listing has become a delicate balancing act between

Figure 1.5
House by Walter Gropius and Maxwell Fry, Old Church Street, London, 1936. The house was overclad in the mid-1970s.

Figure 1.6
Bracken House, City of London, by Sir Albert Richardson, 1959. The building was the first post-war structure to be listed, in 1987.

seeking to protect significant Modern buildings that might otherwise be lost through lack of public support or owner care while also maintaining a sufficient measure of popular consensus to progress a programme of Modern designation at all. As John Summerson presciently observed over 70 years ago:

Preservation by legislation is valid only so long as it retains the constant and earnest sanction of a minority of the electorate, as well as the tolerance of the majority… As a preserver of buildings the State should be reluctant and critical, subject always to rather angry pressure from below, but prompt, firm and open-handed in support of proven causes.[9]

THE ROLE OF GOVERNMENT AGENCIES

In England the agency tasked with preparing recommendations for listing is Historic England (before April 2015, English Heritage.)[10] The agency proceeded to propose further post-war candidates, but it experienced a setback in 1988 when a list of 70 post-war buildings was reduced by the then Secretary of State (who has ultimate power of approval for post-war nominations) to only 18, underlining both the controversial status of Modern 'heritage' and the ultimately political nature of the listing process. The period of reflection that ensued, however, produced positive results, as the methodology for selection then became altogether more systematic. In place of the previous annual 'roll forward' method, whereby buildings were considered for potential listing simply when they passed the 30-year-old mark, from 1992 they began to be evaluated thematically according to type – such as schools, houses, industrial, transport, university buildings, etc. – thereby making for a more objective and comparative assessment process that was convincingly supported by specialist research. This programme has still suffered setbacks and interruptions, with the disbanding in 2002 of English Heritage's expert Post-War Listing Advisory Committee. However, the comparative model remains the preferred methodology, as evidenced in 2015, when following such thematic assessment of commercial office buildings built between 1964 and 1984, all 14 recommended candidates were accepted for listing.[11]

Consolidating this process, English Heritage/Historic England subsequently published a series of *Listing Selection Guides* featuring a broad range of building types (see the Historic England website[12]). The suite currently comprises 20 categories, ranging from Agricultural Buildings to Utilities and Communications. In each guide, a historical introduction is followed by a consideration of designation issues, together with sources of further information. These are not exclusively devoted to Modern buildings; however, they have established the official context in which further Modern designations within each category are likely to be considered.

In addition to the programme of thematic selection, younger buildings may still be listed individually, provided they are at least 10 years old, judged to be 'outstanding' (i.e. to Grade I or II* standard) and under immediate threat of demolition or inappropriate alteration – a process known as 'reactive listing', formerly 'spot listing'. This is very infrequent, but a conspicuous Modern example was the Willis Faber and Dumas (now Willis Corroon) office building in Ipswich (1975), by Norman Foster (Figure 1.7), which was spot-listed at Grade I in 1991 to prevent unsympathetic interventions, little more than 15 years after its completion.

Figure 1.7
Office of Willis Faber and Dumas, Ipswich, by Norman Foster, 1975. The office was the first post-war building to be spot-listed, in 1991.

Figure 1.8
CEMEX House, Egham, Surrey, by Edward Cullinan Architects, 1989. The former RMC headquarters was listed in 2014.

A more recent example is CEMEX House (1989), the former RMC headquarters in Egham, Surrey, by Edward Cullinan Architects, another innovative office complex which was listed at Grade II* in 2014 when threatened with redevelopment (Figure 1.8).

The listing of Modern buildings from the second half of the 20th century has continued steadily and may be regarded as a measure of the increasing acceptance over the last 30 years that recent architecture of outstanding merit has an equal right to be considered as 'heritage' as that of earlier ages. Inevitably there are still high-profile cases where listing campaigns have either not been supported by Historic England (for example Robin Hood Gardens, in east London; see p 71 and Figure 1.9) or, even when proposed, have been rejected at ministerial level (such as the Broadgate office complex in the City of London; Figure 1.10). In the case of both Robin Hood Gardens and the Broadgate office complex, the result was demolition.

Conversely there have been cases where Modern buildings, despite being listed, have then been controversially altered, for example Park Hill estate, Sheffield (Figure 1.11), the Commonwealth Institute, Kensington, London (see p 108) and Ernö Goldfinger's Balfron Tower in east London (see p 112).

Such pre-eminent examples foster a suspicion that while Modern architecture through designation is ostensibly accorded equal status to that of other periods (which could hardly be logically denied), the protocols of listing protection are less scrupulously administered when it comes to alteration and intervention (see Chapter 5). So, although the general trend towards recognition is ongoing, it may be expected that this disputatious atmosphere surrounding specific designations and subsequent change will continue.

Figure 1.9
Robin Hood Gardens, by Alison and Peter Smithson, Tower Hamlets, 1972. The photograph shows the building under demolition in 2017. Balfron Tower can be seen beyond.

Figure 1.10
Broadgate, City of London, by
Arup Associates (Peter Foggo),
1988. Demolition of the office
complex began in 2011.

Figure 1.11
Park Hill estate, Sheffield,
by Jack Lynn and Ivor Smith,
Sheffield City Architects
Department, 1961. The housing
estate was listed Grade II* in
1998; renovation/refurbishment
began in 2009 and has been
ongoing in several phases
(compare with Figure 5.1).

AGE, NUMBERS AND GRADES

The vast majority of listed buildings in the UK date from earlier periods. In England, all buildings built before 1700 which survive in anything like their original condition are listed, as are most of those built between 1700 and 1840. The criteria become tighter with youth, so that post-1945 buildings have to be of exceptional significance to be listed. According to Historic England's own figures, the entire 20th century accounts for only 3.2% of all listed buildings – the 0.2% relating to buildings after 1945. (At the time of writing, estimated numbers of listed buildings in England vary from 400,000 entries to 500,000 individual buildings, of which there are only 62 listed at Grade I dating from 1901 onwards, though these also include selected statuary and built features such as walls and ornamental gate piers.)

It is important to note that it is the building (rather than its architect) that is paramount in the consideration of whether or not to list, though in a few cases of architects of international importance the building's authorship may become a factor. The most listed Modern architect in the UK is the Russian émigré Berthold Lubetkin (1901–90), with over 60 individual buildings to his credit at all grades, ranging from single houses to zoological pavilions to housing estates which comprise whole groups of buildings. Conversely, as noted above in the case of Robin Hood Gardens, a large 1970s housing estate in east London, even the international repute of its architects, Alison and Peter Smithson, was not sufficient to secure its designation despite ongoing appeals by campaigners (predominantly other architects) to forestall demolition (see p 71).

Figure 1.12
The Barbican Estate, City of London, by Chamberlin, Powell and Bon, 1965–1982. The whole estate was listed Grade II in 2001.

Three grades of listing apply. Grade I buildings are of exceptional interest and may be considered to be internationally important; only 2.5% of listed buildings are Grade I. Grade II* buildings are particularly important buildings of 'more than special interest' and account for 5.8% of listed buildings. Grade II buildings are nationally important and of special interest; all remaining listed buildings are in this class and it is the most common grade of listing for individual residential properties. The equivalent grades in Scotland and Northern Ireland are known as Categories A, B, C and Grades A, B+, B, B1 and B2, respectively. The list inventories are now digitised and may be consulted online by accessing the websites of the respective heritage agencies. Some listings, of course, comprise more than just a single building, and this often applies in the case of post-war housing estates where an entire ensemble of buildings may be involved. The Barbican Estate in the City of London (Figure 1.12; see also p 115) comprises many different buildings over an area of several hectares and is believed to be the largest built object ever listed (in 2001), now housing nearly half the City's residents.

The governance of such extensive designations creates challenges of its own, which have in turn led to new administrative instruments, such as management guidelines in the form of Supplementary Planning Documents (see p 61). It should be noted that 'listing' refers to buildings, while in the case of archaeological remains and monuments, the term 'scheduling' applies. Other forms of designation exist for historic parks and gardens, conservation areas, historic battlefields and maritime wrecks. Given the sparsity of Modern buildings covered by listing, the number of these within either of the higher grades, that is Grade I and II*, is vanishingly small – as is the number of modern registered parks and gardens.

LISTING CRITERIA

The test for listing as defined in the 1990 Act is 'special architectural or historic interest', with an additional consideration of 'group value' where the compositional quality of an ensemble of buildings (whether intentional or not) is deemed significant. If a building is judged to meet the necessary criteria, it is added to the list. Usually, it is architectural interest that predominates, but this may include special technical factors and historical associations. The giant radio telescope at Jodrell Bank in Cheshire, (1952–57; listed Grade I) and the Express Lift Tower in Northampton (1980–82; listed Grade II) are examples of structures protected for their technical and historic rarity, rather than architectural interest as such. A degree of confusion in public debate persists, however, in assuming 'beauty' rather than 'special interest' is the criterion. State of repair is not supposed to be a criterion (unless this accounts for significant loss of authenticity), neither are the costs of remedial works, where necessary, or such factors as the potential value of site redevelopment. Everything that exists at the time of listing is covered by the designation (unless specifically excluded), regardless of whether it is original or not. These details may be captured in the List Entry that is prepared as part of the designation process, though until recently the primary purpose of the entry was to identify the exact extent and location of the object/s being listed, not to ascribe significance.

Meanwhile, changes in the mainstream planning system as well as in the specialised heritage protection system are regularly being considered. The Enterprise and Regulatory Reform

Figure 1.13
Preston Bus Station, by Building Design Partnership (BDP), 1969. The structure was eventually listed in 2013. The recent restoration of this building has now received the WMF Knoll Modernism Prize – a change in fortunes unthinkable even a few years ago.

Act 2013 (ERRA) included several measures aimed at improving efficiency without affecting protection. Some of these were promoted in the draft Heritage Protection Bill in 2008 that failed to proceed through lack of parliamentary time, and include heritage partnership agreements (HPAs), which may be made between local authorities and property owners and set out works for which listed building consent is deemed to be granted (excluding demolition). The ERRA reforms also provide that the extent of listing can be more clearly defined by excluding attached buildings and structures and those within the curtilage of the principal listed building from protection, or by stating explicitly that some features or elements of a listed building are of lesser or no special architectural or historic interest. These dispensations can prove decisive in the context of gaining consent for projects involving alteration. The 'direction of travel' in Historic England's current approach may thus be characterised as placing greater emphasis on identifying the essential significance of a heritage asset, rather than treating all surviving fabric as automatically worthy of protection.

Listing proposals can be submitted by anyone, not only the relevant government agencies noted above, but the final decision whether or not to designate is taken at ministerial level. While government guidance exists to bring a measure of consistency to the process, for example the Department of Culture, Media and Sport (DCMS) publication *Principles of Selection for Listing Buildings* (2010)[13] in England, there is inevitably a political dimension. In the case of Modern architecture, this can be critical, depending on the aesthetic predilections of the minister at the time. In a move to narrow the eligibility of post-war buildings, the Secretary of State in 2004 introduced the additional criterion of 'fulfilment of the original brief', which if applied literally could raise considerable complications (it resulted in the controversial loss of Pimlico School, London; see p 82). Hyde Park Barracks in Knightsbridge, London, is another example of a seemingly unassailable listing case being unaccountably rejected at ministerial level (see p 89). On the other hand, the eventual listing of Preston Bus Station (Figure 1.13) in 2013, a huge Brutalist structure in the Lancashire town dating from 1969, followed two previous ministerial refusals in 2000 and 2009, despite the fact that the building itself had not changed during this period – another indicator of the function of age in changing public (and political) opinions.

Assessment for designation of a building can also be triggered by an application for a Certificate of Immunity from Listing (COI) which may be made by a developer in order to remove the element of risk from a planned redevelopment. The case is then considered as if for listing; if the building is not deemed worthy, the COI will provide a legal immunity from listing for five years, thereby removing this uncertainty from a developer's project. Recent examples of COIs include London's Broadgate (see Figure 1.10) and the Southbank complex (see Figure 5.12).

LISTING AND CHANGE

Listing does not, of course, preclude subsequent alteration, or in certain cases even demolition (subject to due process), though this is sometimes innocently (or mischievously) misrepresented. However, the primary consequence of listing is to bring the building/s within the provisions of the relevant Act – the Planning (Listed Buildings and Conservation Areas) Act 1990, in the case of England. This makes it an 'offence' (punishable by fine and/or imprisonment) for someone to undertake (or cause to undertake) work that 'would affect the character of a building, listed on account of its special architectural or historic interest', without authorisation. Obtaining 'listed building consent', as this process is therefore known (see Clause 7: Restriction on works affecting listed buildings), entails making an application to the relevant local planning authority (LPA), setting out details of the proposed works. If the grade involved is II* or above the LPA will refer the case to the government agency – Historic England, Historic Environment Scotland, etc. – for advice. Though this advice is seldom contradicted, it is the LPA rather than the agency that is the decision-maker.

The listing of any building, but especially a Modern one, is not always welcomed by its owner, who is likely to regard designation as a constraint on his or her freedom of action and a potential blight on the property value. For this reason, there have been moves over recent years to make the whole process more inclusive and transparent. Measures introduced from 2005 require meaningful consultation by English Heritage (now Historic England) prior to designation and have also introduced more systematic procedures in assessing proposals for intervention and alteration. Best practice in conservation work now expects a 'Statement of Significance' to be produced as preparatory to, or part of, an application for listed building consent. This will set out the principal features of the building or 'heritage asset' that should inform any alteration works, and ideally should also be independent of any specific design scheme. The scheme proposals themselves will then include a 'Heritage Impact Assessment' explaining how they will preserve or enhance the significance for which the building has been listed and demonstrate their compatibility with the Statement of Significance. This still represents the ideal, however, and remains to be fully assimilated into current practice, especially in cases involving Modern buildings where it is still often, and sometimes wrongly, assumed that high-profile 'starchitects' are appropriately qualified to undertake conversion projects on major historic Modern buildings.

In 2008, in the attempt to be more transparent in its own processes, English Heritage published its *Conservation Principles, Policies and Guidance,* which set out six key conservation propositions, together with recommended criteria for evaluating heritage significance. These were identified under four headings – evidential, historical, aesthetic and communal – the sum of which would represent the overall heritage significance of the asset. This document then laid out a generic procedure for developing conservation projects and is now applied as the 'industry standard' in official conservation practice, whether for modern or historic buildings.[14]

More recently, however, Historic England has been concerned to promote the broader view that the sustainable adaptation of buildings to serve current and future needs can often offer the most effective use of heritage assets for the future, in both social and economic terms. In the longer perspective, this approach, perhaps self-servingly termed 'constructive conservation' and focused more on 'managing change' than preserving original fabric, may be seen to reflect a shift away from earlier norms, and specifically the prescriptive manifesto of William Morris and the Society for the Protection of Ancient Buildings (SPAB).[15]

The SPAB, founded in 1877, was an ethically driven movement against the contemporaneous late Victorian tendency for 'over restoration' of medieval churches and a crusade for the retention of authenticity through 'conservative repair'. This instilled the moral dimension to conservation that has permeated British discourse on the subject ever since. The current debate around Modern heritage in the UK may thus be characterised as an ongoing struggle to seek an equitable balance between those earlier stricter conservation precepts and today's more broadly defined objectives of flexibility and sustainability. This increasing focus on identifying significance, as distinct from preserving original fabric, is indicative of the trend towards a more relative or 'proportional' evaluation of heritage. Indeed, the National Planning Policy Framework, published in 2012 and subsequently updated, introduced the explicit presumption in favour of 'sustainable development', which as far as the historic environment is concerned requires planning authorities to weigh up the public benefits that such development would deliver in compensation for potential harm to heritage assets. The resulting, somewhat elastic, concept of 'less than substantial harm', whereby on occasion considerable intervention is authorised, is one on which many conservationists have their misgivings.

THE DEVELOPMENT OF DISCOURSE

From the late 1960s/early 1970s, the interwar and early post-war period in British architecture was already attracting its own retrospective literature and historiography but, as tends to be the case, it was individual events that suddenly brought its significance – and also vulnerability – to wider attention. In August 1980 the Firestone Tyre Factory (Figure 1.14), a noted 1928 Art Deco landmark in west London, was demolished over a Bank Holiday weekend, apparently to pre-empt a preservation order being considered by the local council and the UK government's Department of the Environment (DoE). Recriminations followed, but within a year the Historic Buildings Committee of the DoE (forerunner of English Heritage) had proposed a list of 150 interwar buildings for designation.

Figure 1.14
The Firestone Tyre Factory, Brentford, by Wallis, Gilbert and Partners, 1928. The Art Deco landmark was demolished in 1980.

The previous year, 1979, one of the largest public exhibitions of Modern design in the UK, *Thirties,* had been staged by the Arts Council at the Hayward Gallery in London, substantially raising the cultural profile of that decade in the extensive coverage of its art, architecture and design.[16] The same year had seen the formation of The Thirties Society (later renamed the Twentieth Century Society), a voluntary organisation with the specific mission to promote and protect significant architecture after 1914 (which had been the cut-off date of its historical antecedent, the Victorian Society). However, C20, as it is now known, is avowedly catholic in its criteria, championing any significant architecture within its period regardless of style, and it was not until 10 years later in 1989 that an organisation specifically dedicated to the *do*cumentation and *co*nservation of *Mo*dern *Mo*vement buildings and sites was formed, Docomomo-UK. This is the UK branch of the international movement to be formally constituted at the Eindhoven Conference, in the Netherlands, the following year, 1990. Scotland, meanwhile, formed its own Docomomo chapter in this organisation, which is now represented in over 70 countries worldwide.

By the start of the 21st century, Modern buildings that had been completed before World War II were now well over half a century old and the promotion of Modern architecture as 'heritage' was beginning to be regarded as a more legitimate proposition, even if efforts to list or preserve certain individual buildings were to remain controversial in particular cases. Most emblematic, perhaps, was the furore surrounding Greenside (Figure 1.15), a Grade II listed house in Surrey dating from 1937, by the pioneering practice Connell, Ward and Lucas, which was illegally demolished in 2003 by its owner, who was duly fined and received a criminal conviction.[17]

Figure 1.15
Greenside, Wentworth, Surrey, by Connell, Ward and Lucas, 1937. The house was demolished in 2003.

Figure 1.16
Alexander Fleming House,
London, by Ernö Goldfinger,
1959–67. The building was
listed in 2013.

Other important examples of post-war Modern architecture – such as Brynmawr Rubber Factory (an outstanding industrial complex in Blaenau Gwent, Wales) by Architects Co-Partnership; the cinema that formed an integral part of the office ensemble at Elephant and Castle, London, by Ernö Goldfinger; and the Peter Robinson Store in London's Strand by Sir Denys Lasdun – were also all lost despite vigorous campaigns to save them. Ironically, the remaining Goldfinger building at Elephant and Castle (Figure 1.16) has since been listed, in 2013 – again underscoring the time-lapse factor in Modern architecture's appreciation (albeit further controversial interventions are still being pursued).[18]

Such episodes have proved a powerful stimulant of modern conservation discourse, but this has also been progressively supported by the government agencies already mentioned and by various academic institutions. In 1992 English Heritage launched an exhibition entitled *A Change of Heart* to initiate debate on the preservation and protection of post-war architecture.[19] Only 29 such buildings had been listed by this time and the issues surrounding Modern heritage were still somewhat ill-defined. The following year, 1993, what is believed to have been the first conference in England to be devoted exclusively to the subject of Modern heritage and its conservation was held at the University of York.[20]

These and other early initiatives began to articulate the philosophical, procedural and technical issues that have come to characterise discussion in the field ever since. 'In what way does, or should, modern conservation differ from the traditional?'; 'Is the conservation of Modernism, a movement supposedly dedicated to the future, itself an inherent contradiction?'; 'Does the repetitive, industrialised basis of much modern construction shift significance away from materiality and craft values towards Modernism's programmatic and intellectual achievement?' – and if so, 'May greater licence be given to interventions in Modern listed buildings than would be tolerated in historic ones?' 'Is listing, which originated as a means of protecting individual buildings, an equally appropriate measure for dealing with large 20th-century developments and estates?'; 'How may specialist techniques of concrete repair, initially a proprietary product-driven market geared to large-scale infrastructure maintenance, be brought within the disciplines of architecturally informed conservation?'

Other typical themes include 'What lessons may be derived from pioneering case studies for wider application?' and 'To what extent should substandard but original technology or design be upgraded to meet current environmental expectations, inclusive access and health and safety compliance standards?' Such are the points most frequently interrogated at conferences and in the journals (see Chapter 8). In practical matters, recurrent questions concern components like early curtain wall systems, or single-glazed steel windows, with their slender sections and elegant sightlines. The debate as to whether, and how, these originally innovative but now underperforming elements may be acceptably replaced by more energy-efficient double-glazed systems or modern thermally broken but thicker frames remains ongoing. Meanwhile, the product industries are increasingly working to develop more conservation-sensitive components for what is now becoming a specialist construction sector.

The repair of reinforced concrete has likewise been the subject of much debate and technical study, featuring as it does so conspicuously in the development of Modern architecture, both pre- and post-war. Here, too, the early reliance of property owners on the recommendations of commercial contractors and producers of proprietary remedies, often coupled with plausible warranties, has begun to give way – at least in several high-profile listed building restoration projects – to more discriminating approaches focused on the retention, or replication, of original and authentic surface characteristics.

Many of these themes have therefore become embedded in modern conservation discourse, as may be seen in the content of conferences and publications. Two such events were organised by English Heritage itself – *Modern Matters* in 1996 and *Preserving Post-War Heritage* in 1998 – the proceedings of both conferences being published subsequently in book form.[21] At the former event, the historian Andrew Saint sought to identify the key factors that might differentiate modern buildings from historic ones – namely number, technique, intention, performance, viability and appeal, headings that have indeed been reflected in the developing discussion. A joint conference of English Heritage with *The Architectural Review*, entitled *Mending Modernism*, was also held in 1996. Meanwhile, the voluntary organisations C20 and Docomomo-UK have also contributed to the debate with themed meetings, short study courses and the publication of regular journals and monographs. A more recent participant, as of 2011, has been the Getty Conservation Institute, Los Angeles, with its international *Keeping it Modern* programme of grant-aided projects and publications.

An exhibition entitled *Modern Architecture Restored* had already been staged by Docomomo-UK soon after its formation in 1989, thereafter travelling to several other venues, including the Bauhaus, in Dessau, Germany, for the organisation's second international conference in 1992. A notable collection of essays, *Modern Movement Heritage*, was also produced under the aegis of Docomomo-UK for the conference of the international movement, held in Stockholm in 1998.[22] Monographs and themed chapters devoted to the Modern cause within general conservation publications have also appeared. Another reflection of this increasing attention was the special book-length issue of the *Journal of Architectural Conservation*, entitled *Conservation of Modern Architecture*, published in 2007.[23]

Alongside these events and publications there has been coverage of leading building restoration and adaptation projects in the professional and technical press, as well as of the various campaigns, controversies and causes célèbres. Though some of these campaigns have not prevented the destruction or disfigurement of important 20th-century buildings – a particular risk where listing campaigns are unsuccessful, thereby supposedly 'mandating' demolition – the cumulative effect of such coverage is gradually to raise awareness of Modernism as a historical achievement as deserving of due care as any other period. All this activity must also surely have been strengthened through the increasing attention given to Modern architecture in mainstream media and television, and through major exhibitions such as *Modern Britain 1929–1939* at London's Design Museum (1999) and *Modernism* staged at the Victoria and Albert Museum in 2006 – though the resulting change in public attitudes remains impossible to quantify.

Meanwhile in Scotland, the particularly unusual and challenging case of St Peter's Seminary, at Cardross near Glasgow – a Category A listed training college for Catholic priests, opened in 1966 but closed only 14 years later and thereafter becoming an abandoned ruin – was the

Figure 1.17
St Peter's Seminary, Cardross, by Gillespie, Kidd and Coia, 1966. This aerial view was taken after site clearance in 2016.

subject of a special symposium at the Venice Biennale of 2010. This contributed to it becoming a government-funded rescue initiative that by 2016 had achieved significant progress in stabilising and decontaminating the site, though the project is now again beset with uncertainty.[24]

To sum up, over the period covered in this review it could be said that from the distinctly bleak picture of Modern heritage in the early 1970s there now exists a recognisable 'culture' – in terms of statutory recognition and discourse, technical knowledge and project cases – that has been registered in professional and institutional circles, together with a wider, albeit more nebulous, interest in the arena of public consciousness. That an exhibition entitled *Brutal and Beautiful – Saving the Twentieth Century* could be mounted in 2013 by English Heritage at Wellington Arch, in the heart of London, featuring many post-war buildings by still living architects, gives an indication of just how far official and public readiness to revalue Modern architecture has grown in the last quarter of a century.

CONSERVATION TOOLS

Over the same period there has also been steady progress in the development of various conservation tools – conservation plans, conservation management plans, listed building management guidelines and heritage partnership agreements, the latter a feature of the aborted Heritage Protection Bill 2008 noted above. These instruments have all been effectively applied to Modern architecture and have now become models of good practice in the management and adaptation of buildings and sites generally. While differing in structure and scope, such tools all seek to focus on the significance of the asset concerned and how best this may be maintained while managing ongoing pressures for change. Although the durability of subsequent application, or long-term 'buy-in', can be variable, the process of preparing and consulting on such documents in itself usually has the beneficial effect of raising consciousness and encouraging more informed stewardship of the asset concerned. The voluntary element in these measures is crucial, as in many cases the alternative of relying on statutory enforcement as a primary management tool would be impracticable. Thus designations such as the Barbican or Golden Lane Estate – large tracts of housing in central London – are now served by listed building management guidelines, which have been formally adopted as Supplementary Planning Documents by the controlling authority, the City of London Corporation. These guidelines now operate as a 'material consideration' in the determination of local planning matters.[25]

In other cases, the voluntary adoption of listed building management guidelines or conservation management plans for significant buildings has enabled owners and conservation authorities to agree 'rules of engagement' identifying which kinds of intervention may trigger formal consent procedures and which need not, thereby allowing both a defined freedom to proprietors and also a measure of confidence to conservation officers in the responsible stewardship of these heritage assets by their owners. Examples include listed building management guidelines for Sir Denys Lasdun's University of East Anglia (listed Grade II*), in Norwich, and the Lloyd's building in the City of London, listed Grade I in 2011.

MODERN ARCHITECTURAL MUSEUMS

One particular development that must surely have advanced the cause of Modern heritage over this period is the acquisition and presentation of select Modern Movement buildings as museums open to the visiting public. The National Trust is the oldest heritage charity in the UK, being founded in 1895 with the object of protecting important historic assets – houses, monuments, coastline, forests, islands, castles, nature reserves, etc. – across the whole country. To the surprise of many familiar with its traditional portfolio of historic properties and stately homes, the National Trust acquired the house of the émigré Hungarian architect Ernö Goldfinger (1902–87) after his death, opening it as a public museum in 1996 following judicious restoration works (Figure 1.18). Designed in 1938 for himself and his family, 2 Willow Road in Hampstead, north London was then occupied by Goldfinger continuously for the rest of his life and was filled with the artworks, furniture and personal effects that had accumulated over 50 years, providing a vivid record of the architect and his milieu. The Trust believed that such an intact and authentic example of 'modern heritage' was just as valid as some of its other properties in illustrating episodes in the nation's history as a continuing narrative, and the ensuing popularity of the exhibit has certainly vindicated this judgement.

Figure 1.18
2 Willow Road, Hampstead, north London, by Ernö Goldfinger, 1938. The property opened as a National Trust house museum in 1996.

This early success was consolidated a few years later when the Trust took possession of another outstanding Modern house, The Homewood (Figure 1.19), near Esher in Surrey, designed by the young English architect Patrick Gwynne (1913–2003) for his parents – also in 1938. Gwynne had returned to the house after World War II and proceeded to live there for the rest of his life (dying there aged 90 in 2003). He adapted and enriched the building and its extensive gardens throughout this period, so that, like Willow Road, the property became a living palimpsest of the man and his times. Following extensive restoration works, this too was opened to the public, though on a different regime from Willow Road as Gwynne had stipulated that the property should be tenanted and continue to be enjoyed as a family home. Taken together, these two exhibits – one the formal London townhouse of a Continental émigré, the other a Corbusian country villa by an Englishman – offer ideal representative pendants of the early Modern Movement in the UK, creating a trail of enthralled visitors, for many of whom these were their first hands-on experience of 'historic' Modern architecture.[26]

Figure 1.19
The Homewood, Surrey, by Patrick Gwynne, 1938. The National Trust opened Gwynne's home as a house museum in 2004.

Figure 1.20
The Isokon Gallery, Camden,
north London, created by
Avanti Architects and others
in 2014.

A more recent Modern architecture museum is the Isokon Gallery (Figure 1.20), created in the former garage of the Grade I Isokon/Lawn Road Flats, Camden, north London (see Figure 1.23) – the pioneering apartment block completed in 1934 and designed by the Canadian architect Wells Coates. Opened in 2014, a decade after the restoration of the building itself, and operated by a private charitable trust, the Isokon Gallery tells the story of this remarkable building and some of its distinguished residents. Original exhibits include several of the specially designed furniture pieces created to complement the apartment designs. A regular lecture programme and changing annual displays help to present the building's stories to a wide audience. To judge by visitor numbers – exceeding 25,000 over the first five seasons – this facility has also engaged the interest of an avid public.[27]

LEADING CASES

Examples of restoration/adaptation projects involving high-profile Modern buildings (e.g. Grade I cases) can also have a beneficial impact on consciousness-raising and the appreciation of Modern architecture as cultural heritage, as well as providing valuable case study material for technical and educational benefit. One of the first such projects was the Penguin Pool at London Zoo, a Grade I icon of the early 1930s designed by Berthold Lubetkin that was to become a sort of mascot for the fledgling Modern Movement in the UK in its 'heroic period'. With funding from the zoo, together with grant aid from English Heritage and private

Figure 1.21
The Penguin Pool, London
Zoo, constructed in 1934, was
restored (with original colours)
in 1987.

benefaction, the pool was fully restored in 1987 (Figure 1.21) and reopened in the presence of Lubetkin himself and the original engineer, Ove Arup, then aged 86 and 92 respectively. The works included comprehensive concrete repairs, renewal of the mosaic pool lining, upgrade of the hydraulic systems and judicious adaptations of the structure in response to the zoo's changing ornithological demands. The project was widely featured in press and film coverage.[28]

The De La Warr Pavilion (Figure 1.22), in Bexhill on England's south coast, was another high-profile rescue project. The outcome of a major architectural competition won by Erich Mendelsohn and Serge Chermayeff and opened in 1935, this recreational and cultural centre also became an icon of the English Modern Movement, with its sweeping International Style

Figure 1.22
The De La Warr Pavilion,
Bexhill, by Mendelsohn
and Chermayeff, 1935. The
photograph shows the pavilion
after its restoration in 2005.

façades and virtuoso staircases. Vital to the rescue and upgrade project was the formation of
the De La Warr Pavilion Charitable Trust, a registered charity with associated tax concessions
that assumed ownership of the building for the project and was able to attract local support
and Heritage Lottery funding to carry out a phased rehabilitation programme, reopening
the building in 2005 as a major arts centre for the visiting public. Once again, considerable
publicity followed.[29]

Figure 1.23 a and b.
The Isokon/Lawn Road Flats, Camden, north London, by Wells Coates, 1934. The apartments are shown here after their restoration was completed in 2004.

Another major building rescue case was the Isokon building (aka Lawn Road Flats) in Camden, north London, noted above, and the first British essay in *Existenzminimum* living, with compact studio flats of 25sq m in a four-storey reinforced concrete gallery-access block that later also included a restaurant and other communal facilities. Although highly successful initially, this building had fallen into a state of acute dereliction following various changes of ownership, and by the late 1990s had become uninhabitable. However, its acquisition in 2001 by Notting Hill Housing Group, a leading social landlord, and sympathetic repair and adaptation to serve a mixed-tenure/shared-equity residential community, has enabled this landmark to become once again an exemplar of compact urban living, accommodating a range of key workers – nurses, teachers, etc. – who normally could not hope to live in such an expensive area of London.[30] In 2018 an English Heritage Blue Plaque honouring the three Bauhaus masters and former residents – Walter Gropius, Marcel Breuer and László Moholy-Nagy – was installed at the Isokon/Lawn Road Flats (Figure 1.23; see also Figure 1.20).

Finsbury Health Centre (Figure 1.24; see also p 182), a Grade I listed building by Berthold Lubetkin, dating from 1938, remains a more intractable rescue mission. This pioneering building, which anticipated the founding of the National Health Service by a decade, has succeeded in maintaining its function as a public health care facility ever since, but more recently became vulnerable to proposals for dispersal of its NHS services and disposal of the building itself. An exemplary, though partial, restoration project in the mid-1990s has been followed by chronic neglect, though the building itself remains essentially viable, having been designed for flexible adaptation originally.[31] While the danger of its disposal has receded thanks to determined local opposition, the full restoration of the building fabric remains uncertain due to the funding difficulties of its current owner, NHS Property Services.

Next in this selective resumé of leading case studies is the Royal Festival Hall (Figure 1.25) – the only permanent legacy of the 1951 *Festival of Britain* on London's South Bank and variously described as Finsbury Health Centre's architectural progeny and the UK's most popular post-war building. Between 2005 and 2007 it underwent a multimillion-pound regeneration that included fabric repairs, services upgrade, rectification of many illiterate accretions and modifications of its concert auditorium acoustic properties. The importance of this exercise (which also included extensive precinct works) as far as Modern heritage is concerned has certainly been magnified through its status as an international cultural and recreational venue in central London.[32]

Figure 1.24
Finsbury Health Centre, London, by Lubetkin and Tecton, 1938. The building was partially restored in 1995.

Figure 1.25
The Royal Festival Hall, London,
by LCC Architects Dept, 1951.
The photograph was taken after
its restoration in 2007.

Last, and perhaps most indicative, in this review of transformative leading cases is the Royal National Theatre (1969–76) by Sir Denys Lasdun, which had been a lightning rod for Modern architecture's unpopularity when it first opened and although listed Grade II* in 1994 had undergone various unsympathetic remedial works to its expressive concrete fabric (Figure 1.26). More recently, however, a much more carefully considered project has been undertaken, correcting many of the earlier interventions and approaching the concrete repair task with the same conservation protocols and sensitivity as would be expected in any historic building context.[33]

All but the last of the above examples are in the tiny category of Modern Grade I listed buildings, but these are now being joined by increasing numbers of other cases of successful restoration/adaptive reuse of significant 20th-century works. Even where these projects have been motivated by other considerations, including economic, social or environmental factors, heritage values have often still played an important part. Indeed, it may be suggested that as most of the very few Grade I listed buildings have been dealt with, the focus of attention is now widening to embrace other and later buildings of lower grades, even if these are of scarcely less significance.

Notable cases of major Modern buildings being adapted to new use include Tate Modern on London's South Bank, originally Bankside Power Station (closed in 1981, reopened in 2000) and now reportedly the most popular art gallery in the world, with some 4.7 million visitors

per year. Its even larger cousin, Battersea Power Station, designed by the same architect, Giles Gilbert Scott, is the scene of a massive mixed-use regeneration after many years of uncertainty and numerous failed projects. Meanwhile, the former Commonwealth Institute in Kensington, an outstanding Grade II* exhibition pavilion opened by Queen Elizabeth II in 1962, has found a new role as the Design Museum (see p 109). Such major publicly accessible adaptive reuse projects cannot but increase awareness of the importance and heritage significance of Modern architecture for both local and international audiences.

Figure 1.26
The National Theatre, London, by Sir Denys Lasdun, 1969–76. The complex was restored in 2015.

EDUCATION QUALIFICATIONS
AND CONSERVATION COURSES

Since the beginning of modern listing in the early 1970s, the development of modern conservation as an academic discipline has also progressed. In many cases this has been added as an elective subject or postgraduate module within an existing conservation course or architectural degree programme. Such courses may lead to a diploma or master's qualification, but there are also a number of shorter vocational courses focused on practical skills with specific materials or techniques. The Centre for Conservation Studies at the University of York has been a leading venue for more than 40 years, and other courses have been conducted at the Architectural Association in London, as well as several university settings including Cambridge, the Bartlett UCL, Bath, Birmingham, Edinburgh and Sheffield. Meanwhile, West Dean College in Sussex has hosted occasional study courses on the repair of reinforced concrete within its well-established traditional arts and crafts programme.

Founded in 1959, the Council on Training in Architectural Conservation (COTAC), a registered charity, has developed a wide range of courses on its digital platform – *Understanding Conservation* – comprising a series of modules derived from the education and training guidelines of ICOMOS (the International Council on Monuments and Sites; see Chapter 3). Although primarily focused on historic buildings and traditional materials, this resource provides much valuable generic guidance applicable to the conservation of heritage of any period.[34] In 1997 the Institute of Historic Building Conservation (IHBC) was formed as a charitable trust by members of the previous Association of Conservation Officers, with branches throughout the UK. As its name implies, the focus is also predominantly on historic rather than modern buildings, but it maintains a wide range of general educational resources and through the Historic Environment Service Providers Recognition (HESPR) agency operates its own accreditation system.[35] The recognition of particular expertise in conservation (historic as well as modern) has also been formalised in the establishment of registers of accredited professionals by various other bodies. Leading examples include those operated by the RIBA, AABC (Architects Accredited in Building Conservation), RICS (Royal Institute of Chartered Surveyors), RIAS (Royal Incorporation of Architects in Scotland) and, in the case of engineers, CARE (Conservation Accreditation Register for Engineers). These qualifications entitle members to use post-nominal letters and may in certain circumstances be imposed as an eligibility criterion in the selection of architects and other building professionals for projects involving public grant aid.

The formation in 2001 of the UCL Institute for Sustainable Heritage, as part of the Bartlett Faculty of the Built Environment, in London, was another milestone in the systematic development of heritage studies, with a wide-ranging scientific scope and connections on an international scale.[36] This acceptance of modern conservation as a subject worthy of formal academic study and specialist accreditation may be expected to continue, albeit there are still misgivings in some quarters over creating too decisive a divorce of conservation work from mainstream architectural practice.

OUTLOOK

This chapter began by noting that the recognition and appropriate stewardship of Modern heritage in the UK is still a work in progress encumbered by controversy, passion, ignorance and neglect. Nonetheless, it can be seen that over the last 50 years the UK has begun to embrace its Modern heritage as a revalued legacy, albeit that embrace has varied from the warm to the distinctly tepid. The cautiousness of this response is not surprising. If one applies a Darwinian analogy, it is self-evident that our inheritance of *historic* architecture from the past consists only of those buildings that have survived, and that these account for but a fraction of all the buildings that existed in earlier periods. In terms of heritage recognition, their struggle has been 'won' (albeit despite survival they may remain vulnerable to other risks), whereas in the case of Modern architecture the process of 'natural selection' is still in full swing. To the extent that popular recognition of the architecture of any period as 'heritage' is commensurate with its age, it may be anticipated that the conservation of Modern buildings for their heritage value (as distinct from economic or environmental reasons) will remain substantially dependent on statutory intervention and the advocacy of 'experts' until the point at which the surviving buildings of modern times can command the equivalent popular affection as their historic forbears. In the meantime, the said experts may find that as much progress in saving and appropriately adapting important Modern buildings and sites may be achieved by deploying economic, sustainability and environmental arguments as by relying on heritage advocacy alone. This prospect is one to which we will return in the final chapter.

2
Authenticity

Chapters 2 to 6 investigate some of the central aspects of modern
conservation discourse and practice as a series of discussions – or
'moot points' – that have typically characterised the debate to date.
The selected topics are referenced to some of the key texts in the field,
including academic studies, official regulations, recommended guidance
and recent controversial cases. The survey seeks to identify aspects of
policy and practice that differentiate the treatment of Modern from
traditional heritage, proceeding from consideration of the more generic
issues – starting with authenticity and charters and moving progressively
'downstream' into matters of listing and protection. The concluding essay
– Weaknesses – highlights some of the principal anomalies and problems
in current practice that call for resolution. We begin our discussion in
Chapter 2 by looking at the hoary question of authenticity.

ONE OF THE MOST VEXED TOPICS in modern — indeed any — conservation discourse is that of authenticity. Sooner or later it surfaces, explicitly or implicitly, in seminars, conferences and learned papers, or conversely is admitted as being so controversial and insoluble as to be quarantined from consideration pro tem, just to avoid becoming engulfed in its difficulties. 'Authenticity is the live rail,' a leading practitioner has asserted. 'Approach with caution, or better still, keep away.'[1] And before long the ghostly figures of John Ruskin and Eugène Viollet-le-Duc appear in the background, alternately intimidating or inhibiting discussion.

The concept of authenticity is indeed so ubiquitous in cultural studies that it takes much preparatory effort to sift the specific from the generic and arrive at any useful analysis for its application to Modern buildings. Ruskin is invariably summoned to provide the predisposing ex cathedra denunciation of replication as an ethically valid response in preserving old buildings. We are back in the company of William Morris and the Society for the Protection of Ancient Buildings (SPAB) again, and its castigation of renewal in preference to continuous gentle repair in the performance of responsible building stewardship. Conversely, if such exemplary practice has not been followed and the building in question is at mortal risk, is outright loss to be preferred to well-intentioned restoration in the interests of ethical purity? In short, should Vézelay Abbey, in France, have been allowed to collapse in order to save it from Viollet-le-Duc's restoration? (And if it should, one might ask, how exactly would this be justified to its Benedictine community?)

THE ELUSIVE CONUNDRUM

The ultimate irony has arisen following the tragic fire at Notre-Dame, Paris, in April 2019 (Figure 2.1), when the spire (*fleche*) – itself a second-generation replacement by Viollet-le Duc of the 13th-century original and dating from 1859 – was completely destroyed, posing the question as to whether its replacement should be a replica of his replacement, a 13th-century pastiche or an entirely new design. Evidently authenticity is a matter of degree, with this particular example providing an exquisite conundrum for generations of future conservationists to dispute indefinitely.

An additional problem with much of this debate is that it tends to be indulged in by commentators who behave as if the eventual decisions can be taken by themselves, when in the context of 'live conservation' they are more often settled in an entirely separate commercial or political arena by others. An old and arguably significant building may, or may not, be everyone's idea of heritage – but it is invariably somebody's property. One of the more noticeable characteristics of conferences on modern conservation is that they are usually completely devoid of perhaps the key actor in the process of building stewardship – the owner or investor. Thus the proceedings, being already predicated on the primacy of conservation per se, tend to have a self-serving academic flavour and reach conclusions *in abstracto*, lacking the vital ingredient that transforms analysis and aspiration into enactment – executive responsibility. Alternatively, they become an exercise in show-and-tell, featuring case studies narrating, and generally seeking to justify, what has already happened. The object of the current investigation is to examine and try to clarify the 'real world' circumstances in which the issues of authenticity are pertinent and played out.

Figure 2.1
The fire at Notre-
Dame, Paris, in April
2019 has presented the
ultimate conservation
conundrum.

After Ruskin and Morris, it is generally the propositions of the Austrian art historian Alois Riegl that provide the baseline for contemporary discussions of authenticity. His essay *The Modern Cult of Monuments: Its Character and Its Origin* (1903) defined a framework of values whereby conservators could achieve conceptual precision to inform their strategies for care and intervention in heritage assets, highlighting 'age-value', with its attendant patina, as the crucial factor in the definition of authenticity.[2]

Riegl's analysis privileged the state of the artefact 'as found' as the primary entity in which authenticity inhered, since the effects of time were an intrinsic part of its evidential essence that could not be re-created. This would become a key influence in the formulation of later 20th-century conservation charters, including the Athens Charter of 1931 and the Venice Charter of 1964 (see p 56), but although the doctrine provides helpful philosophical ballast for arguments against excessive or speculative restoration, it does not enable the practitioner to avoid the difficulties of attributing relative significance to an asset in the context of an actual project. Much that age may have contributed to a Modern building may not be credited as 'age-value'. Moreover, the assumed scenario of a venerable Modern building rich in senile character and in a state of noble abandonment is usually inapplicable. More often than not, the said 'heritage asset' is disfigured through neglect and/or ill-considered interventions, and must prove itself capable of beneficial future use in order to be judged worthy of further investment.

Echoing Riegl's theories, the next most widely referenced 'modern' definition of authenticity is that of Walter Benjamin in his essay *The Work of Art in the Age of Mechanical Reproduction*:

Even the most perfect reproduction of a work of art is lacking in one element: its presence in time and space, its unique existence at the place where it happens to be. This unique existence of the work of art determined the history to which it was subject throughout the time of its existence. This includes the changes which it may have suffered in physical condition over the years as well as the various changes in its ownership. The traces of the first can be revealed only by chemical or physical analyses which it is impossible to perform on a reproduction; changes of ownership are subject to a tradition which must be traced from the situation of the original. The presence of the original is the prerequisite to the concept of authenticity… The whole sphere of authenticity is outside technical – and, of course, not only technical – reproducibility.[3]

Claiming originality of fabric and proof of provenance as his key criteria, Benjamin's investigation was focused primarily on works of fine art, photography and film and sought to highlight the difference between manual reproduction, which of course had persisted for centuries, and 'process reproduction', which he identified as distinctively modern in its implications for authenticity. The former was more commonly associated with forgery, counterfeit paintings and the like where, as we most commonly witness it, the preoccupation with separating the genuine from the fake translates directly into either multimillion-pound value or utter worthlessness. However, even forgery still depended upon 'craft', albeit directed towards dubious ends. (Indeed, we are now familiar with what might be called the Van Meegeren subgenre of forgeries so finely crafted as to acquire significant value – and even forgeries of themselves – in their own right.)

Process reproduction, on the other hand, tended to result in a different type of loss of authenticity inasmuch as it involved multiplication, relocation and a greater independence of the reproduction from the original. In the mid-1930s, when Benjamin was writing, the explosion of this type of reproduction in the proliferation of art (as distinct from industrial products) might be regarded as still in its relative infancy – as compared with, say, the situation some 35 years later when John Berger examined the impact on meaning in art in his famous study *Ways of Seeing*,[4] when any undergraduate could have a 'perfect' facsimile of Leonardo da Vinci's *Mona Lisa* on their study wall for a few pounds. Again, much of Berger's focus was on the changed meanings of fine art in the era of mass 'image culture'. Incisive and ground-breaking, his analysis – though saying nothing specific about architecture, Modern or otherwise – also fastened upon the key factor in Benjamin's analysis – *process* reproduction. Now this does indeed have relevance for the consideration of authenticity in Modern built heritage inasmuch as 'process reproduction' is very likely to have been involved in the resultant asset – i.e. the original building as an assembly of industrially produced repeating components. This was already a feature of Victorian construction that also troubled Messrs Ruskin and Morris through the removal of the craftsman's (author's) hand from direct creation of the eventual artefact.

THE ICOMOS VERSION

Coming closer still in time, one might have hoped that, under the authoritative aegis of ICOMOS (the International Council on Monuments and Sites), the conference of self-declared experts that took place in Nara, Japan, in 1994 to specifically examine the concept of authenticity would have nailed the issue once and for all. Yet when one gets to the crucial paragraph of the ensuing conference communiqué it only serves to underscore the problems of relativism.

All judgements about values attributed to cultural properties as well as the credibility of related information sources may differ from culture to culture, and even within the same culture. It is thus not possible to base judgements of values and authenticity within fixed criteria. On the contrary, the respect due to all cultures requires that heritage properties must be considered and judged within the cultural contexts to which they belong.[5]

It was perhaps somewhat ironic that this declaration should emanate from a conference in Japan, where in the tradition of *Shikinen Sengu*, Shinto shrines are ritually demolished and rebuilt every 20 years, apparently without any inhibition as to loss of authenticity. Much the same conclusion was reached nearly 20 years later in the Xi'an Declaration on the Conservation of Modern Heritage in Different Contexts (Docomomo, China, 2013), when again the relativity of cultural interpretation was reinforced.

Valuable as these critical investigations might be in clarifying the varying interpretations of authenticity in the post-industrial age, they only get us so far in relation to *architectural* authenticity and its role in modern building conservation. This is principally due to the inherent differences in both the production and the consumption of architecture as an art form – assuming this is allowed an identity separate and distinct from 'mere' building. (I will bypass that other gaping rabbit hole posited by Nikolaus Pevsner's famous distinction between a bicycle shed and Lincoln Cathedral.[6])

So, can 'aura' – Benjamin's definitive term denoting the unique quality of an authentic artistic creation – realistically be entirely transferrable to the complex and multifarious processes of designing, assembling, operating and, in due course, restoring a Modern building? The implication is that the attribute of 'significance' demanded by listing criteria, and invariably privileged in conservation charters, would ideally be fulfilled only where either no change whatsoever had occurred in a building following its original completion, or where all the cumulative effects of change from inception up to the point of consideration were honoured as 'age-value'. Yet in either scenario, as practising architects well know, change – intentional or casual, beneficial or malign – begins virtually the day after a new building has been handed over to its owner. How many practitioners, upon conducting the inspection that follows a Defects Liability Period (traditionally one year after Practical Completion), have been confronted by a building that is already no longer quite the one that they either designed or accepted at handover – not on account of the (hopefully few) defects, but due to numerous subtle, or not so subtle, interventions arising from patterns of usage. How are these to be weighed on the scales of authenticity? The notorious interventions of the residents at Le Corbusier's housing estate at Pessac, near Bordeaux (Figure 2.2), are only the best-known example – albeit they apparently did not unduly trouble the architect himself, to judge from his reported reaction, *'Vous savez, c'est toujours la vie qui a raison, l'architecte qui a tort.'*[7] In the light of Le Corbusier's comment, one could debate whether the restorations that since followed are more or less 'authentic' than the first occupants' alterations.

Figure 2.2
Cité Frugès at Pessac, near Bordeaux, by Le Corbusier, 1924–26. The occupants' later interventions can be seen in this photograph.

DOCOMOMO STEPS IN

Like it or not, one is immediately precipitated into the metrics of alteration by degree. At this point, the leading international *Modern* conservation agency – Docomomo (an organisation dedicated to the **do**cumentation and **co**nservation of buildings, sites and neighbourhoods of the **Mo**dern **Mo**vement) – enters the discussion with an important new proposition. In 2001 the UNESCO World Heritage Centre, ICOMOS and Docomomo launched a joint programme for the identification, documentation and promotion of the built heritage of the 19th and 20th centuries – the Programme on Modern Heritage. Having established that the World Heritage List could include nominations for the Modern Movement, Docomomo proposed a wider definition of authenticity to include authenticity of the idea, authenticity of form, authenticity of construction and details, and authenticity of materials. It is the first of these – authenticity of the idea, or concept – that opens up a new dimension. Arguing that the sheer quantity of modern construction, ranging from 'the icon to the ordinary', necessitated particular selectivity, the notion of conceptual preservation by documentation – the Do of Docomomo – acquired a new importance. In the words of its report to ICOMOS:

> As the twentieth century was above all a century of the common, it is important to bear in mind that not everything can be preserved: selection is crucial. Docomomo emphasized that the idea, the concept, is more important than physical form. For the greater part of Modern Movement architecture and town planning, instead of preservation, comprehensive documentation has offered a good alternative to safeguard ideas, heritage and memory.[8]

The proposition that in today's world of virtual reality, authenticity could now validly reside in the digitised record, opens up a whole new dimension of philosophical speculation. Would this mean that, for example, Jørn Utzon's beguiling but unbuildable sketch of Sydney Opera House shared, or even appropriated, some of the authenticity of the actual building itself? Should high-resolution photographs of the original Barcelona Pavilion (Figure 2.3), built in 1929 by Mies van der Rohe (and demolished the following year), be accorded greater weight in terms of authenticity than the exemplary reconstruction undertaken in 1986?

But perhaps these are just recreational riddles, and of greater import is the implication for practical conservation if 'the concept' is to be accorded primacy, for thereby reinstatement of an architect's original design, which involved no speculation whatever, might be regarded as more authentic than the altered version passed down by history, with all its arbitrary ramifications of 'age-value', including worthless patina (at best) or wholesale dereliction.

As an extreme example, the immaculate restoration in 2016–2020 of the Narkomfin Building in Moscow (Figures 2.4 and 2.5) must surely be regarded as of more value than its prior state of 'authentic' (and amply documented) ruination.[9] Indeed one might well ask for whose conceivable benefit would have been such continued 'authentic' ruination other than perhaps a niche clique of architectural tourists seeking physical souvenirs of Constructivism's demise.

Such reasoning would offer welcome justification for the technical interventions usually necessary in rescuing Modern buildings – concrete remediation, window replacement, performance upgrade generally – all of which can be difficult to reconcile with the equation of authenticity with heritage value 'as found'.

Figure 2.3 a and b.
The Barcelona Pavilion,
Barcelona, by Mies van der
Rohe, 1929, re-created in 1986.

Figure 2.4 a, b and c.
Narkomfin Building, Moscow,
by Moisei Ginzburg, 1932.
The building was in a state of
utter dereliction before the
restoration, as can be seen in
these images of the rooftop
solarium in 2006 (2.4a), the
planters on the east façade in
2016 (2.4b) and the east façade,
general view, in 2017 (2.4c).

Figure 2.5
Narkomfin Building, Moscow,
as restored in 2016–2020 by
Alexey Ginzburg, grandson
of the original architect,
Moisei Ginzburg.

THE SHIP OF THESEUS

Figure 2.6
The Ship of Theseus – an ancient riddle of authenticity.

We are heading back to the relativism of Nara, or – to revert to the court of first instance – the Ship of Theseus (Figure 2.6), a thought experiment that addresses the question of whether an object that has had all of its components replaced remains fundamentally the same object.[10]

But tempting as it is to luxuriate in the company of Heraclitus, Plato, Hobbes and Locke (not to mention Noam Chomsky) in seeking to resolve the puzzle as a philosophical task, we must try not to stray too far from the matter in hand, that is, an analysis of authenticity in the context of Modern architectural heritage. Here it must be recognised that a redefinition of great importance has occurred within the period covered by this book. Insofar as 'heritage' is – at least in regulatory terms – what the government, or its advisory agency Historic England, says it is, then it must be admitted that a decisive change took place in 1987 when the age criterion of eligibility for listing was reduced to 30 years (see p 10).[11] This effectively meant that whereas previously the building in question was necessarily constructed before the lifetime of anyone involved in its listing and might also be readily expected to have become an object of popular affection or at least respect, now neither of these conditions could be assumed. Indeed, the primacy of *age* in the eligibility of candidates for listing is explicitly addressed in Historic England's advice that 'all buildings built before 1700 which survive in anything like their *original condition* [author's emphasis] are likely to be listed, as are most buildings built between 1700 and 1850,' whereas 'particularly careful selection is required for buildings from the period after 1945. Buildings less than 30 years old are not normally considered to be of special architectural or historic interest because they have yet to stand the test of time.'[12]

'The test of time' – an expression apparently dating only from c. 1800, according to Christine Ammer[13] – is one to which we will return later. For now, it is the linkage of buildings of previous ages with the criterion of 'original condition' that is key. What this is effectively saying is that the heritage value of such residues, in other words their authenticity, inheres in their *fabric* – and arguably not just fabric but fabric in its *original condition* – a qualification that ostensibly even contradicts the concept of patina as an enhancement of age-value. The test is anyway an objective one, relying essentially on the evidential verification of originality – and of course the accuracy of dating. At the same time, this differentiation inevitably means that whereas the listing of old buildings is usually underpinned by popular consent, the listing of modern ones perforce relies on the advocacy of experts and for that reason alone (apart from others) is likely to be controversial. In the latter case, the statutory criterion of 'special architectural and historic interest' is by no means necessarily synonymous with original fabric. Such 'special interest' may now inhere in all sorts of values apart from that (if any) of original fabric – conceptual, technical, associational, rarity and more. In short, the test has become subjective. Indeed, Historic England itself distinguishes authenticity from integrity, defining authenticity as 'those characteristics that most truthfully reflect and embody the cultural heritage values of a place' while acknowledging that 'retaining the authenticity of a place is not always achieved by retaining as much of the existing fabric as is technically possible'.[14]

It is now that Walter Benjamin's problem of 'process reproduction' becomes entangled with the legislative criterion of special architectural and historic interest. How does the process reproduction that is inherent in the making of Modern buildings affect their authenticity? For example, is the once radical *concept* of a curtain wall of greater 'special interest' than the materiality of its constituent windows? The question is only compounded by the likelihood that many, if not all, of a Modern building's individual components are themselves the product of standard industrial multiplication (i.e. process reproduction), such that any given component within a 'significant' building may differ in no material way from an identical component in another 'insignificant' one – except only by (perhaps) being used in the former in a more interesting or innovative way.

LIKE-FOR-LIKE

A conventional means of easing the difficulty is to suggest that authenticity is a cumulative phenomenon that increases in direct ratio to the quantum of surviving original fabric in the building considered as a whole – in other words the measure of its intactness. This criterion could be said to have been echoed – even reinforced – by the Enterprise and Regulatory Reform Act 2013 (ERRA) which enables the heritage identified in a particular building to be disaggregated into items of greater, lesser or no 'special interest'. As another way of simplifying matters, the conservation authorities routinely apply the workaday rule of 'like-for-like' as an acceptable justification for replacing original components or materials with well-matched substitutes. Indeed this 'joker card' may even be deployed as a mutually agreed means of avoiding the procedures of obtaining listed building consent for material upgrades. Anyone visiting a medieval cathedral in Europe will be familiar with the adjacent *chantier* of the mason's yard, where brand new stones are in a continuous process of production as substitutes for decayed original ones, ideally to matching profiles from identical geological sources. Yet the knowledge that a substantial proportion of Amiens or Reims now consists of facsimile masonry does not seem to cause undue ethical discomfort. A similarly substantial number of windows at Berthold Lubetkin's Highpoint apartment block (Figure 2.7), in Highgate, London, where windows account for nearly half of the façade area, are now also replacements, yet its (Grade I) significance remains substantially undiminished.

In the case of MoMo (Modern Movement) windows in particular, previous replacement with poor-quality substitutes frequently enables their further, second-generation replacement in a conservation project to restore a greater measure of visual – if not material – authenticity (as well as improved performance). Is it therefore not so much a case of *what* is changed, as how well it is done?

Moving from the reproduction of discrete components to the repair of built 'fabric' as such, there has been considerable debate in recent years over the proprieties of what might be termed 'heritage grade' concrete conservation. In 2018 the Getty Conservation Institute, in LA, published its didactic survey *Concrete – Case Studies in Conservation Practice*, promoting a series of model examples in which defective concrete in MoMo structures dating from

Figure 2.7
Highpoint apartments,
Highgate, London, Lubetkin
and Tecton, 1935. Windows
constitute nearly half of the
façade area of this Grade I
listed building.

1928 to 1991 have been remediated with particularly conscientious care to mimic original appearances.[15] More recently still, the Getty programme has been supplemented with a specific 'concrete charter' – *Conservation Principles for Concrete of Cultural Significance* (2020) – which it might be expected would provide definitive guidance on the matter.[16] Admirable and helpful as these initiatives are, however, the same problems remain in relation to judging best practice in the replacement of defective concrete, and the loss of original fabric and surface characteristics (including patina) that this almost invariably entails. The question as to whether concrete patina (in common parlance 'grime' – though often the less benign phenomenon of carbonation-induced spalling) is regarded as a 'significant' contribution to age-value, or merely unsightly, is one that can perhaps only be answered in the individual case, but it is legitimate to ask whether the soiled masterpieces of the early 'white Modern' period – even if not thereby suffering progressive fabric damage – are rendered more or less authentic by the effects of ageing. It might be contested that such visual degradation, by changing their original message of progress and youthful optimism, actually diminishes *conceptual* authenticity and accordingly mandates restitution of their pristine original appearance – cultural significance outranking original (but now degraded) fabric. Such arguments apparently provide quite adequate justification for cleaning the works of the 'Old Masters', where wonderful revelations emerge from the removal of umpteen layers of dirt and varnish. Indeed, the equivalent cleaning of degraded concrete is sometimes simply justified by the argument that it helps redeem this troublesome material from its widespread unpopularity. Alternatively, if the damage wrought by time and (usually) inadequate or ill-informed maintenance is to be privileged as offering greater authenticity, then concrete conservators will have some considerable obstacles to overcome, since most remediation techniques must begin with cleaning and removal of deleterious surface layers to gain access to a viable repair stratum for remediation to begin. Presumably William Morris would argue that continuous gentle care would have retained the original appearance of modern concrete and thereby have avoided the vexed question of whether to remove 'authentic' patina after years of neglect – a theoretical proposition that would cast doubt on the merits of age-value anyway. Unfortunately we can only speculate, as the problems of concrete carbonation were not ones that William Morris was obliged to address.

So, the provisional wisdom seems to be that in cases where the concrete was originally coated (or subsequently overcoated and incapable of effective remediation without coating removal), replacement coatings are legitimate as the remediated concrete they cover would not have been visible anyway. Even here, though, care should be taken to avoid obscuring original shuttering patterns or other authentic evidence of original working practices. The rescue operation undertaken (2001–4) at the (originally coated) Isokon/Lawn Road Flats in Camden, London, while requiring widespread concrete replacement and complete recoating, nevertheless was careful to retain such revealing evidence of the uneven standards of workmanship of 1934 – as is highly apparent in certain lights and viewpoints (Figure 2.8; see also Figures 1.20 and 1.23).

In cases where concrete was originally uncoated, however, the application of new coatings, unless transparent and matt (typically a migrating anti-carbonation corrosion inhibitor), is ill-advised on conservation grounds since such new coatings would obscure the authentic fairface. In such cases this underscores the importance of replicating the original surface, colour and weathering characteristics in the areas of replacement concrete, with only moderate prior cleaning employing all the bespoke mortar recipes and hand-crafted finishing techniques that fairface matching entails. The observation by those involved in recent repairs at Sir Denys Lasdun's National Theatre, London, that 'it is easier to conserve a medieval stone cathedral than an in situ concrete building with a specialist finish' is something to bear in mind the next time we visit Amiens.[17]

AUTHENTICITY IN CHANGE

Yet there are also cases where even the touchstone of 'original fabric' and its extent – as a measure of authenticity – may not be entirely applicable either. The two Modern houses noted in Chapter 1 by Ernö Goldfinger and Patrick Gwynne, both dating from 1938, that I was involved in restoring for the National Trust, had both undergone significant change since their original completion. Elements of fabric, various components, even substantial interior spatial rearrangement to accommodate changing patterns of use, had occurred over the intervening 60-odd years. Yet the distinctive factor in both cases was that all these changes had been conceived and implemented by the original architects themselves, who had also occupied the properties during the whole period. In other words, the changes could themselves be regarded as 'authentic', and rather than detracting from authenticity, might in fact be argued to have enriched the narratives, or age-value, that these properties now reveal to their visitors. By analogy, reverting to the Ship of Theseus and the metaphysics of identity, how would it affect the analysis if all the interventions in his ship had been carried out personally by Theseus himself? And what if, rather than replacing the original defective planking with like-for-like new timbers, he had sought to upgrade his ship's performance by using aluminium or fibre glass? It is here, perhaps, that the debate descends from a philosophical discourse to a parlour game.

It has to be admitted that there is no universal template by which authenticity can be measured and that the sages of Nara may have been right after all. Modern architectural conservation has certainly granted itself more leeway than its historic cousin in widening the definition of authenticity, and some of the arguments and examples considered above can be invoked for assistance. Still, in the picturesque words of one commentary, 'Today authenticity is a challenging term closely connected to conservation ethics, characterised both by high expectations and by a kind of "shimmering vagueness".'[18]

So, in the end, it just has to be argued out in each and every individual case and in each and every cultural context. In short, the responsibility for assessing the merit of authenticity as a factor within a wider calculus of heritage values cannot be evaded. Or, in the wise words of Arthur Drexler, 'The problem of deciding what is important is a function of human intelligence, and to suppose that its difficulties can be avoided is to advocate that we make ourselves stupid.'[19]

Figure 2.8
The Isokon/Lawn Road Flats, Camden, north London, by Wells Coates, 1934. The restoration in the early 21st century retained the original shuttering patterns.

3
Charters

The intrinsic ethical dimension of heritage stewardship, whether historic or modern, is reflected in the proliferation of charters and other guidance instruments across the field. This chapter looks at this phenomenon with particular reference to the extent to which such documents may serve the cause of modern conservation.

AS GOOD A STARTING POINT AS ANY to initiate a discussion on conservation charters – at least in the UK – is the formation of the Society for the Protection of Ancient Buildings by William Morris, Philip Webb and others and their widely regarded SPAB Manifesto. Much of its enduring authority must derive from its date (1877 to be precise – 10 years before Le Corbusier was born) and from the fact that the society's prescriptions were largely focused on the preservation of medieval churches (Figure 3.1), imparting a distinctly moral dimension to its precepts. Indeed, the SPAB ethic of continuous gentle repair and avoidance of speculative restoration so prevalent at the time is still widely regarded as unassailable, not only in the context of historic ecclesiastical architecture, but also that of other ages and building typologies.

However, it must be acknowledged that – the clue being in the organisation's name – the SPAB maxims so eminently applicable to 'ancient' buildings may not necessarily be quite as relevant to Modern ones. The SPAB charter has certainly established its place in history, but it is not immune from critical review now. A century and a half later, the circumstances have to be reconsidered.

THE CHARTER INDUSTRY

The SPAB crops up elsewhere in this book, but meanwhile it may be helpful to make a few general observations about charters, which must surely catch the attention of anyone surveying the narrative of Modern architecture. The first is the sheer proliferation of such documents over the 20th century and indeed beyond. Of course, the MoMo (Modern Movement) pioneers themselves started all this at the outset with their torrent of manifestos and declarations. In his copious anthology of 1964, Ulrich Conrads assembled no fewer than 68 such documents over the 60 years from 1903 to 1963, including examples by Henry van de Velde, Adolf Loos, Bruno Taut, Walter Gropius, Le Corbusier, Mies van der Rohe, Kazimir Malevich, Louis Kahn and Buckminster Fuller – among numerous others.[1] Even this selection was limited just to those examples between 1900 and the date of publication. There could easily have been many more.

So just what is it that impels people, mainly architects in this instance, to write these declamatory texts? To whom are they directed, what purpose are they intended to serve – and do they serve it? The obvious common factor – the urge to proclaim a credo, take a stand, 'plant a flag' or generally to define and self-identify – almost invariably has to do with articulating a particular cause *at its inception*. The inception element is important. All innovators need to believe they are at the beginning of their mission, that it cannot start without them. Almost invariably, therefore, the texts are propositions of what it is deemed will, or should, happen in the near, preferably immediate, future and are written in critical reaction to the allegedly fatal error of prolonging the status quo. Also implicit is the intention to rouse an audience, to recruit support for the cause in question. Indeed, in many cases the declarations emanate from a small group of like-minded souls armed and impatient to commit to a struggle that in the absence of substantive achievement can as yet only be waged in words. The manifestos might be characterised as affidavits of intention, claims on future history, attempts to impose a preferred reading of its outcomes in advance. Often it seems they are the products of frustration at the lack of work of the kind that they propose. Conversely, as expressions of intention they also

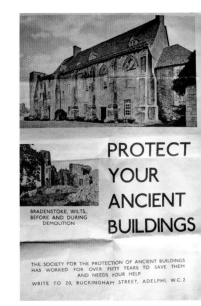

Figure 3.1
A SPAB poster dating from c.1929, campaigning for the preservation of Bradenstoke Priory, in Wiltshire.

become the criteria against which results are later to be measured. In some cases, the creed is vindicated in the realisation, but in many more it is not. Yet whether fulfilled or otherwise, there is something profoundly poignant in the aspirational quality of these texts by the now long-dead MoMo avant-garde. Taken together, it is hard to think of another architectural period or movement that has been launched on such a wave of verbal idealism.

But looking back from this end of the story, the MoMo heritage community likewise has not exactly been idle in producing an equivalent plethora of documents in setting out its stall. Of course, the older examples relate to historic, as distinct from recent, heritage. But they have effectively established the didactic tone and prescriptive structure typical of the genre. The earliest 20th-century example, the Athens Charter of 1931, identified seven objectives that have come to characterise the typology.[2]

- Establish organisations for restoration advice.
- Ensure projects are reviewed with knowledgeable criticism.
- Establish national legislation to preserve historic sites.
- Re-bury excavations which were not to be restored.
- Allow the use of modern techniques and materials in restoration work.
- Place historical sites under custodial protection.
- Protect the area surrounding historic sites.

Thenceforward, to recite only the most familiar from the post-war period, we have the Venice Charter of 1964; the European Charter of the Architectural Heritage of 1975; the Burra Charter of 1979; the Granada Convention of 1985; the Eindhoven Statement of 1990; the Nara Document on Authenticity of 1994; the Intach Charter of 2004; the Xi'an Declaration of 2005; the English Heritage Conservation Principles of 2008; the Xi'an Declaration of 2013;[3] the Madrid Document of 2014; the APT Principles for Renewing Modernism of 2016[4] – not to mention the ensuing later editions of many of the above. Often the product of a conference of experts, they serve as reassuring and tangible evidence of an agreement achieved, in contradistinction to more familiar but less synoptic 'collected conference papers', which may reflect no such unanimity, have no equivalent concision, and are seldom 'campaigning documents' as such.

Another conspicuous feature of the heritage industry's proclamations is their geographical signature. Indeed, we are usually more aware of their origins in place than in time – be it Venice, Burra, Granada, Eindhoven, Nara, Xi'an, Madrid, Seoul, New Delhi, etc., etc. One might mistakenly assume that these territorial labels betoken some local limitation on the respective document's universality of application, but the texts themselves rarely display any such inhibition. On the contrary, to take only the most conscientious recent example, the ICOMOS Madrid Document (now Madrid–New Delhi; Figure 3.2), the fact that it has since been translated into English, Spanish, French, Russian, Italian, Finnish, German, Japanese, Portuguese, Mandarin, Hindi, Basque and Catalan testifies to the apparently limitless horizons of its authors. So, the names of locational origin turn out to be merely for convenience of citation.

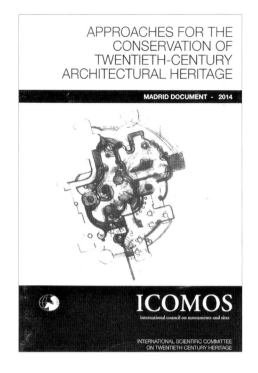

Figure 3.2 a and b.
The Madrid Document, ICOMOS (International Council on Monuments and Sites), 2014 (3.2a), which is now the Madrid–New Delhi Document, ICOMOS, 2017 (3.2b).

MODERN EXAMPLES

Systematic comparative study of this range of documents reveals a generic quality that suggests a striking measure of consistency across the field of heritage, despite marginal differences in style and emphasis. In the case of the Modern Movement, this might not be very surprising given its diaspora across all corners of the globe, notwithstanding the diversity of its mutations in this process. Nevertheless, it may be illuminating to compare and contrast briefly a couple of the most pertinent examples of the type – the Eindhoven Statement originating at the founding conference of Docomomo in Eindhoven in 1990, and the Madrid Document emanating 21 years later in 2011 from an international scientific committee of ICOMOS (with later editions in 2014 and 2017) – as both these endeavours were specifically addressed to those engaged in the field of *modern* conservation. First the Eindhoven Statement which, with admirable brevity, proposes the following six-part credo (in its original 1990 iteration).

1. Bring the significance of the architecture of the Modern Movement to the attention of the public, the authorities, the professionals and the educational community concerned with the built environment.
2. Identify and promote the recording of the works of the Modern Movement.
3. Foster the development of appropriate techniques and methods of conservation and disseminate knowledge of these throughout the profession.
4. Oppose destruction and disfigurement of significant works.
5. Identify and attract funding for documentation and conservation.
6. Explore and develop knowledge of the Modern Movement.

In a later revision of 2014, additional text was included to reflect the growing concern for adaptive reuse and environmental sustainability.[5]

Now consider the ICOMOS Madrid Document (second edition) of 2014, which after a familiar preamble calling urgent attention to the contemporary crisis of endangered 20th-century heritage conveys its (nine) messages in a similar tone.

1. Identify and assess cultural significance.

2. Apply appropriate conservation planning methodology.

3. Research the technical aspects of 20th-century architectural heritage.

4. Acknowledge and manage pressures for change which are constant.

5. Manage change sensitively.

6. Ensure a respectful approach to additions and interventions.

7. Respect the authenticity and integrity of the heritage site.

8. Give consideration to environmental sustainability.

9. Promote and celebrate 20th-century architectural heritage with the wider community.[6]

The document substantiates these articles with several subclauses of more detailed advice, but the whole is essentially summarised in just four overarching themes.

• Advance knowledge, understanding and significance.

• Manage change to conserve cultural significance.

• Encourage environmental sustainability.

• Promote clear interpretation and communication.

Both documents are written in the imperative mood as a series of orders addressed to 'all those involved in heritage conservation processes' who are credited with the executive capacity to enact some or all of them, and who otherwise would presumably go astray if left unguided. But it also becomes clear that the respective documents, while seeking similar end goals, are concerned with distinctly different tasks – an aspect that could be explained by the period of some 20-plus years that separates them. The identification and recording of significant MoMo works as promoted by the Eindhoven Statement was a vital pioneering prerequisite to mobilising the modern conservation movement as such, with the compilation of National Registers being of critical help to the countries concerned in understanding their own recent architectural history and building stock. Any systematic opposition to their destruction would only ever be possible at national and international level if the pre-eminent buildings were first assessed and prioritised. In essence, the Eindhoven Statement was an agenda, a series of self-imposed resolutions, an *aide-mémoire* directed at the new organisation itself. Two decades on, with the modern conservation initiative increasingly well established, ICOMOS was able to focus more on matters of good practice and conservation technique.

Docomomo has certainly achieved considerable progress in the compilation of its registers and has sought to impose a measure of enforcement by requiring evidence of 'homework' on the part of its many national chapters in the two-year periods between conferences as a condition of acquiring voting rights at its biennial council meetings – albeit these sessions are characterised by almost complete unanimity of the attendees and the homework itself is necessarily evidenced by progress of national registers, rather than that of the less measurable objectives.

The ICOMOS documents are at best advisory and have no official status beyond the imprimatur of the sponsoring agency – not that in cases such as ICOMOS, an NGO advisor of UNESCO, this should be underestimated. Formal enforcement – to the extent that it occurs – belongs in a separate sphere of national legislative governance and policy-making. One would be unlikely to see copies of the Madrid Document pinned on the wall of a property executive's boardroom or contractor's site hut, and only marginally less unlikely in the office of a local authority conservation officer. So, while a charter explicitly concerned with '20th-century' architectural heritage must surely help cultivate and disseminate important common beliefs and promote a degree of solidarity across the modern conservation community, it is hard to quantify its precise impact in practice. Reference to its precepts may be assumed to occur in the development and assessment of scheme proposals in a general sense, depending on the conscientiousness of the participants, but it is difficult to cite specific instances 'chapter and verse' and reference is probably more common as a form of retrospective commentary.

THE POWER OF CHARTERS

So, one is left to speculate on the ultimate efficacy of such documents. If one considers the main types of stakeholder in the field – property owners, planning authorities, building users, construction professionals and other (non-statutory) conservation bodies – it might be suggested that they each have a particular kind of 'power', graduating in this line-up from hard to soft. The power of a building owner is self-evident inasmuch as he or she has executive dominion over the assets within the limits of the law; that of a planning authority is both active and reactive insofar as policy may be promulgated *in abstracto* yet remain unfulfilled without the investment of others, while specific development proposals may be accepted or denied, but not necessarily initiated.[7] Building users or tenants (corporate or otherwise) may or may not choose to use or inhabit the buildings that owners/developers – the supply side – make available, withdrawing or relocating their occupation in unfavourable circumstances, or as may be. But what of the other conservation bodies (a wide category admittedly, but one in which surely belong the authors of charters)? Their 'power' – if it may be so called – arguably the softest of all, stems only from the proponents' commitment and the credence attributed to their proclamations and campaigns. Their charters are but the weapons of the dispossessed. The equity which they seek, or for which they struggle, is not real, it is intergenerational and their efficacy resides only in their 'power' of persuasion.

The bid for universality is thus both the strength and the limitation of charters. As aspirational statements they are generally unexceptionable and must certainly help to promote a doctrinal consensus among conservation professionals; as 'how-to' guides they only get you so far. The most frequently used key words – 'significant', 'appropriate', 'sensitively', 'respectful', etc. – which may appear unarguable in abstract, are open to considerable interpretation in a specific context. It is in the gap between such idealistic advice and the realities of project design and site practice that the real challenges of conservation must be worked out. And in this arena the cause of Modern heritage, even if it is designated, can take no special privileges for granted – it must fight its corner against equally pressing, and not necessarily compatible, considerations of operational and commercial viability and the many other claims of a generally unsympathetic culture besides.

However, there have been endeavours at filling this gap between the Olympian tenets of charters and the exigencies of practice in the field. Perhaps the bravest fairly recent (and also official) attempt at nailing the central concept of heritage significance and advising how it may be managed in a context of constant change is to be found in the document produced by English Heritage in 2008, initially for its own internal use, and thereafter by others in the field as an 'industry standard'. This document, *Conservation Principles, Policies and Guidance,* subsequently updated, is presented as a management tool rather than a list of commands, and is generally expressed in the modal auxiliary 'should' as a series of recommendations derived from six generic principles or definitions.[8] In fact, it is possible to apply the document almost as a *mode d'emploi*, following its directions almost as one might with an owner's DIY manual for operating a household appliance.

The much-used and pivotal term in current conservation charters and discourse – 'significance' – is deconstructed into four constituent 'values':

- evidential value: the potential of a place to yield evidence about past human activity
- historical value: the ways in which past people, events and aspects of life can be connected through a place to the present – it tends to be illustrative or associative
- aesthetic value: the ways in which people draw sensory and intellectual stimulation from a place
- communal value: the meanings of a place for the people who relate to it, or for whom it figures in their collective experience or memory.

These four categories turn out to have an impressive pedigree. Indeed, with a little allowance for semantic variation, they may be traced back three centuries through the writings of William Lipe (1984), Alois Riegl (1903) and as far as John Vanbrugh (1709), whose references – 'remains of distant times'; 'historical association with people and events'; 'magnificence or curious workmanship'; and 'linkage to extraordinary occasions' – might roughly be equated with English Heritage's 'evidential', 'historical', 'aesthetic' and 'communal' values respectively.[9] Meanwhile, the Burra Charter of 1979 and Granada Convention of 1985 employ almost identical nomenclature as English Heritage.

Of course, these values also aim at universality and are not specific to Modernism, but English Heritage's *Conservation Principles* go further than the prescriptions of most charters by acknowledging and accommodating the reality that many heritage assets may exhibit both a range of types of value as well as gradations of quality within these types.[10] Also acknowledged is the likelihood of conflicting interests and the need to search for a sustainable balance in their reconciliation – even if this can only be ameliorated through mitigation when otherwise impossible. The description of the change management process in a logical sequence of steps is as pragmatic as could be, yet *Conservation Principles* remains an essentially generic document whose recommendations must still be tailored to a particular project or set of circumstances in order to be applicable in the field.

What this survey of charters (considered in the broadest sense) suggests is that even the best efforts of conservation jurisprudence to lay down rules for the correct stewardship of heritage (Modern or otherwise) perforce ultimately rely on the right reading of 'canonical texts' by those other parties in the process whose motives and priorities may lie elsewhere and may not be taken for granted. So, is there no further means of achieving closer traction between the 'chartists' and the objects of their concern? By what means, if any, may these different types of equity – proprietorial and intergenerational – be brought into closer and more meaningful conjunction?

PRECISION INSTRUMENTS

The answer is supplied by conservation plans, management guidelines and heritage partnership agreements. These tools, properly conceived and systematically applied, can indeed provide a meaningful reconciliation of the potentially diverging interests of various stakeholders in a given 'heritage' project. Such documents, for which there are now well-established templates, may come in many shapes and sizes but they share several crucial features.[11]

- They are effectively bespoke 'charters' for a specific heritage asset.
- They entail analysis of the special architectural interest – or 'significance' – of the specific heritage asset/s involved and active cultivation of stakeholder recognition of these attributes.
- They provide guidance on the management of change and clarity on when formal authorisation is required, when it is unnecessary and when it is unlikely to be given.
- They include, and seek a consensus among, all parties with a legitimate interest in the asset and contributing to the process.
- They provide for regular review of the guidance and its updating as required.

These tasks, perhaps most analogous to negotiating a treaty, effectively bring the generalities of charters into direct engagement with the specifics of the particular heritage asset, preferably in a context of constructive discussion leading to a sustainable consensus. Such undertakings also ideally take place outside the constraints and circumstances of a live building project, when the various parties may have already adopted entrenched positions. This still leaves open the question of document status, which will depend to some extent on the public or private ownership of the asset and the nature of the instrument – whether conservation management plan, management guidelines, heritage partnership agreement or other. In any scenario, there should be a process of 'formal adoption' whereby all concerned (or their representatives) are enjoined to put their signature to the document. In certain circumstances the document may acquire a quasi-legal status, and in the case of assets in public ownership may be incorporated into formal planning policy, by becoming a Supplementary Planning Document – for example as has been achieved in the case of the Barbican and Golden Lane Listed Building Management Guidelines (Figures 3.3 and 3.4).[12]

Figure 3.3
The Barbican Listed Building
Management Guidelines,
prepared for the City of
London Corporation by Avanti
Architects, 2005.

Figure 3.4
Golden Lane Listed Building
Management Guidelines,
prepared for the City of
London Corporation by Avanti
Architects, 2007.

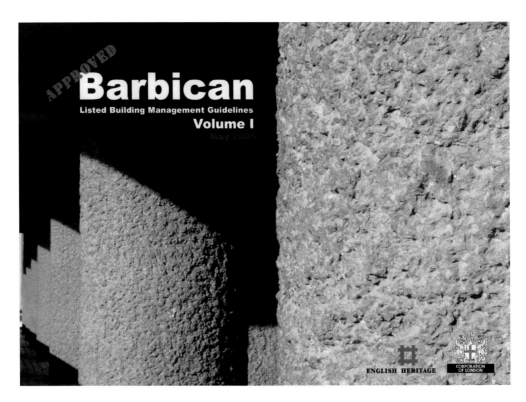

Even here, however, it must be noted that such documents cannot prescribe in a legally binding way what is, or is not, of 'heritage significance' within the meaning of the Planning (Listed Buildings and Conservations Areas) Act 1990.[13] Ultimately, this can only be settled in a court of law.

We seem to have come a long way from William Morris, but in plotting the changing focus in conservation charter documents from his day to ours it becomes evident that their prescriptions have become less partisan, more generic and increasingly preoccupied with 'heritage significance', whether that inheres in authentic fabric or a range of other more intangible values. But it is also evident that for the objectives of charters to be truly realised, a whole other layer of diligence is needed through the production of such instruments as management guidelines and conservation plans, which in effect operate as bespoke mini-charters for the assets in question.[14] Their great advantage over the charters themselves lies not only in their specificity, but also in the mutuality of engagement required of all stakeholders in their creation, especially in the Modern context where many of the said stakeholders may typically start from divergent viewpoints. Such inclusivity, when real and meaningful to all participants, is the key prerequisite of their traction and durability. In the progressive use of such instruments and the transactional processes they entail, must therefore surely lie vital opportunities for the beneficial revaluing and better stewardship of Modern architecture.[15]

4
Listing

The statutory designation of buildings by 'listing' is one of the key instruments in the governance of heritage of any period. This chapter considers the way this powerful tool has been variously applied and withheld in the conservation of Modern architecture, particularly that of the post-war period. A close review of the statutory texts and associated guidance is followed by analysis of a selection of key cases.

IT'S OVER HALF A CENTURY SINCE THE STATUTORY designation of Modern architecture began with the so-called 'Pevsner list' in the late 1960s (see p 8), yet the subject seems to have become hardly less controversial. In his foreword to the document published by English Heritage in 1992, *A Change of Heart – English Architecture since the War – A Policy for Protection*, which accompanied an exhibition launching that organisation's move to grapple with the listing of post-war architecture, Jocelyn Stevens wrote:

Our growing appreciation and understanding of Victorian, Edwardian and inter-war architecture – once derided and despised – have led to general acceptance that the best should be protected. No such consensus yet exists on post-war buildings… People still react passionately to post-war architecture. Many are hostile because of the failures that stick in the mind. But much is excellent and exciting, and it is possible now to assess both contemporary and subsequent criticism and the buildings themselves, especially those down to the late 1970s, with cool detachment.[1]

'Cool detachment' still sounds optimistic, to say the least, and even more than two decades after the 20th century ended those arguing for its architecture to be regarded as 'heritage' can still expect to face a sceptical audience. There are many reasons why Modern architecture remains unloved by so many – its sheer ubiquity and familiarity; the visibly industrialised basis of its production; its frequent technical mediocrity or downright failure; its association with post-war paternalistic forms of central or local government; the disparity between professional advocacy and actual performance; the alienating places and spaces that it so often created; and, perhaps most of all, nostalgia for what it displaced.

In the same booklet, historian Andrew Saint identified three strands in British Modern architecture – modernism of method, modernism of style and modernism of good manners – a simplified taxonomy to be sure, but still quite useful.[2] While public appreciation of Modernism *in toto* has at best been an uneven and disputatious affair, made more so by continual stereotypical media coverage and the disobliging pronouncements of public figures such as the Prince of Wales, there is little doubt that it is Saint's second category – the modernism of style – that remains most troublesome. Unsurprisingly, therefore, the process of elevating conspicuous examples of the Modern style through formal designation is only likely to heighten the controversy. However, it must be acknowledged that in the UK, post-war listing has grown substantially, both in numbers and typologies of buildings over the ensuing 30 years, entries having increased from 29 at the time of that exhibition to several hundred at the time of writing. One has only to compare the burgeoning size of successive editions of the publication *England – A Guide to Post-War Listed Buildings in England* as published in 2000, 2003 and 2015 to get a sense of this progress in the official revaluing of Modernism.[3]

The underlying problem of 'herit**age** recognition' has already been noted (see p 11), and here the clue is surely in the title: that is **age**. By way of illustration, one could juxtapose the superficially similar images of Stonehenge (Figure 4.1) and the Apollo Pavilion (Figure 4.2) – separated by approximately 4,500 years. The first is universally recognised as heritage. The second, though also (eventually) designated at Grade II* in 2011 and conscientiously restored (with public funding from the Heritage Lottery and Durham County Council) remains an object of controversy.

Figure 4.1
Stonehenge, Wiltshire,
c. 3000–2500 BC, is universally
recognised as heritage.

Figure 4.2
Apollo Pavilion, Peterlee,
County Durham, by Victor
Pasmore, 1960. The structure
was eventually listed in 2011.

The dramatic reduction in age brought about by the 30-year rule in 1987 that effectively replaced vint**age** with 'significance' as the primary test of eligibility must be reckoned the key difficulty in approaching the issue of modern listing with 'cool detachment'. So it is unsurprising that even for the cognoscenti there can be confusion as to why and how, for example, a building like Ernö Goldfinger's Balfron Tower can be listed Grade II* while the roughly contemporaneous (and equally Brutalist) nearby housing estate by the Smithsons, Robin Hood Gardens, is condemned to demolition (see Figure 1.9). (Both cases will be considered in more detail below.)

To introduce any sort of order into the discussion it is necessary to get beyond the rowdy claims and counterclaims that inevitably prevail under the permissive aphorism *de gustibus non est disputandum* (there is no accounting for taste) and attempt a more forensic examination of the precise provisions of the relevant legislation. The aim is to generate a little more light than heat by reviewing a selection of cases on which the dust has but lightly settled yet which are sufficiently recent for the underlying issues to remain relevant and offer interesting and hopefully instructive lessons.

First it might help clear the ground by rehearsing the precise criteria which the Secretary of State is obliged (not merely permitted) to apply in reaching a decision whether or not to list. The objective is to identify any aspects that reveal difference/s in treatment of Modern buildings from those of earlier periods. As far as primary legislation is concerned – the Planning (Listed Buildings and Conservation Areas) Act 1990, Section 1 – there are only two stated criteria which the Secretary of State *shall* take into account – 'special architectural interest' and 'special historic interest' – and another that he or she *may* take into account, namely 'any respect in which [the building] exterior contributes to the architectural or historic interest of any group of buildings of which it forms part' – commonly referred to as 'group value'. A further provision allows the Secretary of State to consider the 'desirability of preserving any man-made feature fixed to the building, or forming part of the land comprised within the building curtilage'.[4] The text does not recognise any difference between buildings in respect of their age, so we need look no further for modern discrimination in that respect. The emphasis is explicitly on 'special' – since there may be any number of buildings that are of 'interest' for whatever reason, which however may not be of *special* interest. Stated gradations of 'special' include 'more than special' (Grade II*) and 'exceptional special' (Grade I). Thus the parliamentary legislators, in their wisdom, evidently regarded 'specialness' as the vital prerequisite of listability. Sooner or later, therefore, we are inevitably pitched into definitions of this word 'special' in order to divine the intentions and requirements of the law.

The dictionary contains several shades of meaning of 'special' in adjectival usage, and several more as a prenominal (special constable, special delivery, special effects, etc.). As far as the adjectival sense is concerned, there is a range of synonyms to ponder, whether in the dictionary or the thesaurus, including, to name but some, 'characteristic', 'different', 'original', 'distinguished', 'excelling others of its kind' and 'chosen'. These suggest several interpretations, all of which might be included in the sense intended by José Mourinho (ex-manager of Chelsea Football Club) when he referred to himself as 'the special one'.[5] But in sum, the distinctive feature of the concept 'specialness' ordained by the Act is evidently that of being set apart from others of the same genre, or the manifestation of difference in the most pertinent (i.e. essential) characteristic/s.

So, it seems that specialness should consist of being architecturally (or historically) exceptional either through being pre-eminently representative of a particularly interesting architectural genre or alternatively being wholly sui generis and distinguished by uniqueness. An instance of the former would be Templewood School, Welwyn Garden City (Grade II*), first among equals in the Hertfordshire schools canon, listed on account of its special interest in illustrating that county's progressive post-war educational building programme (Figure 4.3). An example of the latter would be The Skylon, centrepiece of the 1951 Festival of Britain, which we may assume would certainly now be listed (probably Grade I, had it not been dismantled) by virtue of its special and singular iconic identity (Figure 4.4).

Differing criteria, however, have been suggested. In her challenging essay 'What is the point of saving old buildings?' Catherine Cooke argued for representative cultural identity as the primary consideration in selecting works worthy of preservation, querying, therefore, the legitimacy

Figure 4.3
Templewood School,
Welwyn Garden City, 1950,
by Hertfordshire County
Council. The school is now
Grade II* listed.

Figure 4.4
The Skylon, by Powell and
Moya, with Felix Samuely
(engineer), at the Festival of
Britain, London, 1951.

of pioneer British MoMo (Modern Movement) buildings on account of their sparsity, émigré designers and elite clientele, and for clearly not being 'generated by any indigenous cultural factors' – in contrast to the rich legacy of Constructivist works commissioned by the Soviet state in, for example, Ekaterinburg (formerly Sverdlovsk), the city of her studies.[6] Her point is well made. But the rejoinder, of course, would suggest that it is the very exceptionalism of the British examples that makes them 'special'. To revert to the football analogy, the interwar architectural scene might be compared to the English Premier League – most of the star players came from overseas. Either way, the primary legislation goes no further in seeking a more specific definition, and there is no mention of Modernism, whether for or against – leaving 'specialness' to be determined in each and every set of circumstances.

The 1990 Act is, however, supplemented by the Department of Culture, Media and Sport's *Principles of Selection for Listed Buildings*.[7] This document enlarges on the three criteria noted above in a short section entitled Statutory Criteria. In the case of 'architectural interest', specialness *must* 'be of importance in design, decoration or craftsmanship. Special interest *may* also apply to particularly significant examples of building types or techniques (e.g. buildings displaying technological innovation or virtuosity) and significant plan forms. Engineering and technological interest *can* be an important consideration for some buildings.' Still no mention of modern. (Note my emphasis on the distinctions between obligatory and optional characteristics.)

But then comes a game-changing addition in the 2018 revision: 'For more recent buildings in particular, the functioning of the building (to the extent that this reflects on its original design and planned use, where known) will also be a consideration.' (Note 'will', not just 'may', thereby obliging the Secretary of State to apply the new test.) This new criterion, resulting from the notorious case of Pimlico School (see Case Study 2 in this chapter), had already begun to be applied before being enshrined in the 2018 revision of the *Principles*, therefore merits careful analysis. (See further below.) The terms 'more recent' are not precisely defined, but in the ensuing section – 'General Principles' – references to 'age and rarity' specify a range of dates – before 1700, 1700 to 1850 and 'from 1850 to 1945, because of the greatly increased number of buildings erected and the much larger numbers that have survived, progressively greater selection is necessary'.[8] Taken at face value this is surely unexceptionable on purely arithmetical grounds – the more buildings of any age that survive, the more selective one must inevitably be in identifying those of 'special interest'. 'Progressively' does, however, suggest a bias against youth.

Lastly and most pointedly, the Age and Rarity section states that 'careful selection is required for buildings from the period after 1945, another watershed for architecture'.[9] This is reinforced in an additional paragraph:

Buildings less than 30 years old: such buildings are not normally considered to be of special architectural or historic interest because they have yet to stand the test of time. It may nevertheless be appropriate to list some modern buildings despite their relatively recent construction – for example, if they demonstrate outstanding quality (generally interpreted as being equivalent to Grade I or II*).[10]

Interestingly, the 2018 revision omits the word 'particularly' from the original reference to 'particularly careful' selection of post-war buildings.

'The test of time' is also curiously platitudinous for an official document, given the dramatic reduction in age already sanctioned in listing eligibility. Apart from the implication that 30 years is now a sufficient period for Father Time to do his testing, what exactly is this test? It might include a variety of considerations – changing tastes, wear and tear, effects of maintenance (or the lack of it), subsequent intervention and alteration, variation in usage and perhaps others – including, presumably, pure misfortune – though none are spelt out. The implication seems to be that the less a building is affected by any of these, the more 'special interest' it is likely to retain. The virtue of survival appears to be vested in the building itself, rather than the conduct of its owners, stewards, occupants or spectators – premature mortality therefore somehow being a consequence of its own shortcomings. As far as listing is concerned, it seems that the received wisdom of studies like *How Buildings Learn*[11] excludes the alternative interpretation – 'how owners forget'.

The clear differentiation between older and younger buildings might not be regarded as contentious in itself were there no other additional criteria aimed specifically at Modern architecture. It is the additional test of functionality in the latter case that is problematic. Whichever way you look at it, 'specialness', except to the extent of being synonymous with rarity, is no longer the only factor in play and there is a clear intention to narrow the filter for Modern, especially post-war, buildings. This seems to be corroborated by the further series of *Listing Selection Guides* published by Historic England covering 20 different typologies, ranging from agricultural buildings to public utilities.[12] They are referred to in paragraph 8 of the *Principles of Selection for Listed Buildings* mentioned above and described as 'supplementary information', but are not part of formal policy. Modern architecture naturally features more prominently in the guides concerning larger programmes of social building, such as public authority housing and education, where – in the case of guide *Domestic 4: The Modern House and Housing – Post-War Housing* – it is stated, 'Remember that the important factor for any post-war building is whether it fulfilled its original brief. It is important to know what the original intentions were, and what the estate originally looked like.'[13] Similarly, the *Education Buildings* guide states, 'Architectural interest will be determined sometimes by questions of successful functionality, as well as by consideration of design quality.'[14]

Despite the fact that it is explicitly stated in the *Principles of Selection for Listed Buildings* that the content of the guides 'does not form part of the Secretary of State's policy or guidance on listing',[15] these additional texts merit critical interrogation as it does appear that in a (presumably) well-intentioned attempt to provide more background information they have enlarged on criteria for which strictly speaking there is no formal statutory backing. While such commonplace mantras as 'fulfilment of the original brief', 'whether a design was influential', 'successful functionality', etc. may appear plausible reasons for judging the success of a building in common parlance, they do not necessarily stand up to close scrutiny when considered forensically in the context of the legislation, and so through informal repetition create the risk of acquiring a false legitimacy. As already noted, the only criteria recognised by the Act are 'special architectural and historic interest, and group value', while 'state of repair' is explicitly excluded, albeit 'loss of original fabric' is described as 'a relevant consideration when considering special interest'.[16]

So let us now examine a number of these key criteria – 'special interest', 'functional performance', 'irrelevance of state of repair', 'group value' – through the lens of some recent examples of unsuccessful (or successful) listing proposals as case studies of the correct or (arguably) incorrect application of the rules, bearing in mind that it is what the various narratives reveal in the interpretation of policy which is of primary interest, rather than the specifics of the buildings themselves. We start with consideration of the central criterion 'special interest', as applied in the case of Robin Hood Gardens.

CASE STUDY 1:
ROBIN HOOD GARDENS

The campaigns to list Robin Hood Gardens, the late 1960s/early 1970s housing estate in east London designed by the architects Alison and Peter Smithson, contributed to one of the highest-profile cases of recent years, which accordingly merits detailed analysis as a decisive episode in revaluing Modernism. An unprecedented number of architects, as well as such bodies as C20 and others (though not English Heritage – as it then was), took up arms in support of designation – ultimately in vain.[17] The first campaign resulted in the issue of a Certificate of Indemnity in 2009.[18] In 2015, a second initiative by C20 was rejected by Historic England. In the face of such overwhelming and professional testimony – supporters included such luminaries as Zaha Hadid, Sir Stuart Lipton and Richard (Lord) Rogers – how could this refusal be justified? Contrary to most of my professional colleagues, I will argue (as I did at the time) that the minister's decision was a strictly correct interpretation of the rules.

As much of the original estate has since been demolished and redeveloped, a brief description may assist those who can now only 'see' it in photographs – or indeed in the partial relic that was claimed for display by the V&A Museum.[19] The estate, located on a profoundly undesirable site at the northern mouth of the Blackwall Tunnel in east London, comprised two blocks of residential accommodation of unequal length and height, one of seven stories, one of ten stories, cranked along their length with staircases and refuse chutes at the hinge points and lifts at each end.

The dwelling units (213 in total) were accessed from walkways every third level (Figures 4.5 and 4.6), such that typically only the hall and kitchen (though depending on unit type sometimes also a bedroom and small toilet) occurred on the entrance level, where internal staircases then served up or down to the living and bedroom accommodation. Kitchens and bedrooms overlooked the estate interior, the latter having narrow continuous galleries alongside to provide secondary means of escape, while the access walkways and living rooms faced outwards. The standardised reinforced concrete grid produced a repetitive window module throughout, though this was interrupted by a syncopated arrangement of projecting fins, allegedly to mitigate noise travelling across the façades. The blocks were accessed from perimeter roadways lined with underblock garaging, leaving a central grassed area featuring a series of circular sunken playpen enclosures and two large conical mounds formed from construction debris. The site perimeter was protected by a high concrete palisade, the whole estate being completed in 1972.

Figure 4.5 (Opposite)
Robin Hood Gardens, Tower
Hamlets, London, by Alison
and Peter Smithson, 1972.
The long horizontal recesses
mark the outward-facing
access galleries/walkways.

Figure 4.6
Robin Hood Gardens' 'street
in the air' – effectively gallery
access.

This was a particularly challenging case for listing for at least three reasons: firstly, the significant amount of attention it received in the popular and professional press, making it 'a hot issue', which is not conducive to careful evaluation with Jocelyn Stevens' suggested 'cool detachment'; secondly, the reportedly imminent disposal of the site and its redevelopment, which tends to blur the issue of listing with that of retaining and upgrading; and thirdly, the high profile of Alison and Peter Smithson, which tends to confuse opinions about the buildings with the reputation of the architects. As already noted, these factors have to be put to one side if the legal question as to the estate's eligibility for listing is to be considered correctly.

The criteria for listing make it very clear what may *not* be taken into account – for example, the condition of a building, its 'popularity' or the imminence of its possible demolition. Furthermore, the notoriety of the architect is not to be conflated with the concept of 'special architectural interest', which is the key consideration – though it might conceivably contribute to the weight given to historic interest. (For example, it might be suggested that some indifferently laid brickwork at Chartwell might be of historic – rather than architectural – interest if it was known to have been laid personally by Winston Churchill.)

Before coming to the particularities of Robin Hood Gardens, it is pertinent to consider the background and circumstances of the architects themselves, as despite the fact that architect reputation is not an eligible consideration in listing, an understanding of the prior narrative in this case will assist in the precise evaluation of special interest. The Smithsons occupy a particular place in the history of post-war British architecture, being third-generation Modernists belonging to the cohort of architects who had received the impacts of the original Modern Movement but had not practised in the pre-war period. Peter Smithson described himself and Alison Smithson as 'inheritors of three European architectural languages – the Swedish, Le Corbusier and Mies van der Rohe'.[20]

Rather like the slightly older (though also avowedly post-war figure) Sir Denys Lasdun[21] and others of this time, the Smithsons accepted the legacy of the great works of their elders with ambivalence. On the one hand, the generation of Le Corbusier, Mies van der Rohe, et al. were acknowledged as heroic intellectual and architectural pioneers; on the other, they were to be subjected to intense critical reconsideration in the search for new directions. Specifically, the Smithsons' involvement with Team X[22] and their part in the eventual dismantling of CIAM (Congrès Internationaux d'Architecture Moderne), the key international organisation of the 'old orthodoxy', is indicative of their challenging stance towards their immediate predecessors. From the start, the Smithsons were pre-eminent in the effort to articulate a new theoretical platform for the future of Modernism and devoted enormous intellectual and artistic energy in this endeavour.

Meanwhile, their position should also be located within the wider English architectural scene. This may be seen to have reached a bridgehead with the 1951 Festival of Britain, which effectively consolidated and showcased the collective achievement of early British Modernism that emerged from World War II. Light, bright, accessible and classless, the temporary Utopia on the South Bank offered the vision of a new social democratic, rather Swedish-looking Britain that with post-war reconstruction and the New Towns programme would seemingly soon be available to everyone. Indeed, the Festival of Britain, viewed in retrospect, was perhaps the closest ever rapprochement of Modern architecture with the British public – a happy honeymoon before the loveless marriage.

But this comfortable assimilation cut no ice with the Smithsons and others of their coterie who together struck out for different goals as the 'angry young men' (and women) of British architecture. A corrosive compound of surrogate proletarianism and raw materiality, the so-called 'new Brutalism', aimed to capture a rugged existential quality as against the 'petit bourgeois' empiricism of the Festival of Britain aesthetic and its lay popularity.

The Smithsons have acquired almost legendary status as leaders of a particular faction re-energising British architecture in the early post-war period – intellectual, rebarbative, articulate, intensely serious and apparently quite devoid of self-doubt, claiming the role of true representatives of working-class culture as against the false populism of their herbivorous adversaries. We must now consider their fortunes in the world of architectural practice.

THE SMITHSONS' CAREER DEVELOPMENT

Like several architects of this generation – Powell and Moya, Gollins Melvin Ward, Chamberlin, Powell and Bon – the Smithsons got their first big break by winning a competition – the Smithdon School in Hunstanton, Norfolk (also referred to as the Hunstanton School). But unlike these architects and many others, they were not so successful thereafter – losing a whole string of high-profile contests – Coventry Cathedral (1950–51), Golden Lane Estate (1952), Sheffield University (1953), Sydney Opera House (1956), Berlin Hauptstadt (1957) and others later. Competitions, then as now, could be career-changing opportunities – particularly for architects with no particular social connections, like the Smithsons, who came from the northeast. It was the only way, particularly if entries were anonymous, whereby an aspiring architect could bypass social advantage and get ahead by sheer talent.

Figure 4.7
Alison and Peter Smithson, photographed in 1954.

But unlike most unsuccessful competitors, whose schemes are quietly forgotten, who get over the disappointment of losing and move on, the Smithsons' entries received spectacular and lasting acclaim. Virtually every published history of post-war British architecture features the Smithsons' competition schemes for Golden Lane and Sheffield University, with pages of approbatory coverage, while not even mentioning or illustrating the projects that actually won these competitions and were built.[23] It is as though they achieved all the recognition that goes to competition winners without having the responsibility or experience of turning their concepts into real buildings and seeing if they work. Indeed, publications of their own *oeuvres completes* are dominated by drawings of unrealised projects.

This surely suggests a pattern. For here we have a highly ambitious, intellectually intense partnership (a married couple who seem literally to have 'lived and breathed' architecture 24/7), who are initially projected into prominence through a high-profile success – the Hunstanton School – only to find themselves repeatedly rejected in favour of – in their view doubtless – less talented or intelligent rivals, while simultaneously being regarded with awe and admiration by their professional peer group, the architectural critics and a growing audience of dazzled students.

To this unusual predicament may be added what can be discerned about the personality of the architects themselves. The propensity for writing up their own story, for hoarding and exhibiting virtually every scrap of paper over decades, noting every utterance and assiduously recording its date, author, origin and circumstances, presents the picture of an intensely introspective sensibility that in the evidential record is yet further reinforced by a bizarre concern to embellish their published writings with numerous photographs of themselves – usually looking straight to camera – as if to minimise any possible risk of ever being forgotten (Figure 4.7). Although it is not uncommon for architects who are repeatedly denied the opportunity to build, sublimating their frustration on other creative pursuits, it is difficult to think of any other architect of their period who devoted quite so much energy to documenting their own legacy.

IMPLICATIONS FOR THE UNDERSTANDING OF ROBIN HOOD GARDENS

There is surely something in the Smithsons' peculiar professional CV that needs to be brought to the understanding of Robin Hood Gardens. This was their first significant experience of building a large social housing project, and it came nearly a decade and a half after they had lost the Golden Lane competition, their entry for which had by then been assimilated into professional folklore as 'the real intellectual winner' and a radical prototype. In the meantime, the key idea in that scheme – the so-called 'street in the air' – had been taken up and built by others, most notably at Park Hill, Sheffield (see Figure 1.11), on a site more suitable and at a scale more ambitious than anything the Smithsons themselves could have hoped for. Other versions of the idea of communal association 'off the ground' had also by now been explored at, for example, Usk Street in Bethnal Green (1955–58) by Sir Denys Lasdun and elsewhere. Thus, in addition to the professional acclamation of their Golden Lane scheme, its apparently successful realisation at Park Hill must have seemed an irrefutable vindication of its key idea, which in fact was already half a century old, having been pioneered at the Justus van Effen complex in Rotterdam in 1922 and transmitted via Jacob 'Jaap' Bakema of Team X (of which the Smithsons were members).[24]

Now, however, at last given the chance to build out their 'signature concept' (which by then had long since ceased to be radical), it is not difficult to see why the Smithsons would have turned in on themselves and used the Robin Hood Gardens commission to compensate for their loss of Golden Lane, and to some extent also Sheffield University (which in their unsuccessful competition entry had been organised along similar principles). And so, in the profoundly unpromising setting of the Blackwall Tunnel approach, they eventually brought forth their cherished 'streets in the air' scheme – which in reality was little more than a gallery-access housing estate – when the world at large had long since moved on. What we see therefore is a housing project that is cloaked in the elaborate rhetoric of 20 years earlier being represented as the radical way forward, but which most of their acolytes, and probably even some of their peers, were too loyal or too trusting to criticise as an idea whose time had passed. To read the Smithsons' own description of their motives is indeed to witness the extent to which their quest for historical recognition had obscured almost all sense of responsibility to the realities of the opportunity, the situation and the resident population.

This building for the socialist dream – which is something different from simply complying with a programme written by the socialist state – was for us a Roman activity and Roman at many levels:
– in that it takes its stand alongside the heroisms of what has been made before – the port and the roads…
– in that it is as heroic as supplying a Romanised city with water…
– in that it wants to be universal, greater than our little state – related to a greater law.[25]

'Our intention has always been… to turn architecture towards particularity… of place, person, activity: the form to arise from these,' wrote Peter Smithson in 1997, apparently unaware of the irony. 'To use a military analogy, the realised buildings are objectives we have taken; they are not the intention of the war.'[26] Having embarked on their self-imposed mission to supersede the generic precepts of Le Corbusier's unrealised *La Ville Radieuse*, with its insouciant neglect of the particularities of time and place, of *zeilenbau* (the public row housing concept promoted in Germany in the 1920s) and its progeny of bleak estates and rectangular flatted blocks, the Smithsons arrive in their own cul-de-sac – a system of urban morphology that bore no practical relation to existing city fabric, local people or municipal context and that even in its most systematically attempted application (the High Walk system in the City of London) could not be sustained over more than a few bridges around the Barbican.[27]

PARALLEL PROGRESSIVE DEVELOPMENTS

In 1961, five years before Robin Hood Gardens was started, Jane Jacobs published her celebrated and savage attack on Modern architecture and city planning and its arrogant disregard of the real social functions and urban benefits of traditional streets, of diversified use and ground-level movement.[28] But this seems not to have registered with the Smithsons – or at least not in any way affecting the conception of Robin Hood Gardens. And all the time it was being built, the real radical thought in urban housing was moving on – not only architecturally but also organisationally. In place of the large comprehensive redevelopment projects of the 1950s and 1960s of strategic and municipal housing authorities, the more local and responsive activities of the Housing Association movement would shortly arrive, with its growing financial autonomy, dedicated management arrangements and local responsiveness. Inner-urban housing schemes –

with exceptions, to be sure – were generally becoming characterised by more modest cellular layouts, with densely planned low- or medium-rise development overlooking identifiable areas of well-landscaped open space that connected to existing streets and were not predicated on large monolithic megastructures. In terms of the theory and practice of progressive urban housing, Robin Hood Gardens was outdated even before its first tenants moved in.

EVALUATION OF ROBIN HOOD GARDENS AGAINST LISTING CRITERIA

So – to return to the matter of listing – it is for all these reasons that despite the powerful and poignant story that this estate undoubtedly had to tell us, it was strictly incorrect to regard it as 'seminal' or of 'special architectural interest' in the sense demanded by listing criteria. The 'streets in the air', described as 'decks' on the drawings, are certainly wider than the conventional access galleries used in housing schemes of this period – approximately 2m (not counting the recessed bays at entrance doorways), compared with the 1.2m norm.

Figure 4.8
Lillington Gardens, Pimlico, London, by Darbourne and Darke, 1968. The development, with its landscaping and variety of access decks, had a radical impact on housing theory.

But, stripped of architectural rhetoric, they were really just off-the-ground cul-de-sacs, with hazardous blind spots and devoid of social footfall – the very opposite of Jane Jacobs' analysis of a benign public realm. At Park Hill, where they were wide enough to accommodate electric delivery vehicles – arguably justifying the description 'streets' – the natural topography enabled the lower decks to run out at ground level, whereas at Robin Hood Gardens they were accessed only by conventional stairs and lifts – the latter typically broken. There was nothing comparable to the landscaped richness and spatial variety of the access decks at the exactly contemporaneous (and rightly listed) Lillington Gardens in Westminster (Figure 4.8), which certainly *was* seminal and did have a radical impact on housing theory thereafter.[29]

Meanwhile, there was little to commend in the design of the dwelling plans at Robin Hood Gardens, where the absence of any private balconies associated with either kitchens or living rooms was a conspicuous shortcoming. And the use of a single window type throughout the scheme, regardless of which room was being served, seemed to reinforce Peter Smithson's unfortunate military analogy, giving the estate a relentless, regimented aspect only compounded by its woebegone setting.

In sum, while it was fair to say that the estate was certainly of some architectural interest, it is difficult to argue that it exhibited '*special* architectural interest' in relation to the contemporary social housing of its period. One could ponder whether the question would have been posed in quite the same way, or even at all, if the estate had been the work of A N Other architect, rather than the Smithsons – though were it to have been built 20 years earlier, when the principal formative concept was still 'special', this conclusion might have been different. Thus the minister's decision not to list was surely correct in terms of statutory criteria, albeit his reported reason – that 'it fails as a place for human beings to live' – was strictly not.[30] The criteria for listing as stated in the Act make no reference to such considerations; moreover this was in May 2009 – before the introduction of the functionality test. Robin Hood Gardens' performance was certainly questionable, but this was beside the fact that by the time it was built, 'streets in the air', of which it was an unconvincing example anyway, were no longer of 'special architectural interest'.

SAVING, BUT NOT LISTING

This is emphatically not to suggest that Robin Hood Gardens should not have been retained, repaired, upgraded and regenerated in order to reverse the decades of underinvestment that it had certainly suffered. Many of the celebrity testaments argued cogently for the feasibility of refurbishment, yet by conflating listing with retention the campaign adopted a high-risk strategy, as failure to list was then inevitably construed as licence to demolish (the estate was indeed progressively demolished from 2017). Besides the listing argument, there must also have been compelling sustainability reasons for not scrapping such vast quantities of embodied energy – to say nothing of the reported desire of at least some of the tenants to remain. There may even have been useful opportunities to add value to the estate by judicious further development on or around the site, its location being by now transformed by the redevelopment of Docklands and nearby Canary Wharf.

Figure 4.9
Robin Hood Gardens, not listed but surely capable of regeneration.

Who can say whether a lower-key campaign based on saving, upgrading and regeneration rather than listing would have succeeded? One may speculate, but compelling exemplars now exist for high-quality, sensitive refurbishment of post-war housing schemes without the support (or constraints) of listing – and it was this emerging tradition of imaginative Modern revaluation that, in my view, should have secured a future for Robin Hood Gardens (Figure 4.9)[31]. As if to demonstrate the feasibility of this alternative philosophy, equally if not more challenging exemplars have recently been achieved at the original (1922) 'street in the air' Justus van Effen complex in Rotterdam by Molenaar and Co Architecten and Hebly Theunissen Architecten (Figure 4.10), and likewise in Geneva, where the Le Lignon estate, a '*unité*' of 2,780 dwellings and numerous social amenities exactly contemporaneous with Robin Hood Gardens, has also been comprehensively refurbished by Jaccaud Spicher Architectes Associés over the last decade (Figure 4.11).[32] It is such compelling examples as these that surely offer valuable lessons for the future.

Figure 4.10
Justus van Effen estate,
Rotterdam, by Michiel Brinkman,
1922. The estate pioneered the
original 'street in the air' concept,
and is shown in this photograph
after its 2016 refurbishment
by Molenaar and Co and Hebly
Theunissen, with landscape
architect Michael van Gessel.

Figure 4.11
Le Lignon estate, Geneva,
by George Addor, 1964–66.
The estate was refurbished
and revalued by Jaccaud
Spicher Architectes Associés,
completing in 2021.

CASE STUDY 2:
PIMLICO SCHOOL

Our next example addresses the controversial issue of the new functionality criterion that was later formally enshrined in the revised version of *Principles of Selection for Listed Buildings* in 2018, and made specifically applicable to the consideration of post-war buildings. This dramatic new test was the outcome of the case of Pimlico School, Westminster, where arguably unique, albeit contested, 'special architectural interest' was not sufficient to secure listing, having been trumped by the minister's criticisms of the building's functional performance.

Like Robin Hood Gardens, this school – a 1,725-pupil comprehensive designed in 1964–65 by architect John Bancroft of the Greater London Council (GLC) and opened in 1970 – has also now been demolished (by Westminster Council in 2010), being superseded by the PFI Pimlico Academy, so may only be studied in photographs and films. These recall the extraordinary appearance of the original building (Figure 4.12), a concrete and glass monolith some 100m long, situated upon the cleared basement level of the houses it replaced, with a sectional arrangement that placed the projecting array of highly glazed classrooms along the exterior either side of a continuous central thoroughfare that acted as the social spine for the whole school community (Figure 4.13). Larger spaces such as the assembly hall, gymnasia and sixth form room were situated at one end, while sports pitches and games courts were placed in the cleared basement areas around the perimeter.

Figure 4.12
Pimlico School, Westminster, London, by GLC Architects Department (John Bancroft), 1970. The school was demolished in 2010.

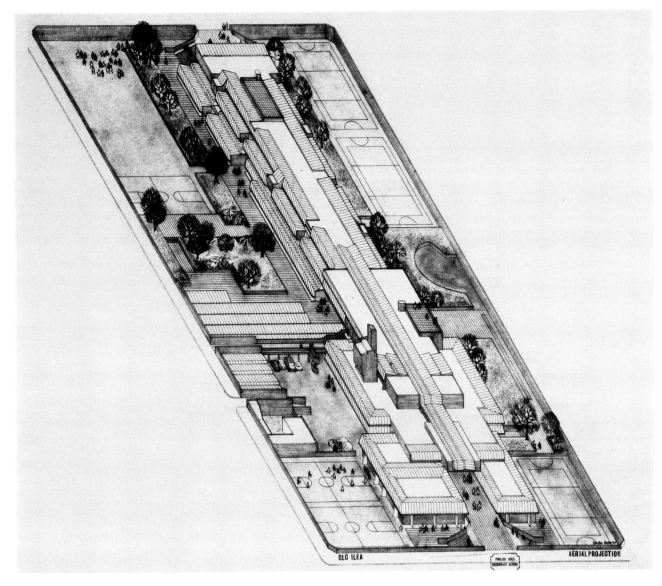

GLC ILEA   PIMLICO AREA SECONDARY SCHOOL   AERIAL PROJECTION

Figure 4.13
Pimlico School, aerial projection showing scheme concept.

Bancroft's innovative design was challenging in every sense — educationally, architecturally and structurally. Most conspicuously, the extent and configuration of patent glazing, calculated to achieve the stipulated daylight factor despite the sunken setting, was hugely ambitious for its time. Unsurprisingly in hindsight, the building suffered various problems — classrooms were subject to undue solar gain, as well as there being maintenance and security issues — and these particularly caught the attention of the minister when a Certificate for Immunity from Listing (COI) was issued in 2004. While such difficulties have not prevented the listing of other cutting-edge educational buildings, it was the fate of Pimlico School to become a test case for the novel and disputed listing criterion of functionality.[33] It is not the intention here to rerun the arguments for and against the school specifically — these can be studied in the case proceedings[34] — but rather to consider the 'functionality test' issue on a theoretical and operational basis, as it has now become a mandatory listing criterion for post-war listings.

Working back from the strict terms of the 1990 Act, it is difficult to see immediately how 'fulfilment of the original brief' could be regarded as a vital test of specialness. It would seem neither indispensable nor sufficient. Indeed, if such a characteristic were to be regarded as a baseline requirement of a building of any age – listed or not – it might be argued that fulfilling its original brief would be its least special attribute. It could be taken for granted. Further, there is the temporal issue of applying the criterion only to buildings 'of recent construction', excusing those of other periods from such examination. One need only consider the application of this test to buildings of other periods to see its absurdity. Applied to a 17th-century castle that was attacked and partially destroyed in the Civil War, it could be said that it had failed in the primary purpose for which it was built. Yet underperforming 17th-century castles are evidently deemed to evade the functionality test simply by being older. The introduction of the 'functionalist' criterion as a formal mechanism in the listing process seems, then, to be a peculiarly English misapplication of contemporaneous discourse that diverts attention from the deeper investigation of historical texts and architectural significance that should properly inform the process of statutory designation.

The concept indeed appears intellectually flawed. Is not the preoccupation with 'fulfilment of the brief' merely a journalistic trope of Modern architectural usage derived from conventional citations of 'Functionalism'? It is now recognised that these Functionalist justifications were widely employed not only by journalists but also, often disingenuously, by Modern architects themselves in promoting their cause, with the consequent migration of this concept into the critical vocabulary that developed alongside the movement as it matured from ideological secession into pragmatic orthodoxy. In other words, might not the introduction of the functionality test as a mandatory criterion in the listing process be simply misappropriating what was originally exploited as a plausible marketing tool rather than seeking a deeper, historically more objective, standard of qualitative assessment. As the historian and critic Reyner Banham put it, describing the consolidation of the numerous early strands of innovative building design across Europe and Russia into the broad river of Modernism around the beginning of the 1930s:

With the International Style outlawed politically in Germany and Russia, and crippled economically in France, the style and its friends were fighting for a toehold in politically-suspicious Fascist Italy, aesthetically-indifferent England and depression-stunned America. Under these circumstances it was better to advocate or defend the new architecture on logical and economic grounds than on grounds of aesthetics or symbolisms that might stir nothing but hostility. This may have been good tactics – the point remains arguable – but it was certainly misrepresentation. Emotion had played a much larger part than logic in the creation of the style; inexpensive buildings had been clothed in it, but it was no more an inherently economical style than any other. The true aim of the style had clearly been, to quote Gropius's words about the Bauhaus and its relation to the world of the Machine Age... 'to invent and create forms symbolizing that age'... and it is in respect of such symbolic forms that its historical justification must lie.[35]

Peter Smithson reached a similar conclusion in summing up the achievements and aftermath of the 'heroic period of modern architecture', writing in 1956:

In the 1930s, through some phenomenon that is too complicated to understand properly, something called functionalism superseded all the separate and distinctive flavours of the heroic period. By functionalism was meant the abolition of ornament and the abandoning of pitched roofs and the Orders. The stylistic void thus created was somehow to be filled by function and sociology. In this way, a rejection of style (and with it consistency and the concept of architecture) and a misrepresentation of the CIAM 'The Four Functions', came to represent Modern Architecture to a generation who never really knew what the original excitement was all about.[36]

The cynical observer, of course, might say that the Modernists have simply been hoist by their own petard. By constantly seeking to promote their cause through functional justifications, they must now face the consequences of being judged by the same criterion. Yet the real question posed in the technical context of designation is whether the tools of assessment employed in selecting buildings for listing are to be derived from the vocabulary of the period from which they originate, or whether they should be framed in the longer historical perspective provided by later, more considered, scholarship afforded by the interval of reflection that is surely precisely what is intended by the 30-year rule.

Then there are other operational difficulties. For a start, what is 'the original brief', against which the functionality test should be carried out – and how is it to be evidenced? Depending on the context, the client and the commission, the 'original brief' might range from a single sheet of paper to several metres of filed documents. (One of my first jobs as a practising architect was the design of 170 housing units for the Greater London Council, the brief for which consisted of a half-foolscap letter specifying merely the site location, the required dwelling mix and the car parking ratio. On the other hand, a typical contemporary health care or educational project will comprise thousands of pages of briefing material – employer's requirements, planning policies, building bulletins, technical memoranda, performance standards, regulations of all kinds, compliance criteria and sundry other demands.) Current procurement protocols typically require specific adherence to, or itemised derogations from, a milliard detailed specifications. Given the repeated emphasis on 'rigour' and 'rigorous assessment' in designation guidance, is this tsunami of documentation to be conscientiously interrogated before a building can be certified as passing the functionality test and considered eligible for listing?

And if so, how are the designating authorities to avail themselves of this information in order properly to undertake their task? Record information of buildings of even quite recent date can be notoriously patchy and difficult to track down – even if it survives. And, incidentally, just supposing the diligent pursuit of such information were to unearth some breach of compliance that had hitherto been concealed or gone unnoticed originally, is it conceivable that what began as a scholarly enquiry could end in a claim on the architect's professional indemnity insurance?

Even if the designation authorities have the resources to do so, how should they construe the evidence that might result? The evolution of even the most simple building is usually a complex and circuitous narrative in which 'the brief' and the design response to it become enmeshed in a process of mutual progressive reiteration until reaching a point where the initial versions of both may have become quite unrecognisable. The subsequent pattern of use following completion and occupation may also depart quite radically either from the designer's formulation or the owner's original expectations (or both) – for wholly benign reasons on either side. In such circumstances, 'fulfilment of the original brief' may have very little to do with a building's special interest – assuming it has it. In short, the retrieval and proper understanding of a building's genesis is a task requiring considerable historical insight and research if it is to be undertaken convincingly.[37]

This leads on to the tricky question of the 'rightness' of the brief itself – howsoever documented and recovered. Is it legitimate to assume that a building which demonstrably 'delivered' its brief therefore passes the fulfilment test? In the case of Pimlico School, was it established through due documentary diligence that the classroom sizes as built could be justifiably criticised for having departed from the original client's formal brief and were therefore noncompliant? Alternatively, could it have been that in dutifully conforming with specifically defined dimensions the design was actually giving effect to an admirable client aspiration for smaller class sizes and an improved student/staff ratio, which was later undone by failure to recruit sufficient teachers? Accounts of the Pimlico debacle suggest that Bancroft delivered scrupulously to a brief that itself may have been flawed. Clearly if listing decisions are to be challenged on matters that turn on ascertainment of, and compliance with, the original brief, Historic England will find itself engulfed in some extremely arduous research.

In the same case of Pimlico School, the issue of overheating resulting from solar gain was cited as a design flaw that disqualified the building from designation. Yet it has to be admitted that this phenomenon was by no means peculiar to this particular school but a widespread characteristic of educational (and other) buildings of the period in question. The Smithsons' celebrated (by some) school at Hunstanton, Norfolk, was famously defective in numerous matters of performance but is now safely listed Grade II*. The daringly overglazed buildings of James Stirling in his 'red trilogy' are likewise all listed.[38] Haggerston Girls School, another Grade II listed group of buildings designed by the architect Ernö Goldfinger in Hackney, of a similar date to Pimlico School, exhibited exactly this problem to the extent that pupils had to be sent home when significant parts of the school could not be used for teaching on hot summer days. But this has not prevented it from being listed and being successfully upgraded (see Chapter 7). So, for that matter, has the Grade II* listed library at Sheffield University (opened by TS Eliot in 1959) – also recently restored and upgraded – where regular overheating of the great Reading Room necessitated complete replacement of its glazed façade (see Chapter 9). The fact is these problems, often attributable to the less demanding building standards of their day, can usually be fixed, with or without the constraints of listed status, provided they are addressed intelligently. They are, or should be, gratuitous to the question of designation.

And is 'the brief' to be limited to matters of design and performance? What about other parameters, such as 'how long' and 'how much'? The conventional mantra that good projects should be delivered 'on time and on budget' assumes that those responsible for determining programme and cost are necessarily right, and that design is the only variable requiring critical examination. But what if the original timescale and budget were hopelessly underestimated? (They so often are that allowance for 'optimism bias' is now officially factored into many public sector projects.[39]) Does this make the building 'wrong'? Or is it the building that is right, and these other parameters against which it is conveniently judged that are flawed? Was the Channel Tunnel 'late'? Or did it take only as long as was actually needed to complete this unprecedented engineering challenge? Would its programme and cost 'overrun' – assuming these were now due to considered integral factors of its original brief – debar this triumphant eighth wonder of the world from designation if and when the time comes? Ditto Crossrail for that matter. (I am reminded of the late, great Sir Denys Lasdun who reputedly, when asked how long it would take him to undertake a new commission, rather than hazarding a finite schedule, would wisely respond to a prospective client with the promise, 'Sir, not a day longer than necessary.')

Then we have to consider the thorny subject of maintenance. This, it was stated in the proposed guidance accompanying the revised *Principles of Selection for Listed Buildings*, was not to be confused with the criterion of technical performance. The fact is, however, that original specification and subsequent maintenance are inextricably connected. The exposed concrete structures that characterised many Modern buildings before and after World War II are particularly reliant on conscientious maintenance in resisting the deterioration that may result from persistent neglect. Their material durability is a function both of knowledge and of ownership. Understanding the process of carbonation (progressive loss of alkalinity through the invasion of atmospheric CO_2) in ageing concrete, and the consequential problems of rebar corrosion and spalling, is still a relatively recent science, yet the degree to which the longevity of concrete structures can be extended is closely dependent on the quality of aftercare. Would a Modern building that was otherwise eligible for listing now be discounted on the grounds that its dilapidation was a direct consequence of compliance with the *original* concrete specification – even if it could be shown that the said specification complied with a standard that was flawed by inadequacies in the understanding of concrete pathology at the time, and/or if routine maintenance had been neglected from the outset? Or would an owner's innocent ignorance of carbonation chemistry be condoned as excusable in light of the contemporaneous extent of knowledge? 'State of repair', it will be remembered, is expressly excluded from the minister's consideration. Dunelm House, at Durham University, provides a pertinent test case (see below).

And what of the varying cultures of maintenance associated with different patterns of ownership? The vast swathe of buildings commissioned by the public sector in the post-war period, when Modern architecture was most dependent on this patronage, has been notoriously badly served by its subsequent maintenance and management – to an extent that goes some way towards explaining its widespread unpopularity. Rarely can so much building work have been commissioned by a proprietor who then proceeded to curate the investment so poorly. Thus the very architectural genre that at least theoretically would deserve consideration for listing as culturally most representative of the welfare state, the public sector 'buildings of recent construction', is uniquely stigmatised by its attendant history of poor stewardship.

So to the question as to why the proposal to introduce functionality as an additional listing criterion might have arisen. This can only be approached from a broader look at the position Modern architecture occupies within contemporary British culture and the ultimately political nature of the listing process. Much of the above commentary has focused on how the difficulties in listing Modern buildings is due to the insufficient critical distance afforded by their recent date. Arguing for the treatment of selected recent buildings as 'heritage' can be an adversarial task, especially when it is undertaken in a context of prospective demolition and the potentially huge rewards of lucrative redevelopment. It should not be assumed, however, that this is unique to our own times. Every age will surely have experienced their equivalent sense of dislocation as new ideas and forms disturb the comfortable pattern of the familiar. The Industrial Revolution and the arrival of the railways were widely seen as a demonic abomination that violated the mythic English idyll that preceded them. In similar vein, one could speculate that had the London Advisory Committee of Historic England existed in 1619 it would surely have rejected Inigo Jones's design for a new Banqueting House in Whitehall on account of 'height, scale and bulk' and its failure to respect the character of its surroundings.

The period 1945–1975, when Modernism arguably enjoyed its greatest hegemony, produced a vast and diverse legacy of buildings, the great majority of which are neither good enough to list nor bad enough to demolish. But insofar as the 'specialness' required of listable buildings 'of recent date' is by definition likely to be controversial, the promotion of Modern designation will continue to challenge ministers to champion unpopular but deserving cases. The fact that ultimate responsibility for listing rests with the Secretary of State, an elective office, means that responsibility for designation is perforce a political matter. What possible considerations might conceivably weigh with the temporal holder of this office other than the diligently researched recommendations of Historic England? The social opprobrium and political dubiety of being seen to confer approval on a troubled housing estate for some abstruse art history pleading? The wrath of an ambitious developer (and potential party donor) seeking to demolish and rebuild a choice inner-city site with lucrative new development? To be sure, there may be few votes to be won by listing an 'unpopular' Modern building, but there could be plenty to be lost.

Yet it is precisely while the outputs of a particular architectural period may be unpopular and controversial that it is desirable to have recourse to statutory measures for their protection until a sufficient consensus may develop to convert such unpopularity into acceptance. Indeed, the attribute of 'rarity' that is routinely deployed as a listing criterion for surviving buildings of earlier periods might be said to arise precisely from the extent to which others in their peer group did not enjoy such protection when they needed it. Misses, and near misses, like the Euston Arch or St Pancras Station, are just the better-known examples. How many more worthy Georgian and Victorian buildings might survive today if they had been afforded sufficient protection during their periods of unpopularity? The conventional wisdom that the survivors have 'stood the test of time' may have very little to do with whether they met their original brief and design, and very much more to do with whether by successive good fortune they luckily escaped the predatory attention of a developer at a time when their heritage value was not recognised.

The determination of what constitutes 'special interest', the residual test demanded by the Act, is ultimately a technical task of historiography and scholarship, but unlike historic buildings where 'specialness' is bolstered by rarity and popular sentiment, in the case of Modern architecture these advantages are often absent. This leaves ministers to choose between professional advocacy as against popular disapproval, and it is not surprising that in controversial cases they will be likely to follow the path of least public resistance. In the light of the above analysis, is it too cynical to suggest that the introduction of 'fulfilment of the original brief' as an additional listing criterion is simply a convenient alibi to make the rejection of difficult Modern buildings appear more scientific?

CASE STUDY 3:
HYDE PARK BARRACKS

One of the more inexplicable cases of listing rejection in recent years must be that of Hyde Park Barracks (HPB) in Knightsbridge, London, designed by the notable architect Sir Basil Spence and completed in 1970 (Figure 4.14). Here surely was a textbook example of all the attributes that endow such an ensemble with a full complement of special interest required for designation – architectural, historic and group value – the latter being especially pertinent in this case.

Group value is defined thus in the *Principles for Selection for Listed Buildings:*

The extent to which the exterior of the building contributes to the architectural or historic interest of any group of buildings of which it forms part, generally known as group value. The Secretary of State will take this into account particularly where buildings comprise an important architectural or historic unity or a fine example of planning (e.g. squares, terraces or model villages) or where there is a historical functional relationship between the buildings. Sometimes group value will be achieved through a co-location of diverse buildings of different types and dates.[40]

Figure 4.14
Hyde Park Barracks,
Knightsbridge, London, by
Sir Basil Spence, 1970.

There would seem to be no possible doubt that HPB exhibits ample group value in the sense described by the *Principles*, presenting in a bespoke contemporary design idiom the entire accommodation for a mounted cavalry regiment on a prominent central London site. It clearly also evinces special interest, both architectural and historic. In terms of rarity, there does not appear to be a single other example in the post-war period of such a building ensemble custom-designed for this purpose. None of the other post-war military barracks that might be cited are comparable inasmuch as, quite apart from issues of architectural quality, none involve the unusual and very particular requirements demanded by the inclusion of cavalry horses as an intrinsic element of the programme. Thus, in addition to the various types of accommodation for service personnel – residential quarters, officers' mess, armoury, rifle range, gymnasium, etc. – HPB also includes stables, a forage barn, a riding school, a forge comprising a shoeing shed and smithy, a saddler's workshop and all the paraphernalia involved in the husbandry of over 250 military horses.

The arrangement of all this accommodation in a coherent sequence of buildings on a significant central urban site raises the likely 'special interest' of the collective complex well above the listable threshold. Its group value might even be regarded as a beneficial consequence of the site constraints, since whereas a larger or deeper plot would surely have produced a squarer, more introverted cluster of buildings further away from, and less visually accessible to, the passing public, the thin strip of land adjacent to Hyde Park produced an enfilade building sequence that presents the whole ensemble as a legible and coordinated architectural narrative to the road frontages on both sides, thereby compensating for the restricted access inherent in a military installation. The series of glimpse views afforded by the distinctive perimeter wall design even enhances this controlled visibility. Indeed, it might be suggested that such is the group value of HPB that a future archaeologist would be able to reconstruct a complete account of this military community and its internal workings just from study of the building ensemble – rather as the discovery of the *Mary Rose* has enabled historical scholars to reconstruct the social relations of an entire ship's company in the era of Tudor England.

As regards authenticity, while there have certainly been alterations to some of the buildings, these are relatively minor in the context of the whole and have not detracted from the integrity or quality of the ensemble. In the case of the Band Room, added in 1994, it could even be argued that the alteration has actually enriched the range of uses represented within the complex. Additionally, substantial elements of the original internal design, most notably the officers' mess, remain intact and of high design and material quality.

As regards functionality, there was no evidence in the assessment that would suggest that it has not performed satisfactorily as a military barracks for mounted cavalry, while anecdotal accounts seem to confirm that the current occupants have no desire to vacate the premises. It may also be noted that the HPB has weathered well over the half century since its completion and that the build quality appears to be of a high order. The use of a restricted palette of materials that were fully understood by the architect and their deployment in a disciplined design vocabulary produces an articulate and integrated ensemble that in its rhythmic repetitive character and predominantly red colouration resonates powerfully with the serried ranks of

Figure 4.15
Falmer House, University of
Sussex, by Sir Basil Spence,
1962, listed Grade I.

horsemen in their red tunics. It is worth noting how Spence adapted his earlier arched spandrel motif from the continuous 'relaxed' horizontal beam treatment used at the University of Sussex (Figure 4.15) to the more staccato 'drumbeat' rhythm of HPB, with its discrete tranches of brickwork and stacked fenestration. These features, together with such details as the hard bricks and raked joints, all combine to project an ethos of order and precision – perfectly emblematic of the institution being housed. In contrast to the pastoral ambiance of Sussex, the whole ensemble at Hyde Park imparts the sense of buildings 'standing to attention'.

Of course, the tower (Figure 4.16) caused controversy at the time of its construction, which was cited as a potential reservation in regard to listing. But current Mayoral, CABE (Commission for Architecture and the Built Environment) or Historic England policies in relation to new tall buildings have no bearing whatever on the consideration of listing a 50-year-old structure – any more than they would be applicable to reconsideration of the arguably far more controversial Millbank Tower or New Zealand House – both built in highly sensitive central London locations and both safely listed decades ago, in 1995. Only its merits in terms of intrinsic architectural interest are pertinent, and in this respect the tower at HPB exhibits distinctive identity and detailed refinement. It is illustrative of the residential component of the military community, serves as an urban marker for the institution it houses (surely more significant as a city landmark than the generic office typology noted above), and with its crowning 'helmet' has become a recognised architectural personality on the London skyline.

The conventional objection that tall buildings on the perimeter of a park 'diminish the park' is difficult to substantiate. They do not do so in Central Park, New York, where the enclosing frame of tall buildings, visible from numerous viewpoints, contributes much of its drama. Conversely, how 'diminished' would St James's Park be if the celebrated view from the Blue Bridge was without the backdrop of Whitehall Court? It might equally be argued that it is the visibility of such buildings in such a context that distinguishes an urban park from mere countryside, and makes it more navigable – just as the sight of a distant church spire becomes an orientation point in the rural landscape. Indeed, to many it is the appearance of a building, or buildings, above the near horizon that intensifies the pastoral quality of the park itself. This is not, of course, to justify the indiscriminate development of towers around parks, but rather to comprehend the particular contribution that known landmarks can make to their environs. Much of the original tower controversy surrounding Hyde Park Barracks could be attributed to its being a 'pioneer' tall building in a prominent London location. But such controversy fades over time, as is evident from the subsequent acceptance of many pioneering buildings that have divided opinions in their day. How very modest, refined, even delicate, might the Mies van der Rohe 'tower' proposed at Mansion House Square (Figures 4.17 and 4.18) have seemed now after the subsequent proliferation of vastly taller and cruder buildings in the City?[41]

Figure 4.16
The Hyde Park Barracks tower, as seen from the park – a view that now includes the Hilton Hotel, the Shard and the London Eye.

PART ONE: RETROSPECT

Figure 4.17
Proposed tower and public square by Mies van der Rohe at Mansion House, City of London, 1984.

Figure 4.18
Mies van der Rohe's Mansion House tower, full-size sample of proposed window.

As to the question of the architect's reputation, Sir Basil Spence has the unusual distinction of being simultaneously lauded and derided for his status as the 'establishment architect' of his period. The building for which he is best known, Coventry Cathedral (now listed Grade I), was admired and criticised in equal measure in its day for being the 'polite' face of Modernism. Likewise, the University of Sussex, with its evident stylistic similarities to the barracks, has also tended to attract popular acclaim while being disparaged by professional critics and 'hardline' Modernists. Yet as the partisan atmosphere of their original reception fades, a more objective stance should be attempted. This surely entails a more nuanced evaluation of Spence's architectural personality than his usual and indiscriminate characterisation as 'Brutalist'. His style is more aptly described as Picturesque – which is to say, he was less preoccupied with the ethical justifications invoked by Brutalist adherents for the rawness of their works and took more explicit responsibility for their aesthetic appearance and scenic qualities. It was his unusually candid defence of formal motivation at a time when this was more often the subject of architectural inhibition that both endeared him to a popular audience and distanced him from the professional one. To the extent that this more subtle reading is an intrinsic, and perhaps under-recognised, aspect of Spence's oeuvre, it could be said to add to the special architectural interest of the HPB.

So, to the other criterion – historic interest. There can be little doubt that HPB embodies historic interest. Barracks for the accommodation of mounted regiments have existed on the site since 1795. The original installation was replaced in the mid/late 19th century with a new scheme that was in turn replaced by Spence's design, the genesis of which dates from the mid-20th century. While the regimental identity of the occupants has altered over the same period – the Horse Guards being superseded by mounted elements of the Household Cavalry – this essential continuity of military use on the same site over such an extended period must be very rare indeed. The location of the site itself and its occupants in operational proximity to Hyde Park, Constitution Hill, Buckingham Palace, the Mall, the Horse Guards, etc. embodies the historic connection of the barracks to the principal ceremonial places of central London and is illustrative of its ritual duties. The retention of these interrelated functions as an active presence in the capital is an important aspect of London's international identity that runs counter to the prevailing trend of traditional institutions, especially the historic markets, migrating outwards from their original central locations – Covent Garden, Billingsgate and soon Smithfield. The Household Cavalry is – to use current parlance – a 'world brand' recognised by millions and at least part of this identity is tied up with the HPB and the extended history of its site. The preservation and re-presentation of the old 19th-century pediment as part of the ceremonial portico on South Carriage Drive is another feature of both historical and evidential interest, and visibly maintains this connection between the current barracks and its predecessors. Provision is made precisely for consideration of such features in the *Principles for Selection for Listed Buildings*:

When considering whether a building is of special architectural or historic interest the Secretary of State may take into account the desirability of preserving, on the grounds of its architectural or historic interest, any feature of the building containing a man-made object or structure fixed to the building or forming part of the land and comprised within the curtilage of the building. The desirability of preserving such a feature is a factor *which would increase the likelihood of the building being listed*.[42] [Author's emphasis.]

In sum, by applying the prescribed criteria strictly in the manner intended by the Act and the *Principles*, the Hyde Park Barracks demonstrably passed all three tests of eligibility for listing. In the light of the above, the rejection of the case was indeed inexplicable – at least in terms of the statutory requirements. Architectural interest was dismissed on the grounds that the creation of 'separate buildings above a podium on such a narrow urban site has resulted in a confusing inhospitable layout'. Even ignoring the fact that the site's location (and therefore shape) is key to the institution's history and relationship to the Palace, the suggestion that 'hospitality' should be the decisive quality of a military barracks is self-evidently daft. Historic interest was dismissed on the inapplicable basis of 'quality of design'. And as for group value, the minister's reasons, that 'the modernist functional ideology of the design resulted in a series of buildings that contrast with, rather than complement their surroundings' is manifestly not supported by the *Principles*.[43] The bizarre reference to 'functional ideology' directly contradicts the self-imposed rule on functionality and the criticism that the ensemble stands in contrast with its surroundings is palpably absurd. A building's contrast with its surroundings, or otherwise, is not a criterion of listing, although in fact the barrack's materials are surprisingly compatible with its context of largely residential and substantial mansion blocks with similar brickwork and stone dressings. The Household Cavalry is nonetheless a major national institution deserving its own architectural identity. One might equally then criticise the Palace of Westminster, St Pancras Station or the National Gallery for contrasting with their respective surroundings.[44] Such reasoning is clearly ridiculous.

But could there be another explanation for the minister's refusal? Could the £650 million estimated land value of the site for disposal by the War Office for private residential development conceivably have had any role in decision? Surely not! (Fortunately, the essential equestrian proximity to the Palace entailed by the regiment's duty of guarding the Sovereign seems to have ensured the barrack's survival, for the time being anyway.)

CASE STUDY 4:
DUNELM HOUSE, DURHAM

Dunelm House (Figure 4.19), the students' union building designed by Richard Raines of Architects Co-Partnership for the University of Durham in 1965 (opened in 1966), is another example of the troubling volatility in modern listing, yielding further important lessons for the future. The case had a complex prehistory, having been already proposed for listing (at Grade II*) in the 1990s as part of English Heritage's thematic review of post-war university buildings – some 20 years before the recent controversy. Though that proposal was not progressed, the case was reactivated as a result of the university's application for a Certificate of Immunity in advance of new masterplan proposals for site redevelopment.[45]

Dunelm House, in a spectacular setting on the banks of the River Wear and within sight of the World Heritage Site of Durham Cathedral, had received several prestigious awards in its day. The drama of its context was further heightened by its relationship to Ove Arup's celebrated Kingsgate Footbridge (completed in 1963 and itself listed Grade I), which it was designed to complement – a powerful example of 'group value'. The streetside views from New Elvet were equally contextual.

Historic England concluded that the building was worthy of listing at Grade II, while C20, which mobilised a vigorous campaign in support, urged listing at Grade II*.[46] The minister, however, determined otherwise.[47] This duly prompted an application for review, filed in January 2017. The minister's initial refusal deserves close scrutiny as an example of the muddled reasoning that is affecting such listing cases since the Pimlico School decision. The principal reasons given below are followed in each case by my comment.[48]

Figure 4.19
Dunelm House, Durham
University, by Architects
Co-Partnership (Richard
Raines), 1966, with the
Kingsgate Bridge in the
foreground.

MINISTERIAL REASON: Design quality: … the building is not stylistically or structurally innovative, despite the involvement of Sir Ove Arup, the designer of the adjacent, contemporary Grade I listed Kingsgate Bridge.

AUTHOR COMMENT: It is not stylistic or structural innovation that a building is required to exhibit to qualify for designation, but architectural and/or historic special interest. This notwithstanding, Dunelm House is in fact innovative in both architectural and structural ways by virtue of the unique manner in which these qualities are fused and customised to its site. There was no precedent in England for a Modern building of this type and use in a setting of such extreme sensitivity. It confounded the popular contemporary misconception that Modern architecture could not positively participate in, and enrich, historic surroundings. There is arguably no other comparable building of its period and sector that better demonstrates this lesson. Dunelm House changed the perception of what Modern architecture was capable of in terms of response to context, and it remains an object lesson in how to behave architecturally at a World Heritage Site.

It is probably unique as a bespoke, modern university students' union that is not simply extrapolated from the generic architectural vocabulary of a larger campus masterplan, a pattern which was typical of the plate-glass university developments of the time. The use of concrete as the principal expressive architectural material in this acutely sensitive context is especially significant in eschewing the easier and less experimental alternatives that might have been adopted by a less progressive client, or insisted upon by a more timid planning authority – ranging from faux medieval, through 'polite' Modern to Geordie vernacular. To suggest the structure is not innovative is also to misunderstand what is being innovated here. It is not in a virtuoso display of structural gymnastics, as might be expected of a purely engineering structure. (The Kingsgate Bridge is an ample example of that.) It is the manner in which the structural negotiation of such difficult terrain is unified with its architectural configuration, employing a series of discrete yet interlinked forms, whose scale is further calibrated through the diminishing volumes up the slope and successive strata of close-mullioned openings. Thus, rather than simply 'conquering' the hillside with a single monolithic retaining wall against which is then placed a conventional building, as would doubtless have been proposed by a less imaginative designer, here the building itself 'becomes' the retaining structure while still expressing the hillside behind it. This approach at Dunelm House, so clearly exemplifying Ove Arup's philosophy of synthesising the disciplines of engineering and architecture, is also why the building sits so comfortably with its Grade I listed neighbour, the Kingsgate Bridge. It is because they both proclaim the same design ethos in rendering it impossible to separate the architecture from the engineering. The involvement in both projects of Sir Ove Arup himself, a 20th-century designer of world stature born locally in Newcastle, makes this place and its associations of very special interest indeed.[49]

MINISTERIAL REASON: Design flaws: the Minister considers that the architectural interest of the building is diminished by design flaws, including: the design of the roof and inability to weather-seal the reinforced concrete lids due to their weight and design; consequent problems with persistent water ingress has led to the degradation of mechanical and electrical services positioned in the void under the roof; the poor distribution and concealment of the building's services that has made their repair difficult; flaws in the building's plan form, including problems with internal access between different levels (that required the installation of an additional staircase to improve access to the upper levels); poor internal planning that resulted in the lack of a lift to provide access from the kitchens to the ballroom, making catering difficult; the building's inefficient use of space – exemplified by the main staircase – resulting in a gross to net ratio of only 56%.

AUTHOR COMMENT: 'State of repair', as already noted, is expressly excluded from the listing criteria. These alleged design flaws are in any case exaggerated. Even if acknowledged as technical issues that may require repair, they cannot be adduced as reasons outweighing the special architectural interest of the building. They are all capable of remedy, as has indeed been successfully achieved in numerous other Modern, now listed, buildings with equivalent experimental features and often far more severe defects. The design of the roof was itself architecturally innovative in conceiving this as a 'fifth façade' – an integral part of the building's visual identity as experienced from higher viewpoints on the World Heritage Site peninsula. It was not demonstrated that the building plan form did not answer the original brief. On the contrary, the original architect confirmed the highly specific spatial requirements stipulated by the client, with which the design duly complied. In fact, the plan form and section (Figure 4.20) are highly ingenious in placing the principal servicing functions – kitchen, servery, storage and prep areas, etc. – at an optimal central position so as to serve all the key communal areas which are gathered on the largest floor plate – the cafeteria and coffee bar, the staff dining room, lounge and bar. Placing these service areas in the heart of the building enables all these surrounding social spaces to enjoy the views and natural light afforded by their perimeter locations.

Equally ingenious is the way the vehicular delivery and service yard is discreetly shielded from all of the key views, whether from the near or far river bank. A later demand to serve food in the ballroom cannot be adduced as criticism of the original plan form. The modification of interior arrangements in response to changing patterns of use is a common occurrence in almost any building, as is also the progressive renewal/redeployment of services installations in answer to new demands. Such interventions often result from later regulatory requirements, most notably in relation to access provision, and it is disproportionate to cite them as obstructions to listing. At the most, it might justify a reduction from a Grade II* designation to Grade II.

The criticism of gross/net ratio at 56% unfortunately reveals another complete misunderstanding of the social functions of such a building – typical of conventional commercial assumptions. A major, perhaps *the* major, purpose of a students' union is to facilitate unscheduled encounters among its users, thereby generating informal contact and interaction within the student community, and it is precisely in such areas as foyers, hallways and staircases that this is cultivated – i.e. intermediate spaces that do not entail specific reasons or prior booking to be in, and which thereby effectively 'belong to everyone'.

Apart from their academic mission, it could be argued that perhaps the key *raison d'etre* of universities as social institutions is to provide the setting for this inestimably productive process, especially for those of the fresher generation whose social horizons may have hardly extended beyond their school peer group. It is precisely because of this vital function that a students' union cannot be judged in the task-based terms or conventional gross/net metrics of other building types, most typically commercial offices where every lettable square metre counts. The special interest of Dunelm House is in the way the main staircase and landings (Figure 4.21), its principal circulation feature, are directly derived from the site topography and exploited and celebrated as the spatial focus for this social interaction.

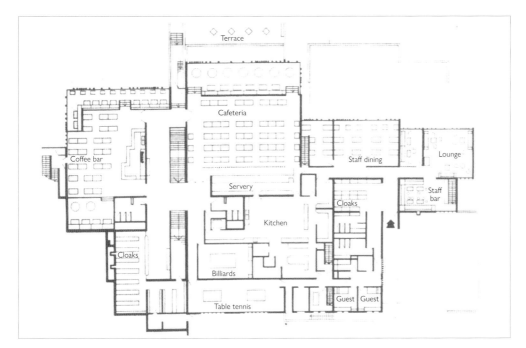

Figure 4.20a
Dunelm House, plan.

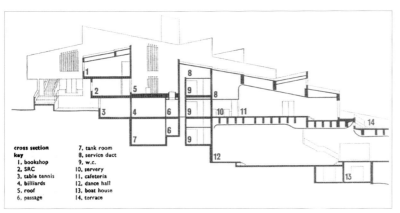

cross section
key
1. bookshop
2. SRC
3. table tennis
4. billiards
5. roof
6. passage
7. tank room
8. service duct
9. w.c.
10. servery
11. cafeteria
12. dance hall
13. boat house
14. terrace

Figure 4.20b
Dunelm House,
section.

MINISTERIAL REASON: Failure to meet its construction brief: the Minister accepts the representations that there is evidence of inadequate concrete cover over horizontal and vertical external surfaces (in places it is under 20mm thick compared to a specified design cover of 50mm), indicating a failure in delivery of the original construction brief and considers this to have a detrimental impact on the architectural interest. The Minister considers that, as a result of the failure to meet the construction brief, the appearance of the external concrete covering has a negative (albeit fairly minor) impact on the aesthetic merits and hence architectural interest of the building. The Minister does, however, recognise the problems with the external concrete could be remedied, but has made the decision on the current evidence and not on any prediction of possible future intervention.

AUTHOR COMMENT: This is self-evidently conflating quality of workmanship with quality of design, which is inadmissible under the listing criteria. The current localised areas of defective concrete (doubtless exacerbated by inadequate maintenance) are made more conspicuous in individual cases only on account of poorly executed past repairs and are entirely remediable.

Figure 4.21
Dunelm House, the communal
staircase foyer (photographed
before the arrival of students;
see endnote 46).

The qualifications – 'albeit fairly minor' etc. – suggest that even the minister recognised the inadequacy of this reason and included it only to bulk out the rejection. In the serial references to the 'construction brief', one can see how the new functionality test can be exploited as an alibi for refusal. Anyway, if millimetres of concrete cover are being cited as sufficient to deny designation, how is one to account for the fact that until the interventions of William Walker in 1906, Winchester Cathedral had no proper foundations? The privilege of age apparently.

MINISTERIAL REASON: Alterations: there is evidence that some of the original interior finishes have been lost following earlier refurbishments.

AUTHOR COMMENT: This presents as another makeweight pretext to avoid designation. The current interior of the building is quite sufficiently intact to reveal the original architectural intentions, and many of the alterations are no more than superficial and reversible interventions that commonly occur in student buildings half a century old, where there has been variable management over the years.

It can be argued that, in refusing designation, the evaluation of the building's importance and special interest was not informed by an understanding of its intrinsic architectural significance, but rather placed undue and illegitimate emphasis on the relatively minor material defects that could be expected from any clipboard survey of a 50-year-old building in rugged student use.

However, this was not the end of the story. The minister's letter of October 2017 was duly challenged by Historic England, C20 and others, and following a further extended period of consultations the eventual decision overturned the previous COI, with the building finally being listed at Grade II.[50] Gratifyingly, many of the minister's stated reasons for rescinding the previous decision echoed my comments above, which formed part of the review request. Specifically, the admission that in making assessments for listing the minister could only consider the terms of the 1990 Act offers hope that Dunelm House result might serve as a vital reference for future contested cases.[51]

As the four pivotal listing studies considered above produce a 'score draw' – two outcomes according with my personal judgement, two against – it might be suggested that this is as equitable an outcome as is reasonable to expect. Yet the investigations are not primarily focused on the tally of case results as such, but on the way in which they reveal the uneven workings of official consideration and public understanding of Modern designation more generally. The specified criteria are critical to the processes of revaluing Modernism correctly in a statutory context yet still evince a precariousness and inconsistency in application that suggests that all is not entirely well.

What becomes apparent is that such issues as architect reputation, performance shortcomings, site disposal value, redevelopment opportunities or the extent and cost of repairs – which may be entirely legitimate matters for debate *after* the question of designation has been settled – are migrating into the listing assessment stage and corrupting the proper application of the statutory criteria. It is the context in which these and other 'issues of intervention' in listed Modern buildings should be dealt with – i.e. that of obtaining planning or listed building consent for repair, alterations and upgrade (or *in extremis* even demolition) – which must therefore be considered next under the broad heading of Protection, before gathering up the various irregularities and identifying the weaknesses that continue to prevail in the system as a whole.

5 Protection

The listing of any building confers certain protective rights and duties on the part of its owner, the planning authorities and Historic England, the government's statutory advisory agency. This chapter surveys some of the ways this protection has been applied, or arguably misapplied, in the case of Modern listed buildings, and considers the impact that increasing development pressures are likely to impose on protected buildings and sites.

HAVING CONSIDERED SOME OF THE ISSUES for Modern architecture raised by listing, we may now move 'downstream' to examine the extent of protection that is provided by formal designation, with particular regard to whether and how Modern buildings are valued and treated differently from those of other periods. Despite the sense of achievement among conservationists when, often after a strenuous campaign, listed status is granted to a significant Modern building, it should not be supposed that its vicissitudes are then over. Rather, the previous endeavours to cultivate sufficient official recognition of the asset in question are now replaced by fresh concerns to ensure adequate vigilance in maintaining its integrity. By contrast, the new protected status is generally not so welcome to the asset's owner, who is inclined to regard it as a constraint on their freedom. Unauthorised alterations to the property may now reward the owner with a criminal conviction under Section 9 of the Planning (Listed Buildings and Conservation Areas) Act 1990.[1]

Even in a 'free country', there are few – if any – freedoms that are not conditional. Of course, many limitations of individual liberty are exercised informally through social mores, whether we call this good manners, inhibition or just plain decency. The recent Covid-19 pandemic presented some unusually explicit examples of the fine line to be drawn between voluntary observance and formal enforcement in matters of public conduct, though those circumstances were surely exceptional. The freedom to do as one pleases with one's own property is one of the more complicated areas of social policy, where, despite the aphorism about an Englishman and his castle, individual or corporate liberty is densely conditioned with interlocking regulations, obligations and constraints. To William Pitt the Elder's 1763 dictum, 'The poorest man may in his cottage bid defiance to all the forces of the Crown,' must be added the suffix – 'but not if his cottage is listed'. This caveat could be said to involve the reconciliation of two kinds of ownership – that is ownership in the sense of legal title, and ownership in the sense of cultural (or in heritage industry jargon, 'intergenerational') equity. Thus the supposed autonomy of de jure possession is made subject to, and must negotiate with, the claims of national patrimony.

The ingenious little mechanism by which the said 'negotiation' takes place is contained in a deceptively simple paragraph of the 1990 Act, Section 7: 'No person shall execute or cause to be executed any works for the demolition of a listed building or for its alteration or extension in any manner which would affect its character as a building of special architectural or historic interest, unless the works are authorised.'[2] Could the parliamentary legislators possibly have imagined the turmoil that this seemingly innocent provision would unleash? The operation of this clause, through which the statutory protection afforded by listing is provided, obliges those involved firstly to ascertain the 'character' of the listed building in question, then to decide whether a proposed alteration would 'affect' it, then (assuming it would) to determine whether such alteration would be benign or detrimental, and finally – having undertaken the preceding tasks – to seek official authorisation for the work. The said authorisation (listed building consent) is normally dispensed (or withheld) by the local planning authority (LPA), following consultation with Historic England in the most sensitive cases, usually Grade II* and Grade I, though even then the LPA is ultimately the 'decision-maker'. An aggrieved owner may appeal an LBC refusal (as with rejected planning applications) or (very unusually) serve a purchase notice requesting the LPA to purchase the owner's interest in the land in circumstances where, as a result of a refusal, the owner is rendered incapable of 'reasonably beneficial use'.[3] Of course, it need not be assumed that all interventions in a listed building will be detrimental; many may 'reveal or enhance' the significance of the asset, for example by removing or correcting later or substandard non-original works, in which case consent is quite straightforward. But just by 'affecting' the 'character' of the asset, consent will still be required. In practice, however, all the trouble arises from contested assessment of detrimental interventions and the extent of resulting harm. The rest of this chapter therefore considers the operation of these procedures, with particular regard to their application to *Modern* buildings.

LIST ENTRIES

In ascertaining the 'character' of listed buildings following designation, the first port of call could be said to be provided by list entries themselves and the grade accorded to the asset in question. It has been well noted in explanations of early list entries that their primary purpose was simply to identify clearly what building or feature was being designated. Addresses and map references were provided for this purpose, with only summary description of the building itself. However, this has changed. As Historic England's website advises:

In recent decades, particularly since the start of post-war listing, greater efforts have been made to explain the history of a building and to outline its claims to special interest. Modern list entries (since around 2005) are thus fuller than earlier ones, and it is fair to say that the more recent the description, the more helpful it is likely to be. More recently still, with the Enterprise and Regulatory Reform Act (2013), it has been possible to be very precise about which elements of a building are included within the listing.[4]

This new provision needs careful understanding, as descriptive reference to a particular feature of a building in its list entry may be neither necessary nor sufficient to secure its protection. Whereas stated inclusions may be conclusive, unstated exclusions may not. As Historic England itself states, 'When the new provisions are invoked, we can be categorical in saying that certain features do not hold special architectural and historic interest and this will be clear in the text; however, silence on a feature does not imply a lack of heritage value.'[5]

Since it has been pointed out that attempts to identify and describe 'special interest' comprehensively in new list entries run the risk that the unintentional omission of particular details might be construed as implying they hold no significance, it would seem advisable for applicants submitting Modern buildings for listing consideration to make specific reference to any aspects they would wish to be shielded by the protection. This may have particular relevance for Modern estates or ensembles where the spatial qualities of the composition as a whole, the importance of their setting, intervisibility and curtilage structures, may all be vital to the significance of the original concept. The conventional concentration on 'features' – decoration, craftsmanship, embellishments generally – that characterises traditional architectural inventory compilation is inclined to overlook these less tangible Modern attributes, yet it is precisely these that are most vulnerable to current-day pressures for densification, infill development and other types of monetisation.

The more significant characteristics of a designated asset's special interest that are captured in the list entry, the better their protection is likely to be, as in the context of a listed building consent application or an eventual planning inquiry it will substantially bolster the conservationist case if reference can be made to specific citations of heritage value in the entry text. A recent study on the future direction of listing, undertaken for Historic England, has laid particular emphasis on the need to update the earlier 'minimalist' entries to match the current more comprehensive standard, as well as progressing the geographic and thematic listing programmes generally. It is notable, however, that while more designations are urged for buildings of earlier periods, including the interwar years, no such recommendation is made for post-war buildings.[6] Historic England's recent introduction of the 'Enrich the List' programme, whereby anyone may contribute additional information on a particular designated asset, provides an opportunity for supplementing list descriptions, though the status of such material (which is curated before uploading) may not equate to that of the official entry.

The relative weight of 'heritage significance' becomes more apparent when we consider the efficacy of the other instruments of protection in order of gravity – starting with the National Planning Policy Framework (NPPF) within which a range of provisions affecting heritage (Modern and otherwise) is included. The National Planning Policy Framework (2012, latest revision July 2021, and supplemented by numerous 'planning practice guidance' – PPG – publications) was undoubtedly beneficial in condensing the maze of previous regulations and policy into a single succinct and accessible document. (Chapter 16, 'Conserving and enhancing the historic environment', is accorded just 19 paragraphs in the 217-paragraph document.) Yet at its heart lies a Faustian bargain whereby the overarching presumption in favour of sustainable development can 'trump' heritage considerations so long as consequential harm is compensated by public benefit.[7] Despite all the warm words about 'conserving and enhancing the historic environment' in the NPPF (paragraphs 189–208), even describing such assets as 'an irreplaceable resource that should be conserved in a manner appropriate to their significance', it is this provision, albeit qualified, that is the key trade-off. Even 'substantial harm or outright loss' – while to be treated as 'exceptional' or 'wholly exceptional' in the case of Grade II or Grade II*/Grade I assets respectively – may be accepted subject to certain conditions.[8] Although there is no stipulation – at least in the words of the Framework itself – in relation to an asset's age that would discriminate against buildings of recent date, it is not hard to see how controversial cases of listed Modern architecture may be particularly vulnerable to this new transactional heritage regime. The degree of harm deemed to be tolerable in the case of an unpopular Modern building may greatly exceed that which might be accepted in a popular old one – even though both are listed. It is therefore in the application of the policy in practice, rather than the policy itself, that we must search for such discrimination against the Modern.

As to the question of how 'harm' is to be measured, a recent interpretation of a High Court Judge was that there are only three categories – substantial (which includes total loss of the asset), less than substantial (in which the judge included 'minimal harm') and none.[9] To judge from custom and practice to date, the threshold of 'substantial harm', notably in several high-profile Modern cases, is very high indeed, sometimes described as harm of such an order that, had it already occurred, it would have prevented the asset in question from being listed in the first place. The majority of contested cases thus tend to rely on the increasingly invoked concept of 'less than substantial harm' – a formally uncalibrated category which can cover anything from negligible harm up to total loss. Its evaluation can therefore become a highly disputatious matter. At a recent appeal case, an apparently exasperated Inspector observed that 'the exercise of identifying the degree of harm within the category of "less than substantial harm" can appear like trying to count how many angels can dance on the head of a pin'.[10]

It is certainly difficult to make sense of some of the instances of harm visited upon listed Modern buildings that have been sanctioned as 'less than substantial' – as we shall see. Experience suggests that all conservation in practice entails making at least some change to the object or 'asset' in question, however minimal. And the rightness of such change/s will ultimately depend upon the designer's creative intelligence in finding a feasible fusion of the contending demands of patrimony and progress – to put it in the most general terms. Yet the provisions of the NPPF surely express in their most acute form the way in which heritage and development are now typically conceived as a contest of opposing values to be adjudicated through the planning system. In an effort to square the circle, English Heritage had already (2008) promoted a new policy called 'Constructive Conservation in Practice', which it describes as follows.

'Constructive Conservation' is the term used by English Heritage to describe the protection and adaptation of historic buildings and places through actively managing change. The approach is positive and collaborative, based upon a shared understanding of the qualities which make a place or building special. The aim of constructive conservation is to achieve a balance which ensures that those qualities are reinforced rather than diminished by change, whilst achieving a solution which is architecturally and commercially deliverable.[11]

Figure 5.1
Constructive Conservation in Practice, English Heritage, 2008. The front cover of this publication illustrates part of Park Hill estate, Sheffield, as refurbished by Urban Splash. Compare with Figure 1.11.

This concept – a double-edged instrument at best – was not specifically aimed at Modern buildings as such, and there are certainly increasing examples of imaginative adaptations from all periods that can be cited. But it is easy to see how it can be exploited as an alibi for legitimising controversial interventions in post-war listed buildings that might be less likely to be accepted in architecture of earlier ages. Indeed, as if to exemplify the policy, the cover of English Heritage's publication *Constructive Conservation in Practice* (Figure 5.1) illustrated the reworked façade of Park Hill, Sheffield, which has been praised and criticised in (almost) equal measure, but in both cases raising the question as to whether the drastic extent of original fabric removal in a listed building may even be described as 'conservation'. The controversy, of course, concerns social economics as much as heritage ethics insofar as a less expensive scheme retaining more original fabric would arguably have avoided the gentrification entailed by the costs of wholesale renewal.[12]

In addition to the Ministry of Housing, Communities and Local Government (now the Department for Levelling Up, Housing and Communities) National Planning Guidance – Historic Environment (updated 2019), which sets out the overall legislative framework, there is the suite of Good Practice Advice Notes (GPAs) addressing such topics as planning, managing significance, the setting of heritage assets and enabling development, and numerous other Historic England Advice Notes (HEANs). All this material, though not of formal statutory force, should still theoretically underpin the conduct of decision-makers, normally the local planning authority, further to consultation with Historic England in higher-grade cases, as noted.

Again, there is generally no bias for or against Modern buildings, albeit many of the illustrations and textual references to timber-framed buildings, thatch and slate suggest that traditional architecture was more likely to have been in the minds of the authors.

Lastly in this survey of instruments through which protection is administered we come back to *Conservation Principles* first published by English Heritage in 2008 (with later revisions pending at time of writing) as 'a clear over-arching philosophical framework of what conservation means at the beginning of the 21st century' (Chairman's Foreword).[13] Here again the emphasis is on 'managing change' with reference to 'constructive conservation' even in the Foreword. Partly an industry standard work of reference for the heritage sector as a whole, partly a 'how-to' guide for the conservation practitioner, this document seeks to establish the basis of theory and practice in an essentially universal manner, without bias to heritage assets of one period or another – even including 'undesignated assets'. Impeccably drafted, it aspires to be future-proof and has no specific reference to Modern buildings, or indeed buildings of any particular age. Its four categories of defined heritage value – evidential, historical, communal and aesthetic – had no direct correlation with the 1990 Act or the *Principles of Selection for Listed Buildings* and strictly speaking may not be adduced as factors contributing to the potential listability of a prospective application. In short, it is a 'downstream document'. However, a recent revision (2018) has substituted the term 'heritage *interest*' for the original four heritage *values* – evidential, communal, aesthetic and historic – and retitled these as archaeological, architectural, artistic and historic. 'Significant places' are now referred to as 'heritage assets', and the role of undesignated heritage assets now has a recognised place in the guidance. The revisions are intended to bring the terminology of the *Conservation Principles* into alignment with that of the NPPF, but there is a subtle – or perhaps not so subtle – shift in the new terminology. Whereas 'value' suggested a quality or qualities that inhered in the object itself, 'interest' arguably describes the measure of subjective appreciation on the part of the observer. Quite how this shift might play out in the treatment of protected buildings remains to be seen, but there is otherwise no specific difference in the manner in which Modern buildings are to be treated.

Now let us consider how these provisions are being applied in practice. In broad terms it might be suggested that the system is working well, since Historic England advise that not only are a very high percentage of their listing recommendations accepted by the Secretary of State but also that many, if not most, listed building consent applications are dealt with satisfactorily, whether or not they involve Historic England or are simply processed by the local planning authority. But if we consider the efficacy of the protection *as actually provided* through the lens of a few recent cases, the picture becomes decidedly less reassuring. Perhaps the two most egregious instances involving Modern buildings being clearly treated differently despite the supposed protection of listing are the former Commonwealth Institute (Grade II*) and Balfron Tower, the Ernö Goldfinger block in east London (also Grade II*). The Barbican Arts Centre in the City of London offers another illuminating example.

CASE STUDY 1:
THE COMMONWEALTH INSTITUTE

The modern Commonwealth Institute (Figure 5.2) was opened by the Queen in 1962, to supersede the original Imperial Institute established by Royal Charter in 1888 but demolished in 1957. The new building, designed by Robert Matthew, Johnson-Marshall and Partners on an open site between Kensington High Street and Holland Park, in London, was intended as an information and education centre to promote mutual understanding among all countries of the Commonwealth. It became a day-trip destination for generations of young people as a teaching vehicle in broadening popular knowledge of Britain's former empire and global connections. Its exterior form, a huge rotated diamond in plan, roofed by a spectacular hyperbolic paraboloid in dramatic contrast with the surrounding urban grain, was reached from a spacious public plaza beautifully laid out by the distinguished landscape designer Dame Sylvia Crowe – one of the very few designated post-war gardens in England. Entered obliquely via a covered walkway, the interior opened into a vast multitiered space displaying and celebrating the national cultures and artefacts of all the participating countries. Other facilities included a separate art gallery, a cinema, stage and lecture hall, back-up workshops and a rectilinear administration block partially

Figure 5.2a
The Commonwealth Institute, Kensington, London, 1962, by Robert Matthew, Johnson-Marshall and Partners. The building is viewed from across the entrance plaza, designed by Dame Sylvia Crowe.

Figure 5.2b
A model of the original design
for the Commonwealth
Institute, showing the extent of
open forecourt to Kensington
High Street, lower left.

engaged with one corner of the 'diamond' through which it passed. Material contributions from many of the participating countries – such as 25 tonnes of roofing copper from Rhodesia (now Zimbabwe) – helped to supplement the parsimonious budget provided by the UK Government.

The building was listed Grade II* in 1988 – indeed the first to be spot-listed under the new 10-year rule – and was reportedly regarded by English Heritage as the 'second most important Modern building in London, after the Royal Festival Hall'.[14] But despite its unique architectural identity and inspirational cultural mission, the institution endured a difficult history during its 40-odd years in operation. Various defects, not unconnected with the inadequate original budget, continued to give trouble, while running costs were a constant struggle. Transfers of responsibility for the building to different government departments led to an eventual decision for disposal in 2002, after several inconclusive remedial projects and a determination that the property was ultimately unviable. As the rich collection of ethnographic exhibits was dispersed, more vicissitudes followed, too numerous to reprise in detail, the final outcome being the Institute's sale for conversion into the Design Museum, following relaxation of some of the listing parameters that had protected the administration wing and the landscaped foreground, in order to facilitate 'enabling development'.[15] Although the original applications for planning permission and listed building consent were granted prior to the introduction of the NPPF in 2012, and so cannot strictly be assessed against its policies, the degree of licence in the

Figure 5.3
The Design Museum, Kensington, London, by OMA (and others), 2016. The museum is obscured by and entered underneath private luxury apartment blocks.

proposed interventions remains extraordinary. The new museum, finally opened in November 2016, while intended to attract greater footfall and commercial activity at the western end of the High Street, has entailed complete evisceration of the original interior and the relegation of the listed building itself to backland status behind three substantial blocks of luxury flats, occupying the foreground in place of the listed gardens (Figure 5.3).

A plausible version of this unhappy narrative would argue that the conundrum presented by the Commonwealth Institute in its original form had reached such an extremity that any response that salvaged even a fraction of it (in the end only the roof and some elements of the elevations) would be a defensible outcome. The nullification of the Commonwealth Institute's protection by listing was considered to be justified on the grounds of unprecedented extenuating circumstances. Having personally witnessed some of the saga at close quarters when it came before the contemporaneous English Heritage committees, there is no doubt that by the time the case had reached the endgame there was a sense of total institutional exhaustion, if not despair. It might even be possible now, as a conscience salve, to invoke the provisions of the NPPF in support of the outcome, by reference to paragraphs 200–202, where substantial harm to a designated heritage asset may be accepted as quid pro quo for commensurate public benefits.

But is that the end of it? Is the case just to be dismissed with that conventional exoneration of past failure, 'We are where we are'? Is there no room for 'not so', or 'yes, but'? This is not merely a matter of 'musical differences' between architects. Surely, even granted the necessity for significant intervention, the Institute's level of statutory protection and English Heritage's

Figure 5.4
The interior of the former Commonwealth Institute.

Conservation Principles should have mandated other possible design strategies. Could the enabling development have been alternatively configured to retain more of the listed plaza as clear public realm explicitly proclaiming the new Design Museum to the street? Could not the residential provision have adopted an orthogonal footprint around the site perimeter, leaving the original building to remain unique in its rotated orientation? Might the new interior have retained a memory of the remarkable original spatial intervisibility (Figure 5.4)?

Did the eventual scheme achieve, or even attempt, an optimal reading and respect for 'special interest' or 'heritage significance'? Manifestly not. Just to enumerate three of the Institute's most important characteristics, or attributes of 'special interest' – its (registered) public realm; its unique rotated orientation, and its interior spatial drama – one can see that all of these have been disregarded. Not only have the residential blocks 'backlanded' the main building, but also their rotation to mimic its diamond orientation, together with their cubic forms, have diminished the uniqueness of its geometrical footprint in the surrounding urban grain. And quite how it was possible to fell the five monumental plane trees that graced the street frontage without requiring Royal Assent defies rational explanation. As for the interior (Figure 5.5), in place of the openness and curvilinearity of the original space that visibly and symbolically interconnected the innumerable nationalities in multiple transverse views, is now a conventional boxy atrium of the kind that could be expected in any suburban shopping centre – Brent Cross being perhaps the most charitable comparison (Figure 5.6).

Any conscientiously prepared Statement of Significance would surely have identified these characteristics, among others, to provide key heritage objectives for the new project. [16] Now, of course, the deed is done and those on both sides can only agree to differ. Yet there is surely a more general lesson to emerge from this tragic story.

The saga of the Commonwealth Institute will stand out as one of the greater losses in the still emergent field of modern conservation. For sure English Heritage cannot expect to win all its battles, but there is at least some sense of closure to be gained from going down fighting. It was not like losing a public inquiry, where even the best arguments may be overturned through due judicial process. The Institute was already listed, and at Grade II*, which in the context of post-war architecture placed it in the vanishingly small group of outstanding buildings of

Figure 5.5
The interior of the new Design Museum, by architect John Pawson.

Figure 5.6
Brent Cross Shopping Centre, BDP architects, north London, 1976.

national – and with all its Commonwealth associations, international – importance. Its setting was also a registered landscape, making the combined designations probably unique in the UK. Given the minefield of policies and guidance that must usually be addressed and navigated in projects involving even the smallest interventions in designated assets, one can only imagine that future historians looking back will find the outcome at the Commonwealth Institute wholly incomprehensible. But then again, perhaps the said future observers will simply interpret it as a pre-eminent example of 'constructive conservation'. We shall have to wait and see. Either way, it is difficult to imagine such an assault ever being countenanced on a historic listed building.

CASE STUDY 2:
BALFRON TOWER

Figure 5.7
Balfron Tower, Tower Hamlets, London, by Ernö Goldfinger, 1965–70. The photograph shows the original façade albeit with cornice removed.

The case of Ernö Goldfinger's Balfron Tower (Figure 5.7) raises similar concerns for the consistency of policy application to listed Modern buildings. This 26-storey high-rise urban landmark within the Brownfield Estate, an extensive redevelopment project in London's bomb-damaged East End, was built in phases between 1965 and 1970. It is now listed Grade II* and epitomises Goldfinger's distinctive Brutalist manner in his ebullient post-war maturity.

A conservation management plan, produced in 2007, to guide a major estate regeneration project provided a detailed statement of heritage significance covering all aspects of the listed estate, including its landscape and setting (also a conservation area), with particular emphasis on the requisite quality of concrete repair and the treatment of façade components, windows and screens, all of which had been meticulously designed by Goldfinger in the original.[17] Specifically, the façade and its fenestration scheme were scrupulously controlled by his characteristic proportional systems and 'classical' ratios, as imbibed during his tutelage in pre-war Paris with the French master Auguste Perret, and were unquestionably a key element of the building's 'special architectural interest'.

However, while the conservation management plan was effective in guiding the first phase of the regeneration of the adjacent block, Carradale House, the project took a new direction when the ensuing phase involving Balfron Tower saw this element become the subject of a joint partnership between Poplar HARCA, the estate's social landlord, and London and Newcastle, an incoming private developer. This has resulted in the complete 'defenestration' of the tower – both literally and socially – with the entire principal façade being replaced in a quite different design idiom and all existing tenants being ejected in the conversion of the accommodation into a luxury apartment block (Figure 5.8).

Figure 5.8
Balfron Tower, as refurbished, 2019. The tower has a completely changed façade (and resident community). The cornice has been reinstated, but in an incorrect colour of white.

The fact that opinions differ on the politics of gentrification and the benefits or otherwise of living in tower blocks is not germane to the matter being considered here, which is the correct and consistent application of statutory planning policy. Whatever one's views on the 'social cleansing' of Balfron Tower, it is hard to imagine that such wholesale physical removal and alteration of an element of such intrinsic 'special interest' as its main façade would be countenanced in a Grade II* building of earlier vintage. Historic England Advice Note (HEAN) 2, paragraph 15, is specific: 'Doors and windows are frequently key to the significance of a building. Replacement is therefore generally advisable only where the original is beyond repair, it minimises the loss of historic fabric and matches the original in detail and material.' The same HEAN, paragraph 42, continues: 'It is not appropriate to sacrifice old work to accommodate the new.' Even if an alternative material (e.g. anodised aluminium) could be justified at Balfron on account of the future-proofing issues associated with maintaining painted timber windows in a high-rise block, the default protocol of like-for-like replacement in terms of *visual* character would surely be applicable.

That such a gratuitous intervention should be consented by the decision-maker – the London Borough of Tower Hamlets – and condoned by Historic England does invite the question whether *Modern* listed buildings, even ones designated at Grade II* as Balfron was, can be assured of the same level of protection as that accorded to those of other ages and styles. The equivalent extent of façade replacement at Park Hill, Sheffield, only reinforces the uncertainty. The justifications in both cases have tended to depend on generalised arguments about meeting the challenges of retrieving degraded 1960s public sector estates. The magnitude of such challenges is certainly undeniable, but the extension of this general argument as an alibi for detailed architectural and social metamorphosis is disingenuous and opportunistic. The more difficult task surely imposed by a rare Grade II* listing context, and arguably a more responsible approach, is to achieve the necessary upgrade *without* compromising a building's essential identity.

As for the 'privatisation' of Balfron Tower and the resulting internal unit reconfigurations, one could argue that Goldfinger's original dwelling layouts were a powerful illustration of Britain's contemporaneous commitment to social housing and as such merited designation not only on grounds of architectural special interest, but also of *historic* special interest now that the early post-war culture of social housing has ceased to exist.[18] As has been well noted elsewhere, the architectural benefits of major regeneration investment must be weighed against the expropriation of welfare state housing that so often accompanies it in neo-liberal economies.[19] Even the handful of units supposedly retained as a 'heritage record' of the original layout have been altered in order to relocate service risers for the re-planned flats above. Of course, there have been vocal objectors to the scheme, not least the Twentieth Century Society (C20), but as with the Commonwealth Institute, the rumpus gradually fades while the built outcome remains, leaving the thin gruel of 'lessons to be learned' as the only return.[20] As the adage has it, 'The conservationists have to win every time, whereas the developer only has to win once.'

CASE STUDY 3:
THE BARBICAN ARTS CENTRE

The Barbican Estate in the City of London was one of the most ambitious post-war urban redevelopment projects in Europe, achieved over nearly 30 years, with a population of over 4,000 and including, in addition to its vast residential provision, an extensive range of public facilities, gardens and other amenities. The last of these to be realised was the Arts Centre, opened in 1982, which as its brief steadily grew during the evolving project, perforce had to be fitted into a plot already tightly constrained by earlier phases of the development. Unlike, for example, the Royal Festival Hall, therefore, where the foyer spaces are 'extroverted' with outward views of the river, at the Barbican much of the interior was necessarily created below ground level such that the principal spatial drama of the foyers occurs internally with limited exterior views (Figures 5.9 and 5.10). Within this Piranesian volume the central orientation point was a spectacular triple-height void originally marked by a huge suspended light sculpture by the Australian artist Michael Santry.

Figure 5.9
Barbican Arts Centre, City of London, by Chamberlin, Powell and Bon, 1982. The original architectural section shows the deep foyer spaces.

The whole estate was listed Grade II in 2001 and is believed to be the largest object ever so designated. But the Arts Centre's unique internal spatial quality, an intrinsic aspect of its 'special architectural interest', has since been significantly altered, with a wide bridge being inserted into the original central void and an additional infill floor being recently introduced alongside it to provide a new enlarged retail offer (Figure 5.11). These interventions, though finely designed in themselves and certainly enhancing the Centre's circulation and commercial operations, have clearly diminished the original spatial character of the Centre and partially obscured the visible presence of its two principal venues, the theatre and concert hall.

Although these interventions are now consented and completed, they do nonetheless – like the preceding case studies – invite a question as to the consistency of 'due process' in the protection of listed Modernism – specifically in the treatment of Modern space. The recently announced multimillion-pound Barbican Renewal project will surely put this matter to the acid test.[21]

Figure 5.10a
Barbican Arts Centre. This original foyer view shows Michael Santry's sculpture in the triple-height void.

Figure 5.10b
Barbican Arts Centre. A view across the foyers, showing interior intervisibility.

Figure 5.11
Barbican Arts Centre foyer, as altered with a new infill retail floor, 2016.

MODERNISM – SPACE VERSUS ROOM

The increasing value of land in urban areas and the disproportionate rewards to be gained by new (and in many cases over-) development are impacting a key aspect of Modern architecture and the importance that it placed on 'space' – especially amenity space. The original pioneers' concern to decongest the 19th-century city and introduce 'space, light and verdure' was as vital a part of the Modern vision as the use of innovative techniques and materials in the development of the new architecture. But the generous surroundings and open aspects that so often formed an integral part of original Modern Movement projects are precisely the 'assets' that are now regarded as opportunities for 'densification' and infill development. What was intended as space for liberation is now interpreted as room for exploitation. A typical and egregious example was Elliott School, in Wandsworth, London, listed Grade II and 'recognised as the finest of the LCC's in-house comprehensive schools', where over half its site was privatised for housing development under the pretext of raising funds in a PFI project for its conversion to The Ark, Putney.[22]

Much the same applies to Modern interiors, at least in the case of large public buildings, where original spatial volume is now evaluated as prospective scope for enclosure or subdivision in the interests of creating revenue-generating floorspace – cafes, retail offers, 'attractions', etc. Does the protection supposedly provided by listing set as much value on 'space' as an integral part of Modern heritage as it does on fabric? And if so, how is this intangible asset to be safeguarded? Of course, the protection of interiors of listed buildings is, or should

Figure 5.12 a, b and c.
Interventions in setting at
London's Southbank Centre.

PART ONE: RETROSPECT

be, subject to the mechanisms of listed building consent, whereas exterior settings are also controlled by other instruments of planning policy. But as 'spatial heritage assets' both are vulnerable to similar predatory pressures for exploitation. Do 'view corridors', conservation area constraints or official heritage guidance criteria provide adequate tools for these purposes when the sites occupied by Modern buildings are often regarded as more valuable than the buildings themselves? The 2005 ICOMOS Xi'an Declaration on the Conservation of the Setting of Heritage Structures, Sites and Areas was a valiant attempt to highlight the importance of, and establish disciplines for management of, the vulnerable surroundings of significant heritage assets, but it would be wise not to assume this could suffice as an adequate measure for their protection.[23] The Southbank Centre on London's River Thames provides as egregious an example as could be imagined. Having already been refused listing on several attempts, the aim now appears to be to make the complex permanently unlistable by a combination of grotesque material and spatial interventions (Figure 5.12). Even the setting of the Grade II* National Theatre has not escaped the seemingly irrepressible invasion of fast-food outlets. To the suggestion that such interventions should not cause undue concern, being usually 'temporary', it could be contended that temporary or otherwise they represent, and eventually encourage, a culture that progressively erodes the significance of the heritage asset from which they siphon their rewards.

There is no statutory definition of 'space' as such, but both the NPPF and Historic England have plenty to say about 'setting', which might be regarded as a close cousin. Setting is defined in the NPPF as 'the surroundings in which a heritage asset is experienced. Its extent is not fixed and may change as the asset and its surroundings evolve. Elements of a setting may make a positive or negative contribution to the significance of the asset, may affect the ability to appreciate that significance or may be neutral.' The NPPF continues:

The setting itself is not designated. Every heritage asset, whether designated or not has a setting. Its importance, and therefore the degree of protection it is offered in planning decisions, depends entirely on the contribution it makes to the significance of the heritage asset or its appreciation. No additional consent is required to alter the setting of any heritage asset. Works may require planning permission and additionally new works within the setting of a listed building or scheduled monument may require listed building consent or scheduled monument consent, as appropriate, if they physically attach to or physically impact upon the building or site… Heritage significance derives not only from a heritage asset's physical presence, but also from its setting.[24]

Historic England's Good Practice Advice (GPA) 3 suggests a checklist of tasks to help in grappling with setting, including its clear identification in the specific case, an assessment of its contribution to the significance of the heritage asset and of the effects of a proposed development upon it, exploration of ways to maximise enhancement and/or minimise harm, and post-factum monitoring.[25] Although the discussion is predicated on setting as an exterior phenomenon, the concept of space as a contributory factor in heritage significance is clearly implicated. Interior space, by analogy, should surely therefore be clearly identified as a component of 'special interest' where it contributes to the significance of a listed building and unlike 'setting', by being enclosed within the asset, could legitimately be treated as designated. Thus, both the former Sylvia Crowe garden at the Commonwealth Institute (the Institute's setting, which actually *was* designated) and the foyers at the listed Barbican Arts Centre (its dramatic interior void) could indeed lay claim to substantive heritage value in the proper assessment of any interventions. But in neither case did such factors evidently influence the eventual outcomes.

These examples, of which more could be quoted, are indicative of some of the most powerful phenomena of our age – the privatisation of what was formerly public, and the marketisation of what was formerly free. It seems that the Marxist dictum, 'All that is solid melts into air' might today be more correctly rendered as, 'All that is air solidifies into air-rights development.' Does the generally positive connotation of 'adaptive reuse' include the redefinition of what was originally a vital Modern idea – the idea of void? Or must we abandon Modernism's defining concept of contemporary space and accept that land, especially urban land, is too valuable a resource to remain 'underutilised'? Is the need for 'optimised development' (external or internal) now an inevitable consequence of 21st-century urban culture and the attendant pressures of growth? Or will existing policies for the protection of 'significant space' be able to hold the line?

The causality of the story in London, as no doubt elsewhere, albeit oversimplified, runs something like this. First, from the 1980s, the stock of social housing is progressively depleted through Right-to-Buy disposals, which failed to redeploy even the marked-down sale proceeds to replace the resulting losses. Then over the years the increasing shortage of affordable homes compels the government to set local boroughs ever more challenging housing targets, which austerity and persistent underfunding make virtually unachievable. Finally, in the absence of adequate resources to acquire the requisite land, the said boroughs have no option but to build on the 'free' land they already own, then selling much of what is built at inflated market values in order to pay for the remaining 'affordable housing', which is both insufficient and too expensive to meet the growing need anyway. The relatively spacious sites of many post-war estates accordingly become increasingly vulnerable to the ensuing 'densification'. Meanwhile, of course, the private sector's incentives for overdevelopment bring their own rewards in an era of ghost ownership, buy-to-let and acute housing shortage.

This discussion can hardly digress into major issues of national housing policy, but simply intends to draw attention to these issues in the specific context of Modern heritage. So, the bigger question remains to be answered. Yet the conflicted state of current planning practice could be summed up in the alternate outcomes of two recent cases less than a mile apart in the City of London. The Golden Lane Estate (1953–63) is celebrated as one of the pioneering housing projects of the early post-war years, designed by architects Chamberlin, Powell and Bon and presenting an entire neighbourhood settlement with numerous amenities in a fully composed urban landscape. The predominantly four-storey arrangement of maisonettes and flats is anchored by the central 'tower block' Great Arthur House, at 16 storeys the tallest building in the UK in its day. The visually and physically permeable nature of the ensemble (listed for its architectural special interest as well as designated in the Register of Parks and Gardens) effectively extends its 'setting' well beyond the site boundary itself, and the importance of surrounding views into and across the estate was recognised in listed building management guidelines commissioned by its landlord, the City Corporation, and formally adopted in 2007.[26]

Figure 5.13
The Denizen, on Golden Lane,
City of London, by Allford
Hall Monaghan Morris and
White Ink Architects, 2020.
The building replaced Bernard
Morgan House.

Figure 5.14
The COLPAI development,
adjacent to Golden Lane
housing (foreground), City
of London, by Hawkins/
Brown, photographed during
construction in 2021.

PART ONE: RETROSPECT

Yet these, and the aforementioned policies on setting, were not sufficient to prevent, or it seems even moderate, a gargantuan development of luxury apartments – The Denizen (Figure 5.13) – immediately adjacent to its southeast corner, replacing an eminently adaptable post-war residential block of sympathetic height and architectural character, named Bernard Morgan House. Together with the even taller COLPAI development (Figure 5.14) at the northeast corner, these two interventions now 'bookend' the modest four-storey residential blocks that originally characterised the street frontage of Golden Lane.[27]

While in the case of COLPAI the inclusion of a new primary school and a quantum of social housing provide worthy justifications for development in principle, there can be little dispute in terms of architectural impact that these interventions neither 'preserve nor enhance' the setting of Golden Lane Estate as a listed (and registered) heritage asset, even if they cause 'less than substantial harm'. But despite vociferous objection from the resident community and others, the schemes have been built.

By contrast, at the nearby Barbican Estate (also listed and designed by architects Chamberlin, Powell and Bon, as well as being 'protected' by formally adopted listed building management guidelines) recent proposals for a substantial extension to the City of London School for Girls, which would have infilled the open undercroft below Mountjoy House (Figure 5.15), one of the estate's apartment blocks elevated on concrete pilotis by the lakeside in a dramatic flourish of Brutalist spatial rhetoric, were withdrawn after sustained opposition.[28]

This benign outcome might not have been wholly attributable to the said management guidelines or even the well-articulated arguments for preserving the space as *space* – the extension itself may simply have been too constrained by its context to fully meet the school's aspirations – but those concerned to protect the spatial qualities intrinsic to Modern architecture and so vulnerable to exploitation and infill must hope that it will serve as a potent exemplar.

Having pointed out some of the inconsistencies in the listing and protection of Modernism, it is time to identify the underlying weaknesses and draw some conclusions.

Figure 5.15
Development plans for the City of London School for Girls extension in the space below Mountjoy House, the Barbican Estate, City of London, were withdrawn after opposition.

6
Weaknesses

Having reviewed in the preceding chapters selected narratives of listing and of the protection that it is expected to provide to the assets concerned, this chapter seeks to summarise some of the apparent inconsistencies of current practice in relation to Modern architecture that suggest the need for rectification.

AS THE FOREGOING REVIEW SUGGESTS, there are some disturbing anomalies in both the listing and subsequent statutory protection of Modern heritage which suggest that 'due process' may not be being followed consistently. Despite the generally benign regulatory framework for the identification and governance of heritage as a whole, the conspicuous variation in its application to *Modern* buildings surely reveals a range of weaknesses which need to be addressed. These might be grouped under the headings institutional weakness, professional weakness and theoretical weakness.

INSTITUTIONAL WEAKNESS

Departmental decisions in many of the cases studied, and others that could be quoted, as well as the justifications provided for them, have often been less than convincing. It is vital as an immediate baseline requirement for the credibility of the modern designation process that ministers' reasons for their eventual decisions are completely transparent and demonstrably derived from the statutory criteria. Of course, outcomes in highly contested cases are unlikely to satisfy everyone, but at least the basis of official decisions should withstand rigorous scrutiny against the terms of the legislation and accompanying regulations. It seems significant that in three of the listing cases considered already in this book – Pimlico School, Hyde Park Barracks and Dunelm House – the ministers' decisions were the subject of subsequent challenge. The original determinations were simply not credible, though at least in the case of Dunelm a correctly reasoned decision emerged at the end.

Starting at the top, it appears that certain ministers in several high-profile cases, such as those mentioned above, have departed from the specified listing criteria in rejecting well-argued application cases that surely merited acceptance, even if at a lower grade than that proposed. To be clear, the weakness does not only relate to the ignorance, indifference or prejudice on the part of politicians – which leaves fine examples perilously dependent on the whim of whichever culture minister is in post at the time. One is simply asking that their department fulfils its statutory duty to correctly apply the rules as written. The more flawed decisions that accumulate through misapplication, or neglect, of the specified criteria, the greater the risk of poor practice becoming engrained, with earlier bad precedents serving as justification for more later ones. Of course, some might wish to take issue with details of the predisposing legislation or regulations, but it is evident that for the most part the problems arise in their application rather than in their content which, in general if not entirely, is 'age blind' and avoids specific discrimination against Modern architecture.

Meanwhile, the most wayward decisions deserve to be appealed. A particularly disturbing pattern in the decision-making, notably in cases originating in applications for a Certificate of Immunity, is the unfortunate practice of building owners commissioning a condition survey that is typically predicated on a prior decision to demolish the building in question. The content of such reports, usually concentrating on state and/or costs of repair and/or the benefits of redevelopment – none of which are legitimate criteria in the consideration of listing – thereafter migrates into the case against designation submitted by the owner, or on their behalf, with the result that much of the reasoning then infiltrates into the official assessment process, and in some instances, directly into the minister's eventual decision letter.

The procedure is further obscured by what might be termed the Apollo 8, or 'dark side of the moon' syndrome, whereby after a case has been submitted to the Department for Digital, Culture, Media and Sport (DCMS) it is processed by officers before a response is formulated on behalf of the minister. As with the inscrutable deliberations of a High Court jury when it 'retires to consider its verdict', external stakeholders are left to divine the reasoning between their original representations and the minister's eventual decision letter without access to the crucial in camera exegesis. Any attempts at discovery must perforce rely on the vagaries of Freedom of Information (FOI) requests (as was the case at Dunelm House). Greater transparency in that part of the process 'within' the DCMS between submission of an application for listing and the determination of the minister is surely vital. As it is, an exemplary and conscientiously researched case submitted by the government's advisory agency Historic England can emerge at the other end as a perfunctory rejection with scant justification. The words of the Planning (Listed Buildings and Conservation Areas) Act 1990 may not oblige the minister to provide reasons, but it surely offends current norms of open government not to do so.

Additionally, consultation on prospective listing decisions and subsequently in the context of a potential development project often fails to engage the relevant voluntary bodies – C20 (the statutory Amenity Society) and Docomomo – at a sufficiently early stage to allow proper account to be taken of these resources of expertise. More timely engagement is surely desirable if eventual decisions are to carry wider support. It should be remembered that the 1990 Act imposes a *duty* on the Secretary of State '*before* compiling, approving (with or without modifications) or amending any list' to 'consult with a) the Commission' (i.e. Historic England), 'and b) such other persons or bodies of persons as appear to him appropriate as having special knowledge of, or interest in, buildings of architectural or historic interest'.[1] This duty – not merely a choice – is not discharged by consultation only with Historic England, nor is it restricted to statutory amenity societies. It embraces any other 'persons or bodies of persons' that have special knowledge or interest etc. Clearly in the context of Modern buildings, this should include C20 *as well as* Docomomo *and* any other legitimate commentators whose locus in the dialogue would 'appear to him appropriate'. If this is not currently 'apparent' then all parties with such 'special knowledge' of Modern architecture would be well advised to bring it to the Secretary of State's attention.

Then, in the downstream context of applications for listed building consent, it would be preferable for Historic England to follow the same procedure of consulting with such sources *before* formulating its response to a developer, rather than the current practice whereby these advisory bodies are usually engaged only later by the local planning authority during the statutory consultation period. At present, typically, a developer having procured a 'letter of comfort' on his proposals from Historic England prior to such wider consultation is unlikely to pay much heed to the informed representations of one or other of these amenity societies. Neither, unfortunately, is the local planning authority, the eventual decision-maker, despite the fact that in England these authorities are obliged to consult the recognised amenity societies on all applications involving the partial or total demolition of listed buildings dating from their respective periods.[2]

There are surely ways of avoiding, or at least reducing, such inconsistencies. In the Netherlands, for example, the role of Rijksbouwmeester, or Chief Government Architect, has existed in one form or another since 1806 and is widely respected as an authoritative advisor in matters of planning and development policy, as well as monuments and public art. More recently, the office has expanded to include equivalent functions covering landscape, infrastructure and cultural heritage, the four together becoming the College of Chief Advisors. Similar models could be considered in the UK.

But beyond the politicians and their immediate advisors, it must be acknowledged that there is a serious lack of capacity and period knowledge in the planning and conservation departments of many local authorities. Even where qualified staff do exist, their competence more often derives from conventional training in historical architectural periods and traditional conservation practices, with little or no experience of Modern architectural heritage. In the current climate of austerity and downgrading of local planning resources generally, it seems unlikely that this weakness will be rectified any time soon.

PROFESSIONAL WEAKNESS

Problems also stem from the propensity of commercial developers to engage high-profile 'starchitects' for significant heritage projects in the belief that their reputation in mainstream practice and track record in gaining advantageous planning consents equips them to deal with Modern listed buildings, with their particular sensitivities. Experience has unfortunately shown that despite all the official guidance and procedural advice, it cannot be assumed that such practices will be conversant with the protocols of preparing conservation plans and Statements of Significance, which should properly be undertaken *prior* to embarking on a particular design programme and be 'scheme neutral' in relation to any ensuing proposals.

More often, one suspects the Heritage Statements accompanying applications for consent are retro-engineered by articulate consultants as a series of alibis for design decisions already made. The due professional skills need not necessarily entail formal conservation accreditation (except when this is a prerequisite for grant-aided or public sector commissions), but lack of any such training or experience whatsoever does constitute a serious risk of being oblivious to the relevant processes and conservation disciplines prescribed by established charters and best practice in the field. Too often it seems that shortage of knowledge is replaced by surfeit of ego. Architects, accredited or otherwise, must cultivate better recognition of the 'special interest' of Modern buildings and acquire greater competence in grappling with the technical challenges involved in their conservation and adaptation. At the same time, the conservation lobby must cultivate a more realistic appreciation of how 'historic' Modern buildings, even where of clear heritage value, often also require upgrade and modification to secure a sustainable future. Architectural heritage, Modern or otherwise, is not always best served merely by knee-jerk resistance to change.

THEORETICAL WEAKNESS

The third weakness is more diffuse, though no less critical. It is the commonplace misrepresentation of Modern architecture as a singular monolithic culture capable of being defined by a number of generalisations that in turn sustain a variety of fallacies and misconceptions – the fallacy of 'Functionalism' being perhaps the most misleading as a criterion of assessment, as already indicated. The reductive account of 20th-century architecture that permeates popular discussion is all too easily absorbed into the still underdeveloped governance of modern conservation in practice. Thus 'Modern' becomes 'Moderne'; almost anything built between the wars not obviously traditional is 'Art Deco'; and almost anything between 1950 and 1975 is 'Brutalism'. The fabulous diversity and complexity of a whole century's creativity becomes reduced to a few stars, villains and 'isms', while a history of unimaginable richness is too often compressed into a series of simplistic clichés. The conscientious and nuanced narration of 20th-century architecture as a complex unfolding story conditioned by myriad social, cultural, economic, artistic, political, technical and legislative circumstances is rarely attempted outside the confines of academic scholarship – where the products generally remain. But it resonates with the alleged lack of an overarching philosophical framework establishing the purposes of contemporary heritage and conservation of which Catherine Cooke complained in her article 'What is the point of saving old buildings?', itself perhaps a manifestation of the notorious Anglo-Saxon aversion to theory and theorising.[3] This is not to berate the public or even the politicians, but rather to chide the mediating interlocutors and the incessant dumbing down of architectural commentary for popular consumption. The infrequency with which building plans or sections are typically illustrated in journalists' accounts 'because the lay viewer cannot read plans' is merely self-fulfilling. Fortunately, the progressive and imaginative use of digital imaging in film and television coverage is beginning to address this weakness. There is some considerable way to go, however, before popular and professional discourse achieve some sort of genuine rapprochement. Meanwhile, the current relationship of the architectural profession to the British public has been likened to that of an out-of-tune orchestra playing to a tone-deaf audience. That a series of propositions such as the following could be promulgated by a leading figure in the heritage field cannot surely be conducive to a deeper understanding of the issues involved.

Late 20th-century buildings are normally functionally inflexible.

They may have been designed for a fixed life span; they may have been completely temporary or they were philosophically designed to self-destruct.

Post-War Modernism at its most utopian built in obsolescence to their structures.

Some architects believed that past generations had encumbered society with ideas and buildings now outmoded that were holding the world back. Therefore, their buildings were to be designed to serve a generation and then be replaced.[4]

The situation is also not helped by the neglect of history teaching in schools of architecture and the relentless tide of image-led architectural publishing that has become such an insidious influence in the formative stages of student development. Forging a more meaningful relationship between the world of architectural practice and scholarly architectural research would also help in the cultivation of a common language of critical discourse. Such challenges may not be susceptible to rapid remedy but require a steady cultural shift over time.

CONCLUSION

This analysis suggests that there are both short- and long-term difficulties affecting the way Modern architectural heritage is being treated. Paradoxically, it may be the long-term ones – the changes in culture and broader public appreciation of Modern architecture – that are less intractable inasmuch as they may be expected to come about 'naturally' as a function of time. The short-term aspects – ill-informed designation refusals, misapplication of the rules, sloppy listed building applications and consents – are going to need more systematic attention from those concerned. Yet there are still some good-news stories to celebrate. The listing in 2020 of Berthold Lubetkin's Sivill House (Figure 6.1) in London's East End following a well-informed application by its committed resident community is unlikely to have occurred even a few years ago, when official opinion might well have dismissed this remarkable late work of the Russian grandmaster as 'just another post-war tower block'.[5]

The eventual decision to abandon the proposed extension of the City of London School for Girls in the Barbican Estate (see p 123) is certainly another. But these may be the exceptions rather than the rule, and it is to be hoped that not too many fine buildings or spaces are lost or disfigured in the meantime. To return to the starting point, perhaps in the extent of its alteration, Bracken House (Figures 6.2 and 6.3), the first post-war designation (see p 11), may come to be seen as uncannily prescient of the permissive culture of intervention that seems to prevail in the treatment of Modern heritage as a whole. It is certainly quite difficult to cite comparable examples of such wholesale changes in listed buildings of earlier periods that are so widely applauded as paragons of good conservation practice.

However that may be, the need to address current anomalies in applying statutory listing criteria, as well as the degree of licence in listed building consents for egregious alterations in 'protected' post-war buildings and their settings under the pretext of 'less than substantial harm', is surely now well overdue.

Figure 6.1
Sivill House, Bethnal Green, 1964, by Skinner, Bailey and Lubetkin. The tower was listed in 2020.

Figure 6.2
Bracken House, City of
London, showing the extent
of intervention by Michael
Hopkins and Partners, 1988–91.
(Compare with Figure 1.6.)

Figure 6.3
Old meets new – detail of a
junction at Bracken House.

131

PART TWO: PROSPECT

7
From relics to resources – the new paradigm

This chapter looks towards the future, beyond the boundaries of conservation considered primarily in terms of 'elite heritage', to address broader issues of adaptive reuse and sustainability as applied to the considerable legacy of ordinary modern buildings that may not be significant enough to list, but are too valuable to demolish. The investigation suggests that revaluing modern architecture beyond the preservation of icons may often be more effectively advanced by embracing a diversity of other motives than pure heritage evangelism.

The dictionary defines a relic as 'something that has survived from the past… kept as a remembrance… treasured as a keepsake'. A resource, on the other hand, is 'a capability… a source of economic wealth, a supply, capital… resorted to in time of need', from the Latin *resurgere* – to rise again.[1] This chapter considers the progress of the modern conservation movement over the last five decades, from the former interpretation towards the latter, and the consequent implications for the future.

THE ORIGINAL MISSION

It was entirely logical that the project of 'revaluing Modernism' – if we define its British inception as the first designations of the Pevsner List in 1970 (see p 8) – should have begun with protecting the most outstanding achievements of the MoMo (Modern Movement) legacy. The task of identifying and proselytising heritage quality in buildings of still contested reputation would always be that bit easier by selection of the finest examples. There was also the concern to provide enhanced security for the rarest works of architecture that in many cases were still vulnerable to ill-considered intervention or even outright loss. As with the national project, so likewise internationally. The Docomomo mission at its first conference in Eindhoven in 1990 assembled delegates from a handful of countries to share their anxiety over the fate of modern architectural heritage across Europe and beyond. In a context of ignorance and neglect, it was a mutual resolve that would grow exponentially across the globe, now embracing more than 70 countries worldwide. Many of the authorities who ought to have known better were heedless of their MoMo legacy, and many of the owners of key buildings and sites had allowed them to fall into varying states of neglect. To those (including myself) for whom this legacy was their inspiration, the situation was unbearable and their response – driven largely by sentiment – was a shared determination to protect the most precious built achievements of the 'heroic' period of Modernism that had fallen into oblivion and were at risk of disappearing altogether, almost by accident.

Figure 7.1
Zonnestraal Sanatorium, Hilversum, the Netherlands, by Jan Duiker and Bernard Bijvoet, 1931. The building was restored by Hubert-Jan Henket and Wessel de Jonge in 2010.

Figure 7.2
The Penguin Pool, London Zoo,
by Lubetkin and Tecton, 1934.
The iconic exhibit was restored
by Avanti Architects in 1987.

What these initiatives ignited was an international movement to ensure that the finest surviving relics of that 'heroic' period were firstly identified and recognised as modern heritage, then protected and conserved. The ensuing paradigm – which I am here calling the 'old' paradigm – was the normative ambition of rescuing and curating these most iconic relics to the highest ethical and technical protocols. Some of the success stories have been heroic in themselves, and perhaps none more so than that of the building that in Docomomo's case started it all – the Zonnestraal Sanatorium, Hilversum, the Netherlands (Figure 7.1), which was eventually saved by Docomomo's founders, Hubert-Jan Henket and Wessel de Jonge. This building, and the monumental task of restoring it, was to become a sort of metaphor for the whole modern conservation movement.[2]

Many of the national groups likewise originated in a particular local rescue campaign, and probably every country in the Docomomo family could identify one building, among all others, that represented their cause. In England, we had the Penguin Pool at London Zoo (Figure 7.2; see also Figures 1.2 and 1.21), which I was privileged to restore in the mid-1980s and which was to serve as an emblem both of English Modernism in its prelapsarian prime, as well as of this new conservation initiative.[3]

All of these projects presented difficult and diverse technical challenges, but in another sense they were all straightforward 'philosophically', inasmuch as they essentially revolved around a shared consensus on the part of stakeholders as to their primary heritage importance, which accordingly became the main project driver. The 'revaluing' consisted of a fresh recognition of their heritage significance. But the new paradigm that we are seeking to address here arises from the developing direction of travel that can now be discerned long after that initial effort. Today, more than 30 years on, it is legitimate to ask whether and how that original paradigm has changed. For it surely has – in at least two respects. The first concerns the modern conservation movement itself, the second concerns its larger context.

To illustrate the first change, the Modern Movement legacy might rather simplistically be imagined in the form of a pyramid where the very few, most iconic, examples are its apex, and as heritage significance diminishes, so the numbers increase (Figure 7.3a). In the centre lies the largest collection of works that may not be of sufficient interest to list, but are certainly too numerous and valuable as real estate to demolish. At the base is the considerable residue of irredeemable buildings that could surely be lost without any regret whatsoever – both in terms of heritage interest and probably also asset value relative to the value of the sites they occupy, discounting issues of lost embodied energy.

Of course, there could be endless and perhaps entertaining debate as to which particular buildings might belong in which category, but that is not central to the matter being explored here. The point is that since many of the most significant icons have now been identified and in most cases (if not all) have been saved, or are at least no longer on the 'critical list', the movement's attention may turn to the other less rarefied but more numerous elements of the legacy. Thus, the first change after these three or more decades is the change of focus that distinguishes between 'the icon and the ordinary'.[4]

Naturally, the chronology isn't quite as tidy as the diagram suggests, but the broad thesis surely holds. In this context we must increasingly confront the 'sub-iconic' modern legacy – buildings about 50 to 70 years old, some listed but more not listable, though still 'worthy' or 'redeemable' for their economic value, and in many cases more. In other words, we are crossing the rather blurred boundary between heritage and something that falls just, or more than just, short of that definition – in the grey zone. Below the level of the iconic (assuming this can be agreed), heritage evangelism alone is increasingly unreliable and in some contexts even counter-productive, as a means of saving buildings that might otherwise be entirely viable and worthy of new investment, upgrade and/or repurposing. Other types of argument and advocacy must be deployed – social, economic, or environmental factors or combinations of these – for their retention and repair (Figure 7.3b). This is also why seeking to save 'sub-iconic' buildings through listing is a high-risk strategy that can often produce precisely the opposite result, since failure to achieve designation becomes equated with licence to demolish – overlooking more subtle intermediate options.

Figure 7.3a
Modern conservation – the direction of travel. It was logical to concentrate on the most significant 'icons' during the first period of modern conservation (notionally 1990 to 2005), before moving on to the more numerous but less 'precious' examples in later years.

Figure 7.3b
The different responses to the Modern Movement legacy. This diagram suggests how different arguments are required depending on the heritage status of the buildings concerned.

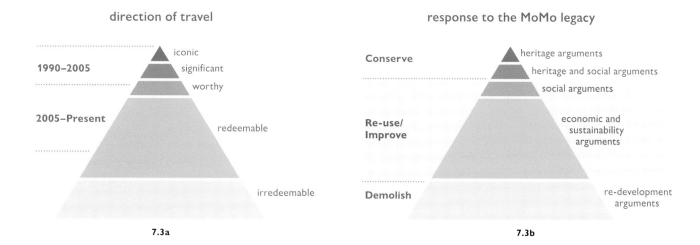

direction of travel

1990–2005 — iconic / significant / worthy

2005–Present — redeemable

irredeemable

7.3a

response to the MoMo legacy

Conserve — heritage arguments / heritage and social arguments / social arguments

Re-use/Improve — economic and sustainability arguments

Demolish — re-development arguments

7.3b

The second change – relating to external context – is the cause of environmental sustainability, which at the inception of the modern conservation movement was little more than a gleam on the horizon, but has now become the single most pressing issue to confront not only building design and construction generally, but also virtually every field of human endeavour in the developed world. It is now unthinkable to embark on any kind of constructive undertaking without the question of its environmental impact and sustainability being at the heart of the agenda. Call it the crisis of climate change, global warming, loss of biodiversity, marine pollution, fossil fuel impact, decarbonisation – it conditions everything from local shopping to international geopolitics. Increasingly alarming statistics tell us that we can no longer behave as if the earth's resources are limitless, and that we must learn how to renew the world with things that exist already. Indeed, it seems as if the Green Agenda is ultimately the only agenda.[5]

These shifts have been identified as two separate phenomena, but their implications in effect combine to create the new paradigm whereby 'conservation' as applied to the built environment as a previously privileged response to the plight of elite icons must increasingly jostle for attention with environmental, operational, economic and other priorities in dealing with that greater majority of modern buildings that are not iconic. Or to put it more melodramatically – the early motivation of 'heritage sentiment' by itself is either inapplicable or insufficient in furthering the cause of modern conservation. In short, the discussion moves from saving relics to exploiting resources, with the role of the actors involved changing from that of curators to that of alchemists.

WIDENING MOTIVATION

This transition connects directly with our earlier consideration of 'heritage recognition'. Whereas the protection of historic buildings can usually be expected to attract instinctive public support, in the case of *modern* buildings, because their status as heritage is still underdeveloped, the arguments for listing must be made by specialists – academics, architectural historians and 'experts'. It is because of the still widespread unpopularity of modern architecture in the UK that listing has remained the conservationists' principal weapon against demolition. If their case is successful then at least the building has the law on its side – even if not public opinion. However, as noted above, this is a game of high stakes inasmuch as if the case for listing fails, then demolition is usually assumed. Certificates of Immunity are sought for precisely this purpose. As we have witnessed, the consequences of failed listing campaigns have played out accordingly on Robin Hood Gardens (see p 71), Pimlico School (see p 82) and Broadgate (see p 14), and are insidiously doing so on London's Southbank complex (see p 119), which has now been turned down for listing four times and is steadily being made unlistable. By relying on listing as the primary defence, and therefore on seeking to convince sceptics of heritage significance, the modern conservation lobby has been attempting to win the most difficult type of argument for saving modern buildings in distress. This is how motivation by 'heritage sentiment' can have precisely the opposite outcome to that intended – since losing the argument for listing becomes synonymous with losing the buildings altogether. It also suggests, in the increasing number of cases where we are not dealing with 'icons' and where heritage advocacy therefore becomes that much more challenging, that exploring and promoting the many other possible motives for keeping a modern building and working with it may prove considerably more effective.

This question of motives merits closer examination because projects which to conservationists may appear to be driven self-evidently by heritage significance are often seen quite differently by the other participants, for whom concern for heritage may come low on the agenda – if indeed it features at all. In most projects involving a building's retention and improvement there are three types of need that require a response – of which only the first may accommodate purely heritage motives. This is 'repair' – the need to shore up or reinstate original fabric to retrieve or prolong authenticity. But beyond this there is typically also 'upgrade' – the need to improve the technical performance of a building or replace engineering systems that have become inadequate or unserviceable. Thirdly, and crucially, there is 'reconfiguration' – the pressure to intervene and adapt buildings and/or their sites in order to add value or accommodate new requirements. (I use the three terms generically to avoid getting ensnared in the semantics of conservation terminology. The glossaries appended to most charters are the place for that.) This pattern repeats so consistently that the architect's role typically involves seeking to bring these three kinds of pressure into a valid and sustainable point of balance (Figure 7.4). However, this will differ with each project, according to differing stakeholder priorities, and may be characterised in a variety of typologies.[6]

Figure 7.4a
Balancing priorities – the old paradigm: repair of original fabric tends to dominate in heritage-led projects.

Figure 7.4b
Balancing priorities – the new paradigm: reconfiguration tends to dominate in 'sub-iconic' projects, accommodating new needs.

The conservation lobby is interested in authenticity and 'significance', and so is biased towards preservation and repair of original fabric. Users and managers are concerned with whether a building is good to work in or live in, and so are inclined to focus on functionality and operational performance. Property owners and investors are interested in their building as a real-estate asset and so are concerned with intervening to maximise its exchange value and market appeal, a priority that usually involves seeking additional floorspace and sometimes also a change of image. The three needs thus tend to be identified with the three key types of stakeholder: repair – conservationists; upgrade – users; re-formation – owners/investors.

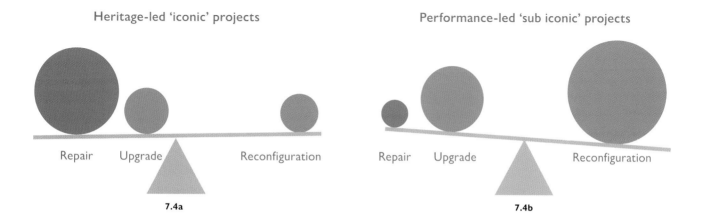

Heritage-led 'iconic' projects

Repair   Upgrade   Reconfiguration

7.4a

Performance-led 'sub iconic' projects

Repair   Upgrade   Reconfiguration

7.4b

Accordingly, the practising architect, especially when seeking to save and work with sub-iconic modern buildings, will be addressing three types of task: designing for new needs; upgrading performance; and identifying and honouring significance. Or to put it conversely, the architect must overcome three types of scepticism:

- the scepticism of owners that their property will retain its market value if it is merely kept and modified instead of being demolished and redeveloped
- the scepticism of managers/users that it can be made fit for purpose and operationally compliant
- the scepticism of conservationists that serving the needs of these other stakeholders can be accomplished without compromising whatever heritage value the building might still possess.

A triple challenge indeed, yet with judicious intervention, technical skill and design intelligence it is, or ideally should be, feasible to satisfy all of these ostensibly competing interests simultaneously, resulting in a genuine synthesis and resolving the seeming paradox of combining continuity with transformation. The weight given to each need can vary considerably. In the few most iconic projects of course conservation is supreme, with upgrade and reconfiguration being admitted only so far as is necessary to secure the key heritage objectives. On the other hand, with the great majority of modern buildings in the middle of the pyramid, it is only realistic to assume that intervention and upgrade will play the dominant role. Since modern conservation in the majority of cases cannot expect to operate in a supportive heritage culture, but must grapple with the science and art of upgrade and adaptation, it is these skills that will assume progressively greater importance. This, of course, is not to underestimate the need for conservation science as such, and the rescue of world-class 'relics' like Zonnestraal, in Hilversum, and Villa Tugendhat, in Brno, provide compelling examples of this discipline.[7] But the point in such projects as these is that the science occurs *within* a conservation agenda, whereas in the kinds of cases being considered here – cases that treat buildings as 'resources' – the science must find its place in a sceptical arena where even keeping modern buildings, and working with them, may not be assumed.

FUSING HERITAGE WITH RENEWAL

The above thesis can be illustrated by rating a series of projects in my experience in descending order of heritage motivation, starting with those that were expressly heritage-led and progressing to those where heritage was increasingly peripheral (though still an important by-product) – in effect, a step-by-step journey from sentiment to science. This surely is the way most 'sub-iconic' modern buildings will be saved – not by pleading the special privileges of patrimony but by demonstrating how they can be revalued and made useful for the future.

At the tip of the pyramid are the two house museums restored for the National Trust – Ernö Goldfinger's house in Willow Road, Hampstead (Figure 7.5) and Patrick Gwynne's house, The Homewood, near Esher in Surrey (Figure 7.6), both dating from 1938 (see Chapter 1). These could be regarded as the most straightforward in terms of motivation – that is, where the key parties (client, conservation authorities, users, architect and professional team) all shared the same priority – preserving heritage for public benefit.[8]

Figure 7.5
2 Willow Road, Hampstead, north London, by Ernö Goldfinger, 1938. The house was restored by Avanti Architects in 1996. Every single item was removed for conservation, then replaced in its original position. The work included formation of a separate curator's flat in the rear ground and lower floors, reconfiguring services to provide a conservation heating regime in the show house and conversion of one of the garages into a small audiovisual space for showing films.

Figure 7.6
The Homewood, Surrey, by Patrick Gwynne, 1938. The house was restored by Avanti Architects in collaboration with Patrick Gwynne, and opened as a house museum in 2004. The work entailed comprehensive fabric repair, reroofing and reprovision of rooftop services, reconstruction of the master bedroom suite to the original 1938 design and restoration of original colours and finishes – with Patrick Gwynne remaining in residence throughout the contract.

Figure 7.7
Berthold Lubetkin's Penthouse, Highpoint Two, Highgate, north London, 1938. The apartment was restored by Avanti Architects for new owners in 1996. The work entailed significant fabric repair and reservicing, restoration of façade sliding screens, reinstatement of lost finishes and original details, including board-marked concrete fireplace surround, decorative door covering and Pollock Theatre prints 'flyposted' each side of kitchen doorway (right). The lace-up composite rug was remade in replica, and original furniture pieces were kindly provided by Sasha Lubetkin, the architect's daughter.

However, by privileging heritage value, the buildings themselves virtually ceased to be private houses. (In fact, both properties still include live-in tenants; at Willow Road the tenancy is separate from the public show areas of the house, which required a new planning-use class of 'museum'. At The Homewood, public visiting arrangements are managed in parallel with residential use.)

The restoration of Berthold Lubetkin's Highpoint Two Penthouse (Figure 7.7)[9] was an almost unique case where heritage priorities and the incoming private owners' objectives were in perfect alignment, but generally there are very few instances where MoMo buildings can survive by fossilisation, or by becoming public exhibits with paid entry. We are in the rarefied realms of the Modernist icons villas Savoye and Tugendhat, Sonneveld and Seidler. By contrast, in rescue missions on modern houses for private owners (Figures 7.8 to 7.13), there have invariably been other priorities — most notably the desire to improve performance and add value, through fabric upgrade, reservicing, spatial reconfiguration and increased floor area. To present these as purely conservation projects in the modern heritage canon, despite being listed in all cases (except The Hill House), would be disingenuous — the economic realities dictated otherwise, and heritage enhancement was simply an added benefit, albeit an important one.

Figure 7.8
Harbour Meadow, Chichester,
by Peter Moro, 1940. Restored
and upgraded by Avanti
Architects for its new owner in
2006. Works included significant
consolidation of the severely
eroded and overpainted original
brickwork, reroofing and
reinstatement of the rooftop
dished screen and other
concrete elements, introduction
of a lower tier of windows to
provide views from the original
servants' area (reconfigured as
a family kitchen seen in shadow
to left of main house), renewal
of original colours and complete
reservicing.

Figure 7.9
Miramonte, Kingston, Surrey,
by Maxwell Fry, 1936. Restored
and upgraded by Avanti
Architects for its new owner
in 2002. Works included
removal of extraneous rooftop
water tower, comprehensive
concrete envelope repairs and
replacement of windows to the
original fenestration pattern,
complete reservicing and
interior fit-out, and addition
of a new library annex, family
rooms and enclosed swimming
pool, located so as to avoid
intrusion on classic 1930s views
of the original house.

Figure 7.10
66 Frognal, by Connell, Ward and Lucas, 1938. Restored and upgraded by Avanti Architects for its new owner in 2006. Works included concrete envelope repair and reinstatement of original colours, replacement of original fenestration, reconstruction of a poorly built swimming pool extension, complete interior refit with spatial reconfigurations to suit client requirements and comprehensive reservicing.

Figure 7.11
Cherry Hill (formerly Holthanger), Wentworth, Surrey, by Oliver Hill, 1935. Restored and upgraded by Avanti Architects for a new owner in 2015. Works included major restoration of the main house, reconstruction and enlargement of outlying extensions to provide a reception suite, additional bedrooms and underground swimming pool facilities. The interior refit entailed complete reservicing and fit-out with high-specification finishes – all undertaken within listing and greenbelt restrictions.

Figure 7.12
The Hill House, Hampstead, north London, by Oliver Hill, 1936–38. Restored and upgraded by Avanti Architects for a new owner in 1998. Works included replacement of a poorly executed second-floor extension with new glazed bedroom floor level and additional rooftop 'lantern outlook', restoration of surviving original features and finishes, and complete reservicing. The house is believed to be the highest residential property in London, the lantern being level with the top of the BT Tower.

North Elevation   South Elevation

Figure 7.13
The Hill House, drawings showing (shaded yellow) additional floors and plan areas added in upgrade.

First Floor

Third Floor

Ground Floor
new build shown in yellow

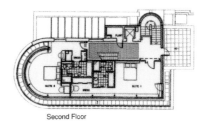

Second Floor

Figure 7.14 a, b, c and d.
The Isokon Apartments,
formerly Lawn Road Flats,
Camden, north London,
by Wells Coates, 1934.
These photographs show
the apartments before
restoration works, 2001.

The challenge was to achieve the clients' required interventions within the formal parameters of designation. In all cases, a combination of neglect and earlier alterations had already diminished the buildings' original character, such that as well as rendering the properties fit for the 21st century there was the aspiration to recapture key aspects of their authenticity – restoring original colours, reinstating correct fenestration patterns, recovering spatial definition and removing or rebuilding poorly executed extensions.[10]

Another residential property, the Isokon (aka Lawn Road Flats), Camden (Figures 7.14 and 7.15; see also pp 29 and 53), which one might assume was saved on account of its iconic status, was ultimately regenerated for its value to Notting Hill Housing Group, a registered social landlord whose project agenda happily dovetailed with the local council's policy to prioritise key-worker housing. The fact that the building was listed Grade I of course meant that observing conservation protocols was an essential element of the project. But after the prior campaign to forestall demolition had achieved its objective, these were not the principal project drivers as such.[11]

What we are witnessing is the changing argument as we move down the pyramid towards the less iconic, more generic elements of the MoMo legacy. In place of heritage advocacy are economic and social drivers – even within a context of designation. Outside that context, the sustainability arguments for keeping and working with mid-20th-century modern buildings come increasingly to the fore.

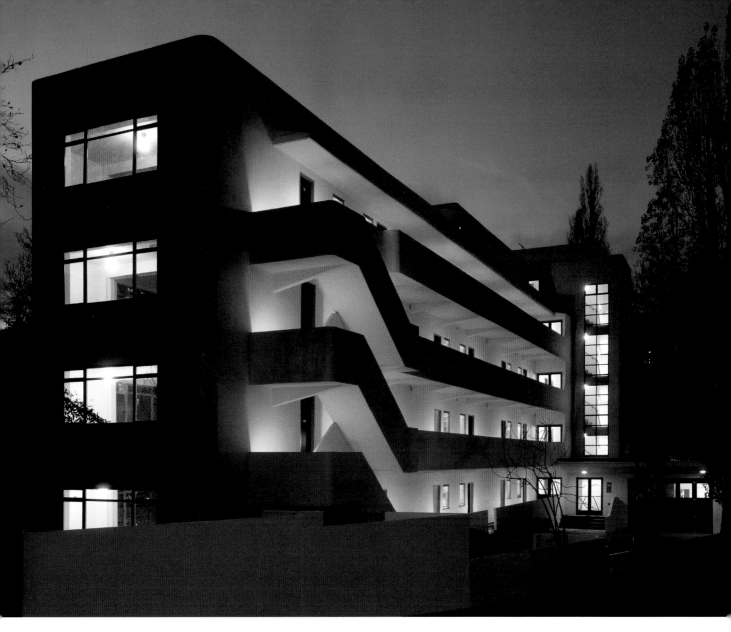

Figure 7.15 a and b.
The Isokon Apartments,
restored by Avanti Architects
for Notting Hill Housing
Group, 2004.

Figure 7.16
New North Court,
Jesus College, Cambridge,
by David Roberts, 1960.

The following studies illustrate two projects where the key drivers had little to do with heritage values, yet where a heritage dividend was still secured. In both cases it was the clients' need for reconfiguration and improved technical performance that triggered the projects – not preservation of architectural heritage. In a communal residential example – a hall of residence at Jesus College, Cambridge University – the underlying requirement, apart from overdue fabric repairs, was to make the building suitable for conference visitor use out of term time, a familiar challenge for British universities. New North Court (Figure 7.16), an originally acclaimed post-war student residence building by the architect David Roberts, had been an ingenious reinterpretation of the Oxbridge college residence typology when it was designed in the early 1960s, deploying a 45-degree rotated plan form with alternating staircases and service zones in a continuous U-shaped block of accommodation that provided full-height oriel windows and individual balconies to every room.

Though listed Grade II in 1993, by the early 2000s New North Court had become degraded, with many service and environmental aspects now being outdated. It was unloved by its users and the original shared bathroom and kitchen cores made it quite unsuitable for conference visitor use. Redevelopment was not a realistic option but the college certainly anticipated the need for radical interventions. The eventual solution entailed complete re-engineering of the service cores to convert all existing study bedrooms into self-contained en suites, with consequential reprovision of the students' communal kitchen rooms ("gyps") that were thereby displaced (Figure 7.17).

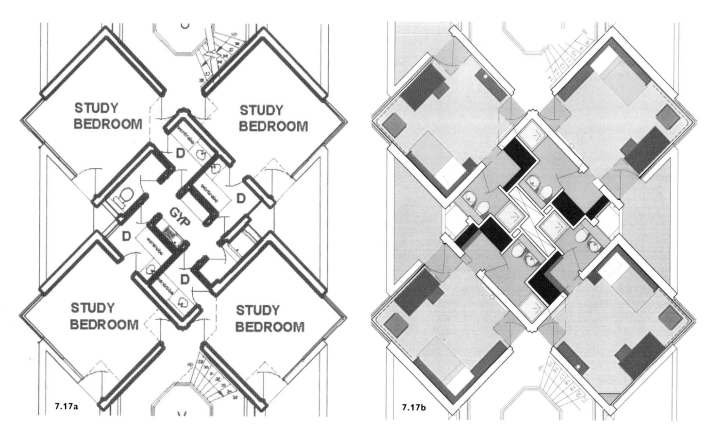

STUDY BEDROOM

STUDY BEDROOM

GYP

STUDY BEDROOM

STUDY BEDROOM

7.17a

7.17b

Figure 7.17a
New North Court, Jesus College, Cambridge. Plan of the original gyp room (kitchen area) embedded in the internal core.

Figure 7.17b
New North Court, Jesus College, Cambridge. Plan of revised service cores with en suite bathrooms to each study. The new pipework installations were 'rehearsed' in advance to check feasibility using an on-site duct mock-up.

Other requirements included provision of a new lift to achieve a sufficient number of compliant rooms for wheelchair users, major envelope improvement with upgraded thermal performance, and complete renewal of roof coverings and maintenance access arrangements. The challenge was to deliver all these improvements without detriment to the special architectural interest for which it was listed. In fact, although the internal bathroom reconfiguration proved to be fiendishly complicated, the final result achieved all the desired results almost without any visible exterior consequences. Heritage sensitivities were observed 'simply' by replacing original components, such as damaged slate copings, on a like-for-like basis, renewing corroded fasciae in tern-coated steel, and 'curating' local areas of concrete repair with a bespoke mortar recipe and an abraded finishing technique so as to blend in with the original fairface finish.

The chief spatial puzzle concerned the reorganisation of the student kitchen areas, known as gyp rooms. The original arrangement had placed these within the bathroom zone that was shared by four study bedrooms on each floor. These areas had necessarily to be claimed for the individual en suites for each room, leaving no remaining area for the gyp function. We explored a range of options, including adding a rooftop floor or creating a sunken communal gyp room in the central courtyard garden, both of which would have been fraught with difficulties as well as substantially increasing costs. The brief indeed seemed to present a problem with no answer. But then one day the solution suddenly dawned. It would be to relocate the gyps into the lower-ground floor store rooms, which offered ideally sized spaces for each group of rooms and which were generally underused (Figure 7.18). The only exterior alteration needed would be the lowering of the existing window cills to these semi-sunken spaces to improve daylighting and afford views in and out. (This strategy even yielded a stock of original bricks that could be used for local repairs elsewhere.)

As well as providing greatly improved amenity (the original gyps being internal spaces uncomfortably juxtaposed with wet rooms), this would establish a visual connection between the gyps and the communal entrance of each staircase, bringing a new social dimension to the building. Returning residents would be able to see if their gyp was in use, if any of their friends were there and join the party if inclined. Those using the gyps would now have a meaningful relationship with the landscaped courtyard, instead of being 'buried' among the communal bathrooms. Externally, the intervention was also arguably an improvement on Roberts' original design, inasmuch as the dominant oriel motif now rises from nearer ground level, opening up the previously blank corners of brickwork to produce a more interactive façade (Figure 7.19).

Figure 7.18
New North Court, Jesus College. Revised lower-ground floor plan with new gyp rooms (kitchens) and trunk stores.

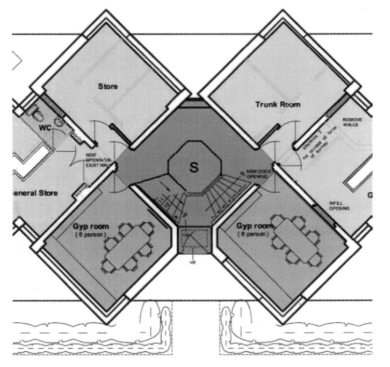

Figure 7.19 a and b.
A view of the oriel windows in their original arrangement (a) and as revised (b), with lowered cills for the new gyp rooms.

To the uninitiated, however, the change in architectural character was so discreet it might even go unnoticed. We were later informed that New North Court, from previously being the least popular residence in the college, had subsequently become the most sought-after. What had been steadily becoming a relic, is now a valued resource (Figure 7.20).

If this transformation at Jesus College had little to do with heritage motivation, as conventionally defined, the project we undertook at Haggerston School, Hackney (Figure 7.21), had even less. This rather bleak mid-1960s all-girls comprehensive school, designed by Ernö Goldfinger, was slated for wholesale upgrading and expansion as part of the Labour Government's ambitious Building Schools for the Future (BSF) educational reforms, before this enlightened programme was abruptly halted by the Conservatives in 2010.

Haggerston's fate might well have followed that of Pimlico School (see p 82) had it not already been listed (Grade II) and earmarked as part of the first BSF batch. Like Pimlico, there were similar problems of environmental performance, with stories of students being sent home early on summer days due to overheated classrooms becoming unfit for use.

Figure 7.20
New North Court, Jesus College, Cambridge, after restoration and upgrade works by Avanti Architects, 2005. Compare with Figure 7.16.

Figure 7.21
Haggerston School, Hackney, northeast London, by Ernö Goldfinger, 1966. The photograph shows the original 1960s view.

Figure 7.22 a and b. (Below)
Haggerston School – typical original corridor view (a) before upgrade works, and with upgrade works in progress (b), showing the resilience of the frame.

Figure 7.23 (Below right)
Haggerston School – typical corridor view after upgrade works.

But major reconfiguration, refurbishment and envelope upgrade of the principal teaching block, as well as construction of a new design technology centre and various other interventions, achieved a transformation of the school at approximately half the cost of the equivalent new build alternative at the time (Figures 7.22 and 7.23).

Furthermore, removal of sundry poor additions that were wholly at odds with the Goldfinger aesthetic and the adoption/reinstatement of his distinctive design idiom in other key areas of the campus resulted in tangible authenticity gains that have also worked to strengthen the school's sense of identity (compare Figures 7.24 and 7.25).[12] Gratifyingly, the outcome was described by a Hackney Design Awards Jury as 'an exemplar of how a building can be regenerated and revitalised, from spatial organisation down to graphic signage'. Thus a brief that was driven essentially by pressing education objectives, also delivered clear heritage benefits.

Figure 7.24
Haggerston School – general view before interventions and upgrade works.

Figure 7.25
Haggerston School – view after interventions (completed in 2012), with the bungalow annexe removed and a new technology centre introduced (right).

THE LARGER LEGACY

The foregoing examples surely help to identify some key features of 'the new paradigm'. Both of these latter projects might easily have gone in a different direction. Yet in both cases, a convergence or synthesis was achieved between new operational demands, improved technical performance and residual heritage recognition – and, despite the initial scepticism of some stakeholders, a renewed commitment and sense of value has been cultivated in the institutions concerned. With the exception of the two National Trust houses (2 Willow Road and The Homewood), all of the above projects were driven by motives other than primary concern for modern heritage. But in every case there has also been a heritage dividend in terms of enhanced authenticity and sense of identity. In other words, the predominance of other motives in projects involving important modern buildings does not mean that heritage considerations cannot play a worthwhile part. This may surely prove to be a pointer for how revaluing Modernism will develop in the future, through a transition from curating relics to exploiting resources. This might seem like merely a re-badging of those interventionist projects promoted as 'constructive conservation' that were noted earlier (see p 20 and p 106). But it involves a much wider interpretation of the modern conservation endeavour, beyond the confines of designated heritage towards that infinitely greater residue of modern building stock that should be understood as representing another kind of legacy – that which Karl Marx described as 'congealed labour' and in current parlance we might refer to as embodied energy.

If protagonists of the modern conservation movement might be described as a 'family', one could speculate that what binds it together is a predisposition to embrace the Modern Movement legacy as a treasure house of heirlooms to be cherished and curated. A characteristic example is the Iconic Houses organisation, an international network that, in its own words, connects architecturally significant houses and artists' homes and studios from the 20th century that are open to the public as house museums. The platform also focuses on conservation, management, policy and cooperation.[13] Iconic Houses is indeed a model of voluntary collaboration and mutual enthusiasm.

Outside the family, however, most people have no such predisposition, especially those whose interest is based on asset value as distinct from heritage value. By all means the family can continue to revere its inheritance, but it must also become better at understanding and exploiting other more 'secular' arguments, beyond heritage advocacy, for keeping and working with sub-iconic modern buildings. There are plenty of arguments to pursue and they are likely to focus on the environmental and economic factors that propel the constant churn of building and rebuilding in cities and towns. Reusing existing buildings is often cheaper and faster than new build, more energy efficient, less socially disruptive, less wasteful of material, less affected by seasonal factors, less onerous in relation to regulatory hurdles and more environmentally friendly. The survival of most modern buildings in the centre of our pyramid (see Figure 7.3) will thus depend not on securing difficult designations, but on developing the metrics to persuade modern heritage agnostics of the advantages and feasibility of upgrading performance, adding value and exploiting opportunities to serve new needs – thereby reutilising existing resources to avoid, or at least reduce, the excessive carbon costs of wholesale demolition and redevelopment.

Except in the highest of high-profile cases, this broader interpretation of conservation will surely outweigh, at least in terms of sheer volume, the more rarefied model typically assumed in the established conservation charters and their preoccupation with surviving authenticity, original fabric and evidential value. Of course, conservative repair and the attendant specialist skills and techniques required in the conscientious restoration of designated heritage assets of any period should still be regarded as the gold standard of conservation practice – *in appropriate circumstances*. But beyond the celebrated icons, the greater challenge will be to find ways of adapting the reusable mass of Modernism's legacy for a sustainable future.

One of the early criticisms of Docomomo was that its conservationist stance towards Modernism was intellectually – even ethically – inconsistent with a movement originally committed to the future and which rejected the 'art-history' interpretation of architecture of the past. In the words of leading iconoclast Martin Pawley:

Through the formation of a quisling organization Docomomo, [the Modernists] agreed to surrender their Modern heritage and endorse its absorption into the art-historical classification system as a style, which it never was. In return they received museum status for many Modern buildings, converting their once-proud revolutionary instruments back into monuments for the delectation of the masses alongside the palaces of the *ancien regime*.[14]

Yet, even if this caricature were true, to follow that 'logic' would mean that we should be bound by the circumstances confronting our forebears when half the world lay in ruins, and should argue that what justified their need to rebuild on a tabula rasa should remain our justification to keep on demolishing. But, as noted earlier, the conditions of our time have surely taught us that 'progress' must now entail learning how to renew the world with things that exist already.

Debate may continue as to the heritage values of the Modern Movement, but what cannot be disputed is that its legacy also represents an incalculably vast investment of labour, energy and material. Inevitably, a fair percentage must be cleared and replaced (ideally salvaging and recycling the proceeds to the maximum extent). To suggest otherwise would be naive. But more, much more, must survive by being intelligently adapted and sustained. The new paradigm would expect that the embodied energy in an existing modern building should make it economically more advantageous and environmentally more responsible to retain and upgrade it, regardless of whether or not it is listed. Increasingly stringent environmental targets will force the pace anyway in achieving a net-zero carbon construction economy within the specified dates – all new buildings by 2030, all buildings by 2050; see the Climate Change Act 2008 (2050 Target Amendment) Order 2019. We will return to this argument in the final chapter.

PROGRESSING THE PARADIGM

Meanwhile, how may this new paradigm be advanced? There are probably three factors that can play a part:

- acknowledging and negotiating with the diversity of stakeholder motivation
- appreciating the effect of the passage of time
- exploiting the evidence.

The first of these – acknowledging and negotiating with the diversity of motivation – as well as widening the criteria for retention and adaptive reuse of modern buildings, surely also has implications for professional training, not in downgrading or diluting conservation expertise as such but rather in breaking out of the silo culture that tends to divorce conservation specialists from 'mainstream' professionals. We need to recognise that all these skills must cohabit and nourish each other if a conservation sensibility is to be brought to sub-iconic projects, where inherent heritage values might otherwise go unrecognised. As noted in Chapter 1, there are certain specialist conservation qualifications and registers of building professionals that hold such accreditations. This is fine, but it should not inhibit meaningful interaction of all disciplines in the construction community. There cannot ultimately be a legitimate separation, since new build work, conservation and environmental engineering all require the exercise of design creativity, historical insight and technical competence.

Coming from the other direction, it may be a generalisation – though probably not an unfair one – to suggest that architects as an occupational group are predisposed towards the creation of new buildings in preference to working with existing ones. To use current coinage, it is 'baked in' to their training and aspirations and underpins a professional culture that tends to value new build more highly as the primary vehicle of architectural achievement, whether in historiography, peer group recognition or academic discourse. I well remember the opening lecture of my own architectural training in the mid-1960s, when as impressionable students we were told by our eminent professor of planning that 'we would be the generation of architects required to build a new city the size of Leeds each year, every year until the end of the century'. Such prophecies were hardly conducive to valuing a career in refurbishment. The profession's heroes are traditionally identified by their new build masterpieces, with projects typically being conceived *de novo* before summoning the resources needed for their realisation. The alternative, whereby their formulation would evolve from an audit of the resources already available, is still the exception, other than – tellingly – in so-called 'less developed cultures', where working with the materials to hand is necessarily the starting point. Clearly this value system is going to have to change for a more environmentally responsible profession.

One could point to signs that it is already beginning to do so. The award of the 2021 Pritzker Architecture Prize to Anne Lacaton and Jean-Philippe Vassal is surely a turning point in the prize's 42-year history of honouring new build work, now celebrating – in the words of the citation – 'a restorative architecture that is at once technological, innovative and ecologically responsive [that] can be pursued without nostalgia' and 'that renews the legacy of modernism'.

The citation continued, '[The architects] have also proposed an adjusted definition of the very profession of architecture. The modernist hopes and dreams to improve the lives of many are reinvigorated through their work that responds to the climatic and ecological emergencies of our time.'[15] The aspect of particular significance is that the 2021 laureates' work is not essentially focused on 'elite heritage' but rather on the types of buildings described earlier as 'perhaps neither good enough to list, nor bad enough to demolish' (see p 88). If only by publicity impact, these shifts help consolidate what has been termed here as 'the new paradigm'.

But it is not only the design professionals who are implicated. Other disciplines, including cost planning, material science, Life Cycle Assessment and others, have an equal part to play. Being able to demonstrate through convincing holistic metrics that retention and adaptive reuse of a substantial modern building, rather than its demolition and redevelopment, could actually be a cheaper option than new build, when taking *all* environmental factors into account, may prove a very much more powerful argument than art-history advocacy in persuading property owners to reconsider their plans. So, likewise, might be the advice that existing substructure, frame, floors and selected envelope components may be viably reutilised without constraining the feasibility of other interventions, most likely renewal of engineering services, that might be needed to upgrade operational performance – seeing as these retained elements usually account for the majority of embodied carbon in a typical modern building.

As to the passage of time – we have only to take stock of what has changed over the 30-plus years since Docomomo's formation to appreciate the different attitudes towards modern architecture today. Notwithstanding the well-noted popular ambivalence, one could point to many signs of progress in public and professional circles – not just in relation to architectural conservation but also in awareness of the wider environmental agenda discussed above. Incentives to go greener are increasingly embedded in regulatory procedures, while disincentives (including penalties) of ignoring such considerations are becoming ever more stringent. According to the Technology Strategy Board, the construction, operation and maintenance of the built environment in the UK accounts for 45% of total UK carbon emissions, 27% attributable to domestic buildings and 18% to non-domestic.[16] The environmental ethics of construction are already being drawn into the centre of 'the Overton window' and will become the subject of increasing regulation, with such measures as Environmental Product Declarations (EPDs) and Building Energy Ratings (BERs) becoming mandatory. Policies for carbon fines, computed on the financial evaluation of the embodied energy lost in redevelopment schemes, are in consideration, along with, conversely, carbon credits for refurbishment, thereby combining stick and carrot. One could legitimately ask how such an evaluation might have altered the calculus of projects like Robin Hood Gardens, Pimlico School or Broadgate, and the extent to which factoring in all their egregious losses of embodied energy as a prior redevelopment levy would have affected the viability of what has replaced them. It suggests that 'the conservation deficit', a term conventionally used where the alleged cost of rescue is claimed as greater than the value of the result – and an all-too familiar pretext for inertia or demolition by a reluctant owner of a difficult existing building – may need to be completely rethought.[17] By promoting such interrogation scientifically and holistically as a prerequisite of obtaining formal consents, the growing impact of the climate emergency on conservation culture will surely be progressed.

Finally – exploiting the evidence. Those familiar with the Docomomo initiative will know that the first of its self-imposed tasks upon formation at Eindhoven in 1990 was the compilation of national registers by member countries to identify the most outstanding examples of modern architecture in every territory (Figure 7.26). This was an essential first step and produced a valuable document of historical record.[18] But it is now time to compile a new register to exhibit the burgeoning number of exemplary case studies involving successful rehabilitation and adaptive reuse, which provide concrete evidence of the movement's three decades of revaluing Modernism.

Many of the examples will doubtless involve revisiting and updating entries on the original register, but they may also feature other outstanding cases involving unlisted buildings that carry equally persuasive but less exclusive messages. Much of the baseline information must already exist in the 'homework fiches' undertaken as a membership obligation, or in the numerous studies presented at biennial conferences over the years, but which become 'lost' in the increasingly bulky publications of collected conference papers. Each local Docomomo chapter could be tasked with selecting and editing its most compelling exemplars.

Such cumulative evidence of what has already been proved possible is one of the best ways to change the minds of sceptics. Indeed, an initiative along these lines is already being attempted in the recent launch of the Docomomo Rehabilitation Award (DRAW), the first results of which were announced in 2021, celebrating the best entries submitted from the international network in a range of different categories.[19] If, as is being suggested, the DRAW becomes a biennial

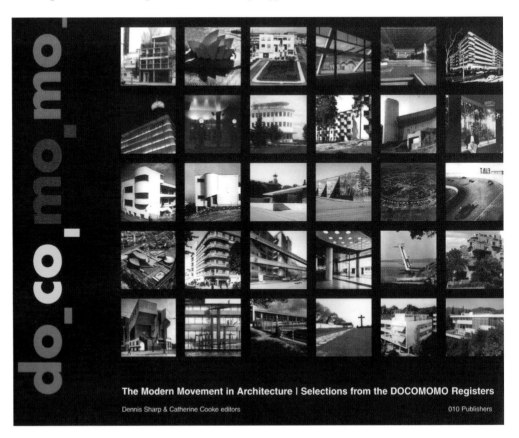

Figure 7.26
Original selections from the Docomomo Registers, 2000. Over 20 years on, it's time for a new selection of exemplary refurbishments.

award, then the wider this growing body of evidence is promulgated, the greater will be its impact. This is not to say that a tipping point for modern conservation will be reached any time soon. Worthy reusable buildings will continue to be spoilt or needlessly lost. But this is only because as far as the modern architectural legacy is concerned, we are still in the Darwinian phase of natural selection. (If it may be called 'natural'.)

Increasingly, however, this new paradigm will surely merge with a still broader scenario – one in which the key distinction is not merely between iconic and sub-iconic buildings, but which acknowledges the utterly changed global context since the original Modern Movement – with its assumptions of limitless energy, perpetual growth and endless material disposability. It is this larger, more secular, and infinitely more ambitious agenda that must surely reach a tipping point, when sustainability and the circular economy in a zero-carbon built environment becomes the new normal. By all these means might the extraordinary *social optimism* of the old Moderns then at last be fused with the new *social responsibility* that global environmental stewardship has made our primary duty today (Figure 7.27).

Figure 7.27
From social optimism to social responsibility.

FROM SOCIAL OPTIMISM TO ➡ SOCIAL RESPONSIBILITY

8
Quickfire Q & A

This chapter offers a concise summary of selected modern conservation issues in a Q & A format. The texts aim to encapsulate and answer some of the key questions that recur in professional discourse and student discussion. But they come with a caveat…

THE GREAT ENGINEER OVE ARUP WAS notoriously noncommittal when answering difficult questions on subjects on which he was an acknowledged authority. It was as though he knew too much to be lured into giving simple responses on matters that he understood were too complex for glib answers. 'On the one hand, there is this to be considered. On the other hand, there is that... On the third hand...,' was the typical reply.[1] This apparent indecisiveness resonates with much of the discourse on modern conservation, which can be complex and equivocal and often tends to lead to the conclusion, 'Well, it depends...'[2] Outside the narrowly defined circumstances of a particular case – and even then – there is frequently no single short answer that can be offered in advance or that will entirely suffice. This, as noted in Chapter 3, can be the limitation of charters and generic advice notes.

But it can also require considerable time and tenacity to absorb all of the official guidance, the mountain of academic and technical literature and the burgeoning collections of conference papers on the subject of conservation generally, including the growing 'subgenre' of *modern* conservation. Becoming immersed in all this material is, of course, essential for those who intend to be fully engaged in the field, whether as officers involved in governance, as consultant heritage advisers or as practitioners, accredited or not. But for those on the edges of the subject, or who are just entering it, there may be some advantage having rough-and-ready answers to some of the issues that crop up again and again in debate and in practice. Eventually, unless the discussion is purely academic, even the most intractable conundrum in practice ultimately requires a decision.

This chapter is an attempt to pull together a range of such questions and offer some 'quickfire' answers. Naturally this runs the risk of oversimplification, so readers are forewarned accordingly. Many of the Q & As that follow have been derived from my interactions with students in the context of lectures and mentoring; others are composites of matters arising from college projects, conferences or interviews. And some touch on issues that are covered in greater detail in other chapters of this book. But all together they attempt a broad overview of the field that it is hoped will prove of introductory value, subject always to 'the Arup caveat'.

The questions are grouped under a sequence of subheadings that proceed from the general to the particular.

PHILOSOPHY OF MODERN HERITAGE

Q. If the Modern Movement was committed to the future and the Functionalist purpose of buildings, is it not a fundamental contradiction to conserve them as heritage – monuments rather than instruments – when they should be discarded as soon as they no longer serve their purpose?

A. No. Firstly it is incorrect to regard 'the Modern Movement' as a singular monolithic phenomenon with a uniform creed directed only towards the future in rejection of the past. Filippo Tomaso Marinetti and Adolf Meyer may have been Modernists – but so were Igor Stravinsky and Hans Scharoun, El Lissitsky and Sir Denys Lasdun. Anyway, many of Modernism's creations were consciously intended as 'monuments', built statements of lasting principles, and should be treated as such. Many of the movement's founding fathers – Auguste Perret, Mies van der Rohe, Le Corbusier, et al. – were profoundly influenced by the architectures and architects of previous ages and were ready to acknowledge it – think Julien Guadet, Auguste Choisy, Karl Friedrich Schinkel, Le Corbusier's *Le Voyage d'Orient* – as were leading second-generation masters in the UK – Berthold Lubetkin, Ernö Goldfinger, et al. – who wholeheartedly embraced the challenge of 'metabolising' the past in their work.[3]

But regardless of original intentions, a culture of such vast creativity, diversity and global reach as the Modern Movement cannot uniquely be singled out for redaction from history. Its belief in progress, as evidenced in its architecture, was itself a historical product of its time and has left a unique cultural inheritance which later generations must evaluate but have no prior right to destroy. The deliberate erasure of historical remains – 'cultural cleansing' – is no less reprehensible in the case of Modern heritage as in any other. Modern Movement (MoMo) buildings cannot be treated merely as a property inventory for selective disposal by self-appointed iconoclasts under the assumed justification that 'this is what the original proponents would have wanted'. In any case, as elements of existing real estate they are subject to legal title and numerous other provisions and must usually continue to earn their living by remaining in beneficial use. Very few MoMo buildings can survive merely by becoming museum exhibits with paid entry, and even an important but redundant 'instrument' should be documented before being lost. But much Modern architecture that is of little or no special interest is abandoned, adapted or redeveloped without issues of heritage even arising, so selectivity is already assured.

Q. Which is more important in Modern heritage – the concept or the fabric, essence or substance?

A. It's a false question – they are interdependent. Heritage significance is defined as an amalgam of evidential, historical, aesthetic and communal values – not just one or other of them. Design concepts, for example Le Corbusier's *Cinq Points*, were crucial in developing the new syntax of Modern architecture, and the materials and techniques (the fabric) were equally crucial to its realisation. The touchstone of heritage value 'significance' may inhere equally in a building's intellectual achievement as in its materiality. Marcel Breuer once stated, 'The basis of modern architecture is not the new materials, nor even the new form, but the new mentality; that is to say, the view we take and the manner in which we judge our needs.'[4] The resulting 'judgement' becomes a cultural footprint. The related question as to which should be given priority in a given conservation project can only be settled in the context of that project. Ideally, both concept and fabric will be honoured, but fabric may be obliged to yield if its retention would cause progressive damage to the asset. In such cases there is no shortage of good guidance on how to reconcile the apparent conflict.

Q. What if, after all reasonable attempts have been made and failed, a significant Modern building just can't be preserved?

A. Well, the question really answers itself. Short of demolition, curated decay or 'managed atrophy' may offer a solution subject to curatorial resources and issues of public safety.[5] But beyond that, the answer must lie in conscientious documentation. 'Do' is, after all, the first syllable in Docomomo's acronym. The scope for high-quality digital recording and accessible archiving is now considerable and the obligation to undertake such forms of 'virtual preservation' can and should be a condition of any listed building consent to demolish.

Q. If technology and components used in the early to mid-20th-century buildings were experimental and imperfect, should they now be preserved?

A. If they're critical to 'special interest', ideally yes, provided their retention is not contributing to progressive damage or is wholly unsustainable. A pioneer's errors or the technical limitations of their time may be just as significant and worthy of preservation as their successes, provided they are not actively detrimental to heritage fabric. Otherwise, good practice would direct that one should aim for discreet repair or like-for-like replacement. It's worth remembering that not all technology or components of pre-20th-century buildings were perfect either. How many stones, bricks, services or roofing materials of Victorian and Georgian buildings have had to be replaced? This is not ethically controversial if carried out responsibly, in accordance with well-informed conservation practice and conscientious documentation.

Q. Is it in the spirit of 'Functionalism' to upgrade/replace defective original building components whenever possible?

A. Not necessarily – assuming this refers to 'buildings of special interest'. 'Functionalism' has become a term used in casual commentary, or can be a promotional mantra deployed (often disingenuously) by architects in justification of their work. The implication behind the question appears to reinforce the culture of disposability which no longer holds in today's world of recycling, reuse, decarbonisation and the circular economy. Our grandparents' need for wholesale clearance and comprehensive rebuilding in the early post-war period, when the world lay in ruins, cannot serve as our justification for indiscriminate demolition. But discreet upgrade of fabric, components and services in buildings of special architectural interest can be justified quite pragmatically in the interests of prolonging useful life, if carried out sensitively and with due respect for the original design intentions. In any case, the 'spirit of Functionalism' has now been superseded by the 'spirit of sustainability' (as argued in Chapter 7).

Q. Do Modern Movement buildings need their own principles of conservation?

A. No, not 'principles' as such, which imply *a priori* validity. The principles set out in many traditional charters are still applicable to significant Modern buildings – for example the Burra Charter of 1979, or Historic England's *Conservation Principles*, which are 'vintage neutral'.[6] But these documents tend to address conservation at the level of ethics and be generic in nature. They may not address certain attributes particular to Modernism. To identify these attributes, it is necessary to go beyond – or beneath – the level of 'principles' and consider specifics. The ICOMOS Madrid–New Delhi Document (2017; see Figure 3.2) is intended for application to Modern heritage, but sensibly uses the term 'Articles' rather than 'Principles'. At the *technical* level, Modern buildings *do* bring their own issues and *do* need their own technical toolbox – just as, say, Tudor buildings or Gothic buildings need their own toolbox in turn. But not to forget, even charters are also susceptible to changing ideology. Note how often they are reissued with revisions. The Venice Charter (1964) was challenged as unduly Eurocentric and defective in various other ways in little over a decade after its adoption, while the Burra Charter has already been revised numerous times.[7]

MODERN LISTING AND PROTECTION

Q. Are Modern buildings treated differently, in terms of listing and subsequent treatment?

A. To judge from recent practice, the answer to this is a clear double 'yes' (see Chapters 1 to 6). There are specific provisions in official policy for Modern, notably post-war, buildings that do not apply to others of previous ages. This is legitimate to the extent that a minimum time interval must necessarily elapse before reasonably impartial evaluation is possible – even if the length of the interval is debatable. But there are also now enough cases in the application of policy to corroborate this different treatment in practice. The related question as to whether they *should* be treated differently following listing is (in my view) a double 'no' – that is in terms of statutory controls and official procedures for protecting listed buildings, as argued in several of the previous chapters. Once a building is protected by listing there is, or should be, no statutory discrimination relating to age.

Q. What weight should be given to age, virtuosity and fitness for purpose?

A. As far as regulations are concerned, the issue of age is simply as currently specified in the statutory guidance – 30 years minimum for eligibility for designation, but 10 years in very special circumstances where the asset is of national significance and under immediate threat. The date banding included in official guidance suggests that significance is considered to increase with age over the long term. 'Virtuosity' depends on whether this is intrinsic to 'special interest'. It is in cases like Lubetkin's Penguin Pool (see Figures 1.2 and 1.21, and p 173) or Arup's Kingsgate Bridge (see Figure 4.19), both Grade I. But architecture displaying no obvious virtuosity might still be of 'special interest' for being simply the best of its type, for exhibiting 'special interest' in some other particular, or for being historically significant – for example, listed buildings by Taylor and Green or McMorran and Whitby. As for 'fitness for purpose', this, and its close cousin 'meeting the original brief', were simply introduced as an alibi for declining to list a building that a particular minister didn't like. Careful analysis casts considerable doubt on the logical validity of this test (see Chapter 4), but unfortunately it has now become embedded in statutory criteria. So its application should be forensically interrogated to verify its relevance when being argued as critical to a particular case. But beyond the specifics of statutory regulation, it must be recognised as a societal convention that – all other things being equal – greater age, as such, will almost invariably confer greater weight in terms of heritage recognition.

Q. Does listing reduce the marketability, value and attractiveness of a home?

A. Not necessarily. In most listed estates or large apartment blocks there is often more than one demographic or 'culture' within the resident community. While some – often the older residents who were in occupation before designation and not predisposed to regard their property as 'heritage' – consider listing as an imposition that reduces value by disincentivising potential purchasers, there are others – often a younger cohort – who are more aware of the building's historical interest and importance and who regard designation as a badge of prestige and an added attraction. Evidence from local estate agents often confirms that authentically preserved flats actually tend to attract higher resale values. However, there does ultimately need to be sufficient 'good fit' between a listed building and its owner/occupier for the attendant restraints not to feel burdensome.

Q. Should a building's 'success' be measured against the designer's stated intentions, or the views of critics and historians?

A. If this question relates to designation, then 'success' is not strictly a relevant criterion for listing, and anyway is likely to be evaluated differently by designer, owner, user, architectural critic, historian and the general public. 'Special architectural and historic interest' should be assessed by the relevant agency – Historic England, et al., and by suitably qualified historians and relevant amenity groups, but with due regard to the views of owner, critics and the general public. It is also important to consider the building's original and current reception, in order to reach a balanced judgement. Merely accepting the stated views of the original architect as definitive contradicts the purpose of a 30-year rule – or an interval of any length – which provides time for the revaluation of a building within the wider context of its peer group to develop and crystallise. However, the designer's recollections and direct knowledge, just like original documents, when available, can be of considerable assistance in the context of a live conservation project, albeit they may not always be regarded as definitive. What was intended and what was drawn are not always what was built (see Chapter 9).

Q. Is listing an insupportable burden in an 'Age of Austerity' that can no longer afford monuments to 'Welfare'?

A. Of course not. The process of selecting and protecting important heritage, Modern or otherwise, cannot simply stop because of a topical policy of a particular government. Listing need not be a 'burden' anyway. At its simplest, it is merely a way of obliging the stakeholders involved to be more careful and conscientious with the building/s concerned than they might otherwise be. The financial consequences of listing are, strictly speaking, a matter to be addressed 'downstream' after the consideration of listing itself is settled. Listed status may also yield opportunities for grant assistance, community support or private benefaction.

MODERN CONSERVATION WORK

Q. The conservation of Modern buildings is often described as being more a matter of managing change than when dealing with older buildings. Is this true?

A. Up to a point – it depends on the particular building/project. Almost all conservation work involves change of some sort, regardless of building age. Victorian houses routinely undergo substantial modification to accommodate current requirements. Conversely, a rare 'monument' of Modernism may invoke conservation protocols just as rigorous as would be applicable in an older historic building. Such restoration projects as the Zonnestraal Sanatorium (see Figure 7.1) and Villa Tugendhat (see p 140) provide model exemplars of the latter. But as a generality, it is indeed true that, with the shift in focus in conservation doctrine from 'retention of original fabric' to 'preservation of cultural significance', the emphasis has moved towards the management of change. Moreover, the increasing attention now given to *performance* is likely to stimulate pressure for ongoing upgrade of fabric, servicing systems and building components in the interests of future-proofing and sustainability.

Q. Conservationists usually have quite different objectives for dealing with a Modern building from those of its owner. Whose view should take priority?

A. Ideally the views of both – as well as those of other stakeholders – should be reconciled. This will obviously depend on the extent of divergence, but even projects primarily driven by economic and/or operational requirements can usually also yield heritage dividends if approached intelligently and creatively. Conservation cannot always (or even usually) be assumed as the principal project driver, so definition of a stakeholder's project objectives is essential in order to determine the extent to which these can be balanced with saving what is of significance that should and can be protected. If options are available, one must always remember to include the 'do nothing' option before making decisions. But doing nothing as a *parti pris* is the luxury of the armchair preservationist and may not always be sustainable without seeking to add value by development or extension. Often the overriding criterion is to identify what strategy is likely to prove more sustainable in the long term. Timing may also be critical. The investment opportunity for a project may occur only at a particular moment and it is important to optimise it.

Q. What is the best way of conserving a redundant building?

A. Usually by finding a viable use for it. In seeking an alternative use – if the original one is no longer feasible – remember that the old adage 'form follows function' is often best reversed, so that 'function follows form' (i.e. allow the original design to suggest compatible new uses, rather than seek to impose an ill-fitting new use on a reluctant structure). The objective is usually to preserve as much of the original significance as possible. This will most likely be achieved by opting for the least intervention in the essential formal identity and spatial character of the building as is compatible with establishing a viable use.[8] However, sometimes 'mindful monitoring' can lead to a positive outcome by allowing an alternative use to emerge before premature intervention or unnecessary demolition. There is little benefit in imposing a wrong answer early.

Q. What should be done if the budget is inadequate?

A. The conservation work that is affordable should be either limited and exemplary in order to serve as a model for future works, or should secure enough of the significant fabric at risk to survive until further funding is available. This may involve unglamorous tasks such as sealing a roof or propping a wall, but these may be essential to retain a future opportunity for saving the building in the longer term. If holding measures are necessary, always consider the design of the eventual permanent works before designing the temporary ones. Remember that 'temporary' has a habit of becoming permanent. The first priority is invariably to arrest progressive damage. There is no benefit in retouching details of the interior if the roof leaks. For particularly sensitive works, it is always advisable to reserve part of the budget for trial samples. In considering the possible phasing of work, it can be important to account for the costs of access, and address as many tasks as possible (including prior survey work) while a scaffold is available.

Q. Is it necessary to use specialist contractors for modern conservation work?

A. It is preferable, though not essential – there are few who could be described as such anyway, outside certain particular specialist trades for Modern buildings, such as concrete or window repair.[9] Genuine contractor commitment, caring and diligence go a long way. But certain precautionary measures are definitely recommended. Most contractors will not be predisposed to regard a Modern building, even if listed, instinctively as 'heritage' – as they would in the case of an obviously historic one. It is desirable, therefore, to include effective information on the architectural and historical significance of the building in tender preliminaries, and underscore these in precontract briefings. Assuming it has not been possible to survey the property comprehensively before the inception of works, it is vital to ensure the contractor understands that nothing should be removed from site without permission. The building 'as found' is a primary source of heritage evidence and must be allowed to yield all its available information to inform design, specification and restoration works. A diligent contractor may also need advice to resist overcleaning or eliminating irregularities where these may contribute to heritage value. And – patronising as it may sound – one should never assume that something is so obvious to a building contractor that it does not need to be pointed out.

CONSERVATION MANAGEMENT INSTRUMENTS

Q. The report *Streamlining Listed Building Consent: Lessons from the Use of Management Agreements* (2006)[10] states that in the formulation of listed building management guidelines (LBMGs) the process of constructive dialogue between stakeholders is more important than the formal document itself. Do you agree with this?

A. Not literally, though the underlying sentiment has some validity. Both the dialogue and the document are important. Certainly, the process of producing any of the various kinds of management documents is one of the best ways of promoting consciousness-raising and the sense of shared responsibility that help to cultivate a tradition of care. But without the document as a focus there would be no ongoing point of reference, no 'objective' platform from which to rethink, if necessary, and build further understanding. Also, those involved in creating the original guidelines often later disperse, so the document may be the only tangible record that ensures that what was achieved is not lost.

Q. Do management guidelines impose excessive bureaucracy, or curtail people's freedom by telling them what they can and can't do?

A. No, on the contrary, they should reduce bureaucracy by effectively triaging listed building consent queries, avoiding unnecessary applications and expediting ones where precedents have already been established. Note also that apart from general advice on heritage legislation and consent procedures, management guidelines don't tell people 'what they can and can't do' – they tell them *what they are, or are not, likely to need consent to do.*

Q. Can guidelines protect what is architecturally significant about building exteriors and settings?

A. Good drafting in management guidelines should certainly help protect architectural significance from detrimental intervention or neglect, and this should extend to definition of any significant spatial qualities in a building's setting and surroundings, to deter opportune infilling or detrimental 'densification'. Clear and convincing description of how context contributes to the special interest of the building in question is also highly desirable. But as a listed building's setting is not itself listed, and may often lie beyond the listing boundary, its protection will ultimately depend on the commitment of the local planning authority and the support of other planning instruments such as a Spatial Development Strategy and/or conservation area status. Experience suggests that even the best guidelines may not by themselves be sufficient to deter untoward interventions. In such circumstances, they must be supported by local action to optimise their leverage.

Q. How can guidelines establish and protect what is architecturally significant about building interiors?

A. This goes to the heart of any conservation management project – i.e. reaching a workable consensus as to what is significant. The objective is to establish a workable balance between formal enforcement and voluntary observance. Public buildings are generally easier to deal with than domestic interiors. Much that is significant will be self-evident and beyond dispute. But special interest can also inhere in the variety and ingenuity of dwelling layouts even though their individual components and materials may be of no intrinsic value or rarity. It would be theoretically possible to 'deconstruct' an interior into its various constituents – skirtings, architraves, doors, plaster, paint – and then argue that few or none of these were significant in themselves. Yet the quality of 'intactness' may still confer significance on an interior as an authentic entity. The line may be drawn where formal consent is only required where proposed interventions would result in alteration of spatial character or planform. In large estates it may be possible to reduce the pressure of wholesale preservation by identifying a small number of intact 'heritage units' where no earlier changes have already taken place and where the form of tenure provides a measure of landlord control over future resident interventions. This 'representative heritage' may be regarded as a compromise, but it is generally of more value than none at all.

Q. Do guidelines impose additional and unnecessary listed building consent (LBC) restrictions?

A. No – the management guidelines could not do this even if desired. Guidelines by themselves neither authorise nor prohibit any specific works – they simply indicate (by identifying 'significance') which kinds of work are likely to require and receive listed building consent, and which are not. Also, provided they are well drafted, guidelines offer clarity to existing and incoming residents who may be unsure of the implications (and obligations) of living in listed property.

Q. Do guidelines require comprehensive stakeholder agreement?

A. Not necessarily, but the greater the consensus, the better. The process of producing management guidelines will itself reveal the range of differing opinions among stakeholders, and the task of identifying, locating and documenting 'special interest' will indicate whether they can all be reconciled. Some initial resistance by residents may be due to earlier dissent on the original designation, but guidelines and conservation plans cannot alter the fact of listing.

Meaningful consultation to ascertain the extent of agreement or otherwise across the widest number of issues is a vital means of progressing dialogue and arriving at a result that is as fair as possible to all viewpoints. But it is seldom possible to 'score a hole in one' and consultation feedback is invaluable in demonstrating responsiveness on the part of the guideline authors in refining the eventual document. Producing such documents is analogous to negotiating a treaty inasmuch as a degree of flexibility on all sides may be needed to achieve a workable result. As to formalising final agreement, this may be possible through representative consent, rather than seeking individual sign-off by all. Either way, it is vital that all concerned have a sufficient sense of ownership of the final document to be motivated to use it.

Q. How can guideline documents remain relevant and active after they have been finished?

A. Firstly they have to be perceived as fair and reasonable by all stakeholders. Without this, there can be no meaningful consensus. Formal adoption by the local planning authority in conjunction with the building/estate owner is also helpful in giving the document 'existential' permanence. The Enterprise and Regulatory Reform Act (ERRA) 2013 allows heritage partnership agreements to have legally binding force.

Then they must be user-friendly. Large and unwieldy documents will quickly be shelved and forgotten. While the necessary underlying research cannot be short-circuited, it may not all need to be included in a single document. The essentials may be formatted in a concise user guide that encourages easy and regular reference. The so-called 'traffic light system', pioneered by the City of London at the Barbican Estate in 2005, provided guidance on which kinds of intervention would, might or wouldn't require listed building consent in a manner that was immediately understandable by all. Lastly, such guidelines must remain resilient. This entails not only including provision for regular review, but also developing a habit of usage that is initially deliberate but eventually becomes instinctual – a process that might be described as cultivating heritage 'muscle memory'.

Q. Are management guidelines just about regulating applications for listed building consent?

A. No. They should go beyond this and deal with day-to-day 'minor' works that accumulate over the years and which, if not undertaken with due regard for the significance of the heritage asset, can have a profoundly damaging impact. This refers to the many small operations that would not require listed building consent individually but which cumulatively can have just as great an effect as major interventions in listed properties and estates – such items as mismatched paving repairs, improvised signage, surface-fixed cables and pipework, randomly installed security alarm boxes, satellite dishes, aircon units, aerials, etc., all contributing to steady loss of authentic character and visual hygiene. Guideline documents and conservation management plans should include simple practical advice for the effective management of all these 'below the radar' items.

Q. Will conservation plans and listed building management guidelines become more widespread? Would a template or model agreement produced by the Department for Digital, Culture, Media and Sport/Historic England be useful?

A. Yes – there are already many such documents in operation, both for individual buildings and for larger estates, though there is unlikely to be a 'one size fits all' answer for situations where management guidelines are applicable. There are consistent themes but the outcome needs to evolve from the circumstances of the particular case. Much valuable work on this already exists and more can be expected.[11] To the extent that Modern designations often involve larger communal assets, management guidelines, functioning effectively as 'mini-charters', should have a particularly useful part to play.

Q. Do management guidelines have the potential to streamline the listing process or are they an unnecessary extravagance? Can the intelligent use of the listing system as it exists now offer the same (or better) results? What role can guideline documents play in the future of listed building practice? Is there a better way of managing listed buildings than listed building management guidelines?

A. It is difficult to imagine how such documents could 'streamline' the listing process. Designation would always occur higher up in the regulatory process than the production of guidelines, which occurs 'downstream'. An advisory note at the time of designation could recommend that the asset being designated would benefit from the managerial support of guidelines, but this could hardly be enforceable. Greater clarity and detail in list entry descriptions may also be helpful in articulating significance and will doubtless grow following the Enterprise and Regulatory Reform Act 2013 and the more recent Saunders report.[12] But the traction of guidelines (and other tools, such as conservation management plans) will continue to depend on availability of resources, their relevance to the case in question and the degree of commitment among stakeholders. Conservation area appraisals also have an important part to play in managing heritage significance in the wider local context beyond the individual building, albeit their degree of traction can be uneven.[13]

Q. The two main aims of management guidelines – to identify the significance and special interest of a building and to reduce the incidence of listed building consent – appear mutually exclusive. Studies to enhance understanding of a building are surely likely to identify more elements that warrant protection, not less. With this in mind, are the aims of guidelines really achievable?

A. The premise that more study must necessarily lead to greater restriction is false. Following detailed research and comparative evaluation, such study could equally produce a greater understanding of what is *not* significant. Management guideline aims are certainly achievable, but they don't just work by themselves. They still need to be understood, user friendly and operated willingly by the various parties involved. Also, it is not strictly correct to suggest that reducing the incidence of listed building consent is an *aim* of listed building management guidelines (although they should certainly reduce the number of unnecessary applications). The aim is to cultivate understanding of when and why formal consent is needed, and when and why it isn't, which is not quite the same thing.

THE FUTURE OF *MODERN* HERITAGE

Q. What developments are likely to be most conducive to the revaluing of Modern architecture as a whole? What are the main obstacles?

A. Progress will surely be a combination of formal regulation and voluntary action. That is, statutory protection will continue to play an important role in the more significant individual cases, but 'organic' change in public attitudes will also alter the context in which Modern architecture is perceived. As the achievements of the post-war Welfare State are increasingly eroded, appreciation of its better built residues and their message of altruism may eventually increase. Moreover, the growing imperatives of environmental sustainability will steadily oblige public authorities, building owners and developers to supersede the culture of disposability and adopt longer-term models of building stewardship, including retrofit, performance upgrade and adaptive reuse – all of which should result in better use of what already exists.

Q. It is said that in order to prevent the important buildings of tomorrow from being lost, listing must stay one step ahead of fashion, meaning that it will always be unpopular to some degree. Does their emphasis on stakeholder consensus mean that management guidelines entail a dumbing down of the listing system?

A. Consultation in the pre-designation stage is now part of the process anyway, and guideline documents are downstream of listing, so they could hardly 'dumb down' the listing system as such. But the extent to which any actual guidelines project supports the degree of protection intended by listing will depend on the quality of the guidelines that are produced in the individual case. It should be remembered that the stakeholder group that produces any such management document should include representation of the local planning authority as well as the relevant amenity society so that there should always be a strong voice to argue the case for protecting significance.

Listing will continue to be controversial in the case of 'challenging' Modern buildings because in the UK (perhaps more than most countries) there is still prejudice and ignorance about the tradition of Modernism (as well as widespread misunderstanding of what listing itself actually entails). MoMo enthusiasts might help their cause by being more realistic about buildings that are *clearly not* of heritage significance, or that need substantive alteration in order to survive, rather than defending any threatened Modern building indiscriminately. Attitudes are changing but only slowly. Perhaps if Britain was a republic, things might progress a little faster….

9
Lessons learned

This chapter is written as a series of vignettes illustrating a selection of episodes from the author's professional experience, offering insights and lessons drawn directly from the practice of modern conservation. Each story concludes with a hopefully useful lesson for practitioners to keep in mind for the future.

BERTHOLD LUBETKIN AND THE PENGUINS

One aspect of modern conservation that must surely, by definition, be unique to it is the possibility that the original architect of the building to be conserved or restored is still alive and available for consultation. This would surely seem to be an unqualified advantage in offering authentic insights into the background and original intentions of a design to guide the conservation team. No need here for the wishful speculation, 'The architect would surely have done it like this,' typically used as an alibi for a conservator's own preferences. I have been fortunate to meet several of the Modern pioneers in pursuit of my interest in Modern British architecture – a privilege that has vouchsafed many a first-hand revelation or colourful insight, as well as bringing a sense of 'real life' into the essential preparatory work of site archaeology and desktop research that is required for any properly informed rescue project.

But there are also circumstances where the involvement of the original architect can risk incorrect decision-making in evolving an authentic design strategy. This was an early lesson learnt in the restoration project for Berthold Lubetkin's celebrated Penguin Pool at London Zoo, which I led in the mid-1980s when Lubetkin (Figure 9.1) himself was in his mid-80s.

In addition to the necessary concrete repair work on the structure itself, the zoo authorities had instructed a number of interventions they wished to make in the original building in the light of more recent ornithological knowledge of the birds' habits and wellbeing. These included the provision of additional nesting boxes, upgraded hydraulics and enlargement of the diving tank above the spiral ramp on the south side of the pool to provide greater water volume for the birds. The last of these called for some challenging amendments to the 1934 design in order to achieve the desired increase in tank capacity.

Lubetkin had drawn a rough initial concept for the amendments – a sketch dated 15 August 1985, and the last drawing of his career (Figure 9.2) – but it needed considerable refinement and detailed development before it could be used for construction, or even as a basis for obtaining listed building consent.

This was the start of an intensive conversation, initially between the two of us, then later with the conservation authorities – Westminster City Council and English Heritage – the pool being listed Grade I and accordingly requiring formal consent for any such alterations.

In the course of developing Lubetkin's sketch towards a fully resolved design, it soon became clear that there were numerous possible permutations of the initial idea. In the best tradition of Tecton, the pioneering partnership Lubetkin had founded in 1932 shortly after his arrival in England, I proceeded to explore a whole series of alternatives (Figure 9.3). These quickly began to divide into two distinct types – those developing a slanting profile from Lubetkin's basic sketch and those maintaining the orthogonal outline of the original design.

Lubetkin became increasingly enthusiastic about the former (Figure 9.3 Options A, C and E), while those in the latter category were my own preference (Figure 9.3 Options B, D and F), for being not only aesthetically 'quieter' but also on account of the considerably simpler constructional implications, since canting the enlarged tank on the diagonal axis of the ramps

Figure 9.1
Berthold Lubetkin, portrait
by Snowdon, 1985.

Figure 9.2 (Right)
Lubetkin's initial sketch for the
Penguin Pool amendments,
dated 15 August 1985.

Figure 9.3 (Below)
Comparative studies of the
Penguin Pool diving tank
alteration.

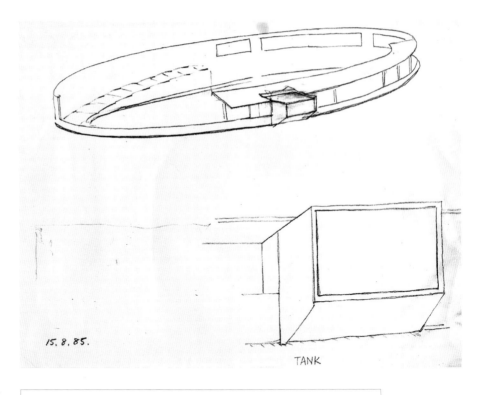

15. 8. 85.

TANK

ORIGINAL DESIGN
1934

OPTION A
ORIGINAL LENGTH
INCREASED WIDTH
CANTED FACE
CANOPY OVERSAIL

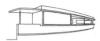

OPTION B
INCREASED LENGTH
ORIGINAL WIDTH
VERTICAL FACE

OPTION C
INCREASED LENGTH
INCREASED WIDTH
CANTED FACE
NO CANOPY OVERSAIL

OPTION D
ORIGINAL WIDTH
EXTENDED TANK UNDER
CANOPY

OPTION E
INCREASED LENGTH
INCREASED WIDTH
CANTED FACE
CANOPY OVERSAIL

OPTION F - AS CHOSEN
INCREASED LENGTH
INCREASED WIDTH
VERTICAL FACE
CANOPY OVERSAIL

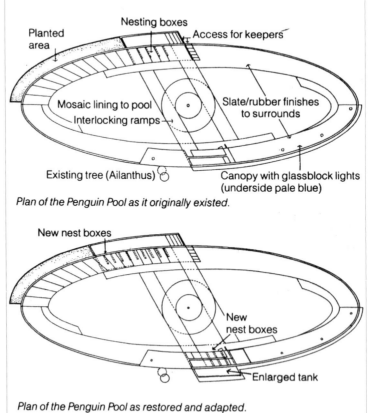

Plan of the Penguin Pool as it originally existed.

Plan of the Penguin Pool as restored and adapted.

Figure 9.4 (Right)
Penguin Pool comparative plans:
1934 above, 1987 below.

would produce oblique geometry in both plan and section, resulting in a rhomboid-shaped viewing window. (The 50mm-thick laminated glazed panel and bespoke stainless-steel frame required to withstand the water pressure of the enlarged tank was already challenging enough, even in a rectangular format, weighing as it did nearly one tonne and costing some £16,000 at 1987 prices.)

I drew up the shortlisted options in a comparative format in readiness for the decisive pre-application meeting at Westminster City Council. Around the table were the Westminster conservation officer, the English Heritage officer, Lubetkin and myself. The alternative solutions were presented in turn, and after much close interrogation the officer from English Heritage expressed a definite preference for one of the straight-sided options (which was also my own undeclared favourite). Considering we were in the presence of the original architect (and by now Royal Gold Medallist), the officer's reasoning was commendably brave, arguing that the versions involving canted geometry appeared to him to reprise a slightly later motif in Lubetkin's developing 1930s canon — for example the canted entrance portal at Finsbury Health Centre (completed in 1938; see Figure 1.24) — which he felt was alien to the purity of the Penguin Pool of four years earlier. Inevitably, the ensuing discussion was prolonged, but the orthogonal version favoured by the officer ultimately prevailed (Figure 9.3 Option F and 9.4).

Reflecting on the experience, I realised that Lubetkin had — perhaps subconsciously — seen the zoo's new requirements as an opportunity to 'improve' his original design and introduce a more favoured stylistic feature from his evolving architectural vocabulary — not an unreasonable ambition in itself, perhaps, but one that would have arguably changed an already significant alteration into an unduly conspicuous one in such a sensitive context.

And the moral of this tale? That even when the original architect is still alive and by your side, it may be that in the conservation of such a unique masterpiece it is the original building, rather than its creator, that ultimately suggests the most appropriate solution. In subsequent lectures on the project, I used to compare the Penguin Pool to Donato Bramante's Tempietto (in the courtyard of the church of San Pietro in Montorio, in Rome) in being an architectural conception so complete and perfect in itself that almost *any* alteration seemed inconceivable.

Figure 9.5
The Penguin Pool as originally built, in 1934, with diving tank far right.

Figure 9.6a
The diving tank before the start
of works, 6 April 1987.

Figure 9.6b
The diving tank works in
progress, 15 May 1987.

Figure 9.6c
The diving tank works in
progress, 23 July 1987.

Figure 9.6d
The diving tank works nearing
completion, 5 August 1987.

Figure 9.6e
The diving tank works
completed, 28 September 1987.

Figure 9.7
The Penguin Pool as restored
and modified in 1987, with an
enlarged diving tank, far right.
Compare with Figure 9.5.

With this in mind, and in view of the later fortunes of the pool (which is another story[1]), one could say it might have been better to make no alterations to the original design whatsoever. But the politics of the project that caused it to be mobilised at all relied upon the zoo achieving what at the time it regarded as essential improvements in ornithological husbandry within the larger context of vital and long overdue repairs.

Rebuilding the diving tank was still a fiendishly complicated operation (Figures 9.5 and 9.6), involving no less than 14 separate concrete pours, but I remain convinced that in 'listening' to the building in this particular instance, rather than to Lubetkin, the correct decision was made (Figure 9.7).

NO RIGHT ANSWER

Sometimes in modern conservation work – indeed in conservation work of any age – one is confronted by, and must knowingly accept, a compromise – that is to say, making an unenviable choice between the lesser of two evils. This commonly (though not always) results from limitations of the budget which effectively constrain the scope of work that it is possible to accomplish within the immediate project, a situation often aggravated by the uncertainty of there ever being a sequel that could provide an opportunity to properly resolve the issue.

It is not splitting hairs to distinguish between a 'compromise' and a 'synthesis'. The former is the product of a contradiction in the situation in which there can be no entirely satisfactory outcome. The latter is quite different, involving a balanced reconciliation of competing issues – an objective that (in my experience) runs through virtually all conservation work since, as already explained, the several stakeholders in any given project invariably have slightly – or

Figure 9.8
The White House, Haslemere,
Surrey, by Amyas Connell,
1933, photographed before
it was white, showing the
staircase enclosure in a dark
frame colour.

more than slightly – different objectives. Typically, the building investor (the client) is interested in enhancing the value of his or her real estate; the building users are concerned with issues of amenity; the conservation authorities are preoccupied with authenticity and the retention of original fabric. But in the best conservation work, insight and imagination can reconcile these seemingly differing aims within a sustainable consensus that neglects none of them. The compromise, on the other hand, must just be confronted for what it is.

Such a dilemma occurred in a project involving an early work of Amyas Connell, the pioneering New Zealander who, with his partners Basil Ward and Colin Lucas, proceeded to blaze a radical and controversial trail through English architecture in the 1930s. The house, known variously as New Farm, Aldings and now the White House (Figure 9.8), was Connell's second venture in Modern design, completed in 1933 on a fine open site just outside Haslemere, Surrey, following his notorious debut 'High and Over' in Amersham, completed in 1931 (see Figure 1.3).[2]

The owner at the time of my involvement was an elderly, frail and charming lady who had lived in the house for many years and loved it dearly, though I dealt with the project mainly through her son. I vividly recall our first meeting on a golden summer afternoon when she arranged for us all to have tea in the garden. The occasion was somewhat formal, with best china, a silver cake stand, etc. It was made clear that the budget, and therefore my brief, was necessarily limited and would accordingly comprise only replacement of the large glazed staircase enclosure (and one other window), together with general repairs to the exterior concrete shell and roof terrace. Even this was not inconsequential as the said staircase enclosure was the dominant feature of the house – as similar variations would prove to be in many of the later works of the partnership. Located at the 'root' of the fan-shaped plan and rising the full three storeys to cap the roof cockpit, the enclosure wrapped two sides of the main stairway, which returned around a central concrete chimney that also supported the staircase itself.

The original steel window framework was savagely corroded (Figure 9.9), with many of the opening sashes rusted shut and several fixed glazing areas patched with adhesive tape and polythene bags bearing the insignia of a well-known supermarket chain. Being also single glazed (where glazing still survived), the staircase window constituted a massive thermal breach in the building envelope, such that most of the boiler's energy was spent in heating Surrey, rather than the house. There was no question that it had to be replaced *in toto*, but here the conundrum arose. Connell's original creation had rendered the house in a daring shade of 'sugar-almond pink', with the window and staircase frames all painted a dark colour – reading as black in the contemporary black-and-white images.[3] These original 1930s coatings had long since been lost in subsequent redecoration works, the exterior and all the windows now being white – by which colour the house itself was now indeed known and named. It was naturally tempting to specify a dark powder coating for the replacement staircase window in a bid to restore authenticity, hoping that all the remaining windows would eventually be recoated to match at some point in the unspecified future if and when funds became available. However, all the other windows had only recently been repaired and repainted and the client had no inclination (or budget) to change them again. In such a context, the replacement of such a major feature as the staircase window in a dark colour, howsoever justifiable on 'heritage grounds', would simply look absurd. And so it was perforce decided that the staircase window should be replaced in powder-coated white to match the rest of the house as it stood (Figure 9.10).

Figure 9.9
Typical condition of the staircase windows at the White House, 1992, showing corrosion-induced glass fractures.

Figure 9.10
The staircase enclosure at the White House, replaced in white, 1992.

Figure 9.11
Other windows at the White House, as later repainted turquoise.

And the moral of this tale? That sometimes it is necessary to make a decision that is less than ideal but which is governed by the circumstances and timing of the project as they happen to occur. Yet the tale is not without a twist, as many years later and following further changes of ownership, all the windows except 'my' white powder-coated staircase screen have since been repainted in… turquoise (Figure 9.11).

A GIRLFRIEND'S HAIR

The partial restoration of Finsbury Health Centre (Figure 9.12), which I had the privilege of leading in the mid-1990s, became a live project in the most unexpected way. Several years previously, in preparation for the 50th anniversary of the centre in 1988, Avanti Architects had been commissioned to undertake a general survey of the building to scope out the range of repairs and upgrade work that should be implemented to secure its continued future in beneficial NHS use.[4]

The anniversary was marked in fine style with a celebratory lunch in the centre itself, with Berthold Lubetkin himself in attendance as guest of honour. All the omens were favourable and we were led to expect an imminent commencement of the job. However, the celebration was followed by a curious silence. The ensuing hiatus extended from weeks to months to years, until without warning a few days before Christmas 1993, I received a telephone call from an unknown officer in the Health Authority accountants' department. They had identified a £350,000 underspend while preparing the end-of-year accounts, and coincidentally had unearthed a copy of our 1988 report. Could we possibly find a way of committing this money on work at the Health Centre before 31 March 1994 to avoid it being lost from their budget? This was probably the easiest client request I ever received in my entire professional career.

By March a contract had been duly organised to take the project on site with a strategy to utilise this slender allocation in such a way as to address each type of conservation/repair work that would later be required to complete the whole building when further funds became available. The partial project would thus serve as a heritage research vehicle, and a worked exemplar for reference in the ensuing sequel – which at the time was assumed would follow shortly afterwards and hopefully would also be led by ourselves.[5]

Our earlier investigations had laid much useful groundwork, enabling the detailed design and specification to progress briskly. But until the site was secured and the building was scaffolded, it had been impossible *literally* to get to grips with the existing exterior fabric – a vital

Figure 9.12
Finsbury Health Centre, London, by Lubetkin and Tecton, 1938. Note the reflectivity of the spandrel panels in the wing façades.

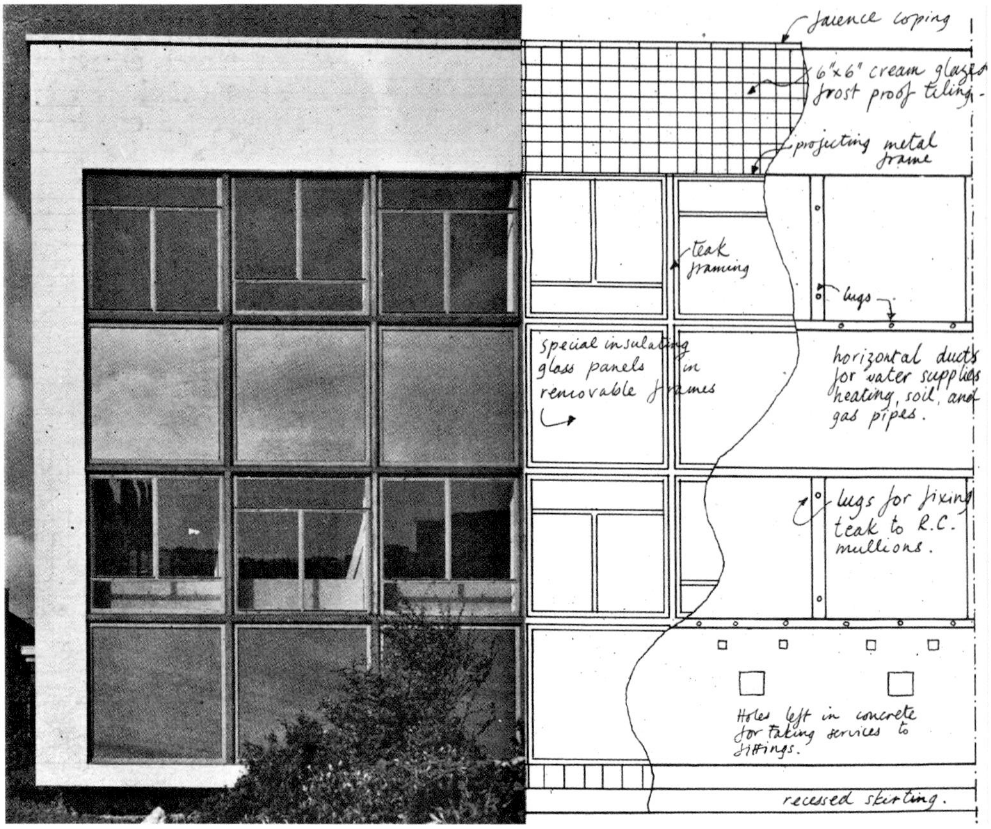
faience coping
6"x6" cream glazed
frost proof tiling
projecting metal frame
teak framing
lugs
special insulating glass panels in removable frames
horizontal ducts for water supplies heating, soil, and gas pipes.
lugs for fixing teak to R.C. mullions.
Holes left in concrete for taking services to fittings.
recessed skirting.

Figure 9.13
Tecton's original curtain wall diagram, 1938.

preparatory task in any conservation work. A particular difficulty was presented by the curtain walling of the clinical wings (Figure 9.13), a pioneering construction of the 1930s combining regular arrays of steel windows with a unique glazed spandrel panel system, all held in place within a gridded teak framework.

This had been severely damaged during World War II, when the building was repurposed as a casualty dressing station and the exterior façades were sandbagged from ground to parapet level, the weight of the steadily saturated sandbags eventually breaking many of the original glazed panels. We had advised that the existing spandrel panels, which were now an uncoordinated miscellany of first- or second-generation post-war substitutions in various unmatched materials, should all be replaced to replicate the originals. We knew from the pre-war documentation that these were a material called Thermolux, a composite glazed insulating panel comprising two sheets of glass within which was sealed a coloured spun silk interlayer. But what was the original colour? The 1938 photographs were inconclusive, and in any case only in black-and-white. Some, taken against the light (Figure 9.14a), suggested the panels had been a reflective shade of… grey? Others, taken with the light behind the camera (Figure 9.14b), indicated a darkish shade of… copper?

Naturally, when working on the original report, I had consulted Lubetkin, by then in his late 80s, in the quest to determine the exact colour. But his reply – 'I can't remember my dear, all I can tell you is that they shone like a girlfriend's hair' (Figure 9.15) – didn't get us much further.

As the contractor's preparatory works proceeded on site, we gained access to the cavity behind the curtain wall – a continuous longitudinal recess created by reinforced concrete channel beams originally devised by Ove Arup and supported on structural mullions to support the full floor width, thereby enabling the external walls to serve as pipe ducts while also maximising operational flexibility by avoiding any load-bearing internal partitions.

Then came a eureka moment. We discovered some small fragments of the original Thermolux panels in the cavity, surviving from the time when they had been broken and replaced. Though tiny and damaged, these remnants provided sufficient evidence for a laboratory analysis to determine their original colour. It now became clear why Lubetkin's recollections had been so allusive. The material indeed consisted of two sheets of glass formed in sealed units with an interlayer of spun silk. But the colour, imparted by this interlayer, was an almost indescribable bronzy, silvery grey, with different tints predominating depending on one's viewpoint relative to the light. Specifically, the interlayer introduced a lustrous 'angel hair' texture that amply corroborated Lubetkin's description.

This thrilling discovery solved one problem, but now presented others. Although Thermolux was still manufactured in Europe, the interlayer was now available only in white. So, while we could reproduce the original 'angel hair' texture of the panels, we had still to find a way to replicate the original colour. The eventual solution entailed adding a sheet of laminated safety glass of the appropriate colour in front of the white Thermolux panels, thereby superimposing the original colour upon the original texture. This strategy also provided a welcome benefit of additional protection to the Thermolux, an expensive material to replace in the event of breakage.

Figure 9.14a
The original curtain wall of Finsbury Health Centre, as viewed against the light.

Figure 9.14b
The original curtain wall of Finsbury Health Centre, as viewed with the light behind the camera.

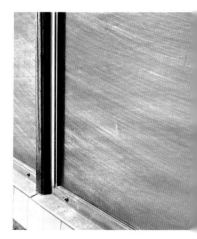

Figure 9.15
'Like a girlfriend's hair' – the visual texture of Thermolux.

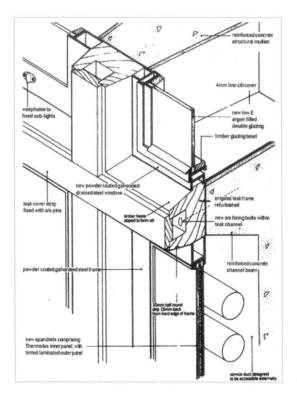

reinforced concrete
structural mullion

4mm lino cill cover

new low E
argon filled
double glazing

timber glazing bead

weepholes to
fixed sub-lights

original teak frame
refurbished

new powder coated galvanised
drained steel windows

new s/s fixing bolts within
teak channel

teak cover strip
fixed with s/s pins

timber frame
sloped to form sill

powder coated galvanised steel frame

reinforced concrete
channel beam

10mm half round
drip 15mm back
from front edge of frame

new spandrels comprising
Thermolux inner panel, with
tinted laminated outer panel

service duct designed
to be accessible externally

Figure 9.17
Finsbury Health Centre's
curtain wall, with third-
generation panels, before
restoration works.

Figure 9.18
The curtain wall as restored to
its authentic appearance.

The result is as near to a perfect replication as is now possible (Figures 9.17 and 9.18).[6] Moreover, the work undertaken all those years ago can now serve as a full-scale sample to guide the eventual project for restoration of the remainder of the building – as was always intended.

And the moral of this tale? Never underestimate the archaeological value of a building in disrepair, or the carelessness of previous contractors in cleaning up after earlier work operations. An incoming contractor must be explicitly prevented from prematurely and overzealously clearing debris from your site at the inception of the job. There may be vital evidence to be discovered that no amount of desktop research could provide.

THE WINDOW WORKER IN WALSALL

Now here is another lesson learned from the experience of (partially) restoring Lubetkin's Grade I masterpiece Finsbury Health Centre in the mid-1990s. The previous account described the challenge of replicating the original curtain wall spandrel panels. These, of course, constituted only one element of the curtain wall, the other principal component being the windows themselves (Figure 9.19). As might be expected, the originals were a beautifully designed composite consisting of offset friction pivot outward-opening casements set within a larger frame that included alternating fixed toplights and sublights. The casements were painted steel with an espagnolette operating mechanism using fine silver-bronze handles that folded down within the width of the central mullions, thereby avoiding any intrusion on the window sightlines. The French casement configuration of the windows enabled either one or both sashes to be opened to any angle and secured by friction pivots, while the offset position of pivots themselves allowed easy cleaning of the outside panes from inside via the gap between the sash and the frame.

Figure 9.19
The original double casement window design, Finsbury Health Centre, 1938.

Figure 9.20
Typical condition of the Finsbury Health Centre windows before works began.

Figure 9.21
Original silver-bronze handles were refitted to replacement frames in the windows at Finsbury Health Centre.

Figure 9.22
Detail of reused friction pivot ironmongery in the windows at Finsbury Health Centre.

Altogether they presented yet another elegant and typically inventive solution in Lubetkin's illustrious window design canon – following on from the retractable vertical sashes at 25 Avenue de Versailles, in Paris, 1931, and sliding folding concertina windows at Highpoint, Highgate, London, 1935 (see Figure 2.7).[7] But after decades of neglect, almost all those in the section of curtain wall we were due to restore (a total of 22 windows) were beyond economic repair (Figure 9.20).

I say 'almost' because with a lot of very skilled and costly craftwork repair, it might just have been possible to enable reuse of one or two of the original frames. This in itself posed a nice question of conservation ethics. In the interests of evidential authenticity, should we have sought to retain and repair the one or two frames that might have been capable of refurbishment, or replace these along with the unsalvageable majority to achieve consistency across the whole array? Original fabric versus original concept – a familiar Modern conundrum. Applying the ultimate heritage test – 'What is significant here, what are we trying to preserve?' – we took the view that it was the curtain wall as an integrated composition (in fact one of the first of its type in the UK) that was significant, rather than individual window frames as such. It was agreed that to restore the curtain wall with a consistent suite of replica new windows was a more important conservation objective than producing a hybrid of mainly new frames and a few, slightly unmatched, old ones. Two additional factors weighed in the decision. Firstly, that we were seeking also to upgrade thermal performance by incorporating double-glazed, argon-filled, low-e units into the replacements, and that these benefits would be compromised by retaining a few single-glazed units. And secondly, that there are other locations in the building where windows are used singly, and where, therefore, there were still opportunities to retain salvageable original frames in the pursuit of authenticity without corrupting the consistent fenestration of the curtain walls. But I digress slightly. As replacement of windows – however many – was unavoidable, the question arose as to how faithful to the originals (as supplied in 1938 by the company Williams and Williams) the replacements could be. The well-established conservation maxim of substituting 'like-for-like' sounds unexceptionable, but when it comes to the details, how 'like' *is* like?

The new windows were to be sourced from a metal window company in Walsall which could supply steel sections almost identical to the originals, while also being able to accommodate the double-glazed units. Naturally we took the opportunity to visit the factory to inspect their operations and settle final details. By this time, a number of the original windows had been removed from the building (though not from the site), so I took the opportunity to take examples of the original silver-bronze handles and friction pivots in my pocket – having been previously advised that the replacement windows could only be supplied with standard new ironmongery.

The factory visit was highly informative – as such visits invariably are – but as we were being squired around the workshops, I noticed an elderly craftsman at one of the workbenches and paused for a chat while the rest of the party moved on. I showed him the original handle and friction pivot and asked whether it really was impossible to reuse these in the replacements that were now being made for our job. 'Leave them with me for 20 minutes', was the response. And behold, when we returned some 20 minutes later he had made a sample section of frame that incorporated both the original handle and the pivot. 'Aha', we cried in unison (including the incredulous sales rep who was our host and had previously advised otherwise), 'so it *can* be done!' And indeed it *was* done – at no noticeable extra cost (Figures 9.21 to 9.23).

And the moral of this tale? Although one is often advised by product manufacturers that today's component designs are constrained by standard current specifications, it is sometimes possible to customise items through a combination of a little goodwill and surviving artisanal experience. In fact, it is often the case that skilled tradespeople who for years may have been limited to the repetitive production of routine designs enjoy nothing more than to be given the opportunity to demonstrate their capabilities in rising to a particular challenge. This latent potential constitutes an important conservation resource that should not be overlooked.

Figure 9.23
General view of the restored façade at Finsbury Health Centre, with authentic colours and details, 1995.

SINGING THE MARSEILLAISE

Important Modern buildings are often at their most vulnerable not on account of their actual state of repair as such, but because of loss of morale on the part of their owners. Morale, as everyone instinctively knows, is a potent ingredient whether in personal or public affairs – as vital as it is elusive – and also has a crucial part to play in the fortunes of buildings. I remember how Lubetkin used to explain that the turning point in Napoleon's victory at the Battle of Jena was achieved not by force of arms, but when his army started to sing the Marseillaise. Absence of volition in the feasibility of refurbishment can be an infinitely more intractable obstacle than lack of funds. If sufficient will is there, funds will usually follow. In short, the 'culture' and mindset of property owners is pivotal to building conservation of any period, but especially for Modern buildings, where 'heritage instinct' is still so underdeveloped. The following vignettes offer some lessons learned in this regard.

Several situations that were to become conservation/upgrade projects for Avanti Architects have arisen from the prior belief on the part of our prospective clients that the difficulties they confronted could be solved only by redevelopment, drastic intervention or disposal. The Grade II* listed Western Bank Library at the University of Sheffield (Figure 9.24), originally designed by

Figure 9.24
Western Bank Library,
University of Sheffield, by
Gollins Melvin Ward, 1958.

Gollins Melvin Ward as the state-of-the-art centrepiece of its competition-winning post-war university masterplan and opened by TS Eliot in 1959, had been slated for complete demolition and replacement shortly before the commission to reconsider its future came to us in 2007.

The Head Librarian even admitted that they had become too ashamed of the library to risk bringing important visitors or potential donors to see it, for fear of losing vital benefactions. The project had a particular resonance for me personally, being an alumnus of the university, having studied architecture there from 1966 to 1971, when the library was still virtually brand new. There had, of course, been enormous changes both in the university generally and in patterns of library usage in the intervening half-century. The student population had increased some sixfold and library management techniques had moved from the age of the card-index to the age of the computer. The scene that we encountered at the inception of the commission bore all the familiar signs of a building that had lost its way. Perceived problems of the original design had been 'solved' by makeshift interventions; each solution being improvised without any overall coordination or controlling vision, and all the amendments were additive, producing an ambiance of hectic clutter and confusion (Figure 9.25) in complete contradiction of the original Miesian aesthetic of Gollins Melvin Ward. Other issues needing attention included major environmental upgrades in the main Reading Room and various further interventions to achieve wheelchair access compliance and enhanced means of escape.

A key strategy in changing the opinions of a demoralised owner is being able to demonstrate how the various problematic parts of their building will look when transformed, and much effort was spent creating CAD imagery to this end. Visual evidence of feasibility can be a powerful promotional tool in changing the mindset of a sceptical client. In the event, with careful interrogation of the librarian's requirements and intense investigation of the building itself, it was possible to deliver all the desired improvements within a fraction of the originally anticipated cost, the budget even being nearly halved during the contract as a result of other

Figure 9.25
The catalogue hall in the Western Bank Library, photographed in 2007 – a scene of chaos before the restoration. Note the replacement false ceiling, contradicting the original design.

university expenditure elsewhere. Moreover, with careful operational planning it was found possible to maintain the library in continuous use throughout the contract, an important aspect in avoiding academic disruption for the students.

Works included radical re-presentation of the entrance area and reconfiguration of a later ungainly control point, adopting the minimalist idiom of the original design. A makeshift computer study area clumsily obstructing the spacious mezzanine floor was removed altogether to create a generous new open gallery for temporary exhibitions (Figure 9.26), and the main

Figure 9.26
The new mezzanine exhibition area at the Western Bank Library.

Figure 9.27
The catalogue hall at the Western Bank Library, after reordering and refurbishment by Avanti Architects, 2009.

catalogue hall – originally a principal set-piece space of the GMW design – was completely cleared out and reorganised, reinstating the fine illuminated false ceiling that had been obscured by an illiterate subsequent installation (Figure 9.27; compare with Figure 9.25).

It was even possible to create much needed additional study areas within the original bookstack spaces by introducing 'daylight boxes' that provided a satisfactory working ambiance for prolonged periods of study in what, as a consequence of the ground section, was otherwise a windowless environment with limited headroom (Figures 9.28 and 9.29).

Figure 9.28a
Library plans showing adaptive interventions (shaded areas).

Figure 9.28b
The library section, showing the underground bookstacks.

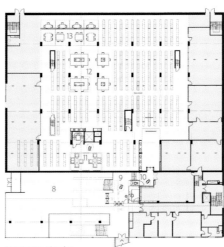

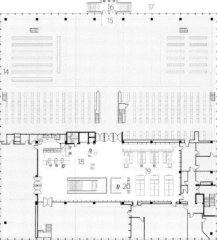

Ground floor / Stack 2

1 Entrance Lobby
2 Reconfigured entrance foyer
3 New Porter's Desk
4 New disabled access ramp
5 Newly installed lift
6 Screened refreshment vending and notices
7 New seating area

Mezzanine / Stack 4

8 Extensively refurbished mezzanine exhibition space
9 Re-ordered welcome desk and entry control point
10 Platform lift access to Stack 4
11 New informal seating area
12 New study carrels in book stacks
13 New group study area

Catalogue Hall and Reading Room

14 New perimeter heating strip in matching marble facing
15 New disabled access ramp in matching marble
16 Improved escape route
17 New facade glazing and fabric conservation of building envelope
18 Reconfigured reception and bespoke catalogue search points
19 Concealed reprographic and issuing equipment
20 Reconfigured seating area and map display

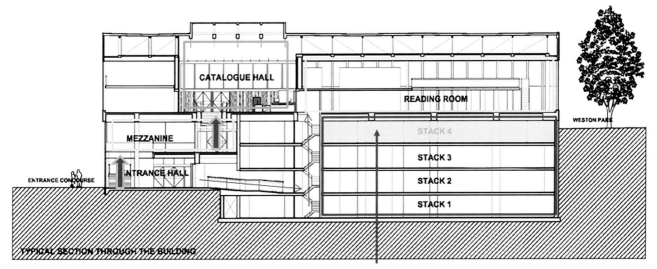

NEW STUDY AREAS INTRODUCED

With these and various other improvements, including new furniture and signage, the Western Bank Library, University of Sheffield, has been upgraded for an extended future by judicious architectural and environmental intervention, and now bears a more authentic relationship to its original identity than at any time over the previous half-century (Figure 9.30).[8]

Exaggeration of a building's structural disrepair can have an equally damaging effect on client morale, with a potentially critical impact on strategic decisions. Such exaggeration may be deliberate and even mischievous, or merely misinformed. The fragment of spalled concrete that

Figure 9.29
View of the library's new 'daylight box' underground study areas.

Figure 9.30
The Great Reading Room at the Western Bank Library, University of Sheffield, refurbished with new glazing and a new heating system.

Figure 9.31
Model of Priory Green,
Islington, London, by Lubetkin
and Tecton, completed in 1957.
Wynford House is the tripartite
nearest block.

one day in the mid-1990s fell from one of the blocks at Priory Green (Figure 9.31), Lubetkin and Tecton's large housing estate undertaken for Finsbury Borough Council in the early post-war years, set in train a succession of consequences quite disproportionate to the original incident.[9]

That the said fragment allegedly narrowly missed a passing pedestrian only added impetus to the chain of ensuing events, the building immediately being suspected as fatally unsafe and perhaps even at risk of imminent collapse. By then in the ownership of Islington Borough Council, the trio of interconnected buildings, known collectively as Wynford House (Figures 9.32 and 9.33), was decanted and in 1996 the whole northern section of the larger Priory Green estate was offered to the market in a move to rid the council of this allegedly intractable liability. No option was excluded, be it rescue or demolition and complete redevelopment. Teaming up with Community Housing Association (as it then was), Avanti Architects submitted proposals for the estate's comprehensive regeneration and were eventually selected as winners of 'The Wynford House Challenge'.

Here there was no question of heritage driving the agenda – on the contrary, the council owner was quite amenable to complete demolition and redevelopment if the bidder so chose – as indeed was proposed by one of the shortlisted contenders. The more sustainable approach was clearly to retain and rehabilitate the estate, which could have been achieved in various ways as the buildings were not listed. The typical reflex of overcladding and replacement plastic windows might well have been accepted as the client was more concerned with residential viability than how it was attained. Indeed, the desire for a deliberate change of image is sometimes a key motive in such 'turn-around' projects, as evidenced by the proliferation of postmodern accessories and garish colours often used to 'transform' degraded council estates.

Figure 9.32
Wynford House as built, 1957.

At Priory Green, the heritage ambitions were only the architect's personal aspiration as a Lubetkin devotee. But there were also many significant interventions, both in the buildings and the site landscape. These included conjoining several ground- and first-floor flats to provide more family accommodation in the form of maisonettes with gardens, the addition of penthouse units on the principal block to add value to the estate, removing troublesome bridge links between the original buildings and inserting freestanding stairflights in their place in order to achieve three independent blocks. These interventions, as well as considerable earthworks to provide level entry arrangements to all ground-floor units, also reduced the number of units accessed from each communal staircase. Extensive remediation was applied to the exposed aggregate precast cladding and brick panels using novel repair techniques to retrieve the original contrasts between the concrete, tiling and brickwork so characteristic of Lubetkin's dynamic façades (Figures 9.34 and 9.35). Additional features included a new concierge facility and conversion of a disused tenants' hall into a children's nursery for the whole neighbourhood (Figures 9.36 and 9.37).

Figure 9.33 a, b and c.
Views of Wynford House, showing the condition of the unoccupied buildings in 1996, before regeneration works.

Figure 9.34
View of the main façade of Wynford House, showing the new penthouses, after restoration of the contrasting tile, brick and concrete elements.

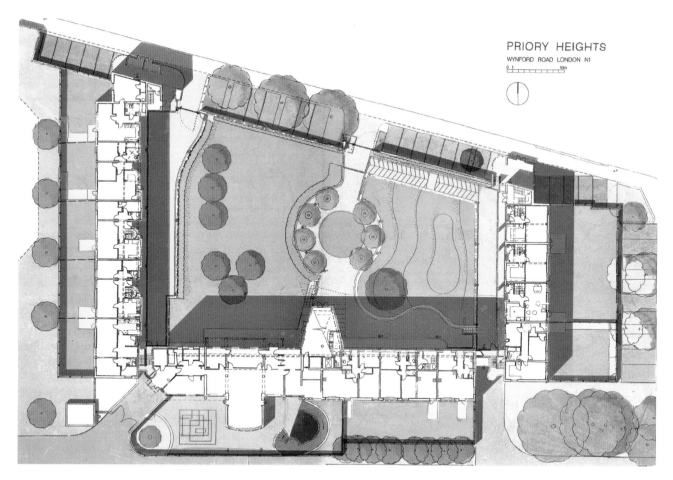

PRIORY HEIGHTS
WYNFORD ROAD LONDON N1
0 1   10m

Figure 9.35 (Opposite)
View of the main gable and
side block of Wynford House
after the regeneration works,
showing the tile, brick and
concrete restoration.

Figure 9.36
Reformed landscape plan at
Wynford House, based on
Lubetkin's original concept and
showing the location of the
new neighbourhood nursery,
lower left.

Figure 9.37
View of the reformed landscape
at Wynford House, with new
concierge point. (Photographed
before new tree planting.)

At one level, Wynford House might be described as 'simply' a comprehensive housing regeneration project, yet it also delivered a substantial heritage dividend. Indeed, such was its reception when completed in 2000 (Figure 9.38) that it caused the local authority to designate the whole of the Priory Green estate as a conservation area (Figure 9.39).[10] This in turn opened the way for Heritage Lottery funding through the Townscape Heritage Initiative, which enabled grant assistance to be provided for what were described as 'Lubetkin friendly' conservation-grade works to be undertaken, as an enhancement to the essential regeneration project being funded by the Estate Renewal Challenge Fund. These works were now brought forward by Peabody Trust, the social landlord taking over the remaining part of the estate relinquished by Islington. Whether one could claim that the fragment of fallen concrete had brought about the total transformation of several acres of inner London housing is perhaps a matter of debate. But it does add poignancy to the admission of one of Islington Council's officers after it was all completed, 'If we'd only known that this was possible, we'd never have sold Wynford House in the first place.'

And the lesson of these tales? A demoralised building owner should always be encouraged to consider the feasibility of an improved future for his or her property through adaptation and upgrade before assuming that disposal, or demolition and redevelopment, is the only option. The owner may be surprised to discover that a transformational result can be achieved at a fraction of the cost and time.

Figure 9.38
Wynford House regenerated, 2000. Compare with Figure 9.32.

PART TWO: PROSPECT

Figure 9.39
The local authority designated
the whole of the regenerated
Priory Green estate as a
conservation area.

10
Changing conservation culture

The final chapter is presented as a selective and speculative survey of current trends and initiatives that may be expected to shape the future direction of modern architectural conservation in the age of climate crisis.

THIS BOOK BEGAN BY DESCRIBING THE recognition and appropriate stewardship of Modern heritage in the UK as 'a work in progress still affected by a mixture of controversy, passion, ignorance and neglect'. While modern conservation culture has clearly progressed over the 50-year period of review, this description still seems broadly applicable if the disputatious atmosphere surrounding many high-profile demolition, listing and COI cases is anything to go by. Yet if the story has necessarily focused largely on the local narrative of Modern heritage as it has played out in the UK, and most specifically England – the main territory of my experience – it is impossible not to be aware of 'shifting tectonic plates' in the wider world of international conservation discourse and its predisposing political context. This chapter accordingly selects just a few straws in the wind that seem likely to foretell of possible developments in conservation that are already unfolding or will surely do so in the near future.

MEANINGFUL METRICS

The changing culture within the construction professions has already been indicated in the growing prominence of environmental sustainability as the key driver in reordering the industry's priorities. The merger of 'conservation' as the common currency of heritage discourse with 'Conservation' as key driver of the Green Agenda is becoming ever more self-evident. The suggestion of a demolition tax – computed on the financial evaluation of lost embodied energy and levied on buildings slated for demolition – was met with distinct scepticism among an American conference audience that I addressed in Arizona several years ago, but would surely be unlikely to occasion such scepticism now. Leaving 'elite heritage' on one side for the moment, what will increasingly force the argument for keeping and upgrading Modern buildings, as against demolition and new build, will be the imperatives of reducing carbon impacts. The Intergovernmental Panel on Climate Change (IPCC) Climate Report, published in August 2021, is such a clarion call as surely to be unignorable by any responsible government the world over.[1] If the first objective is to instil wider acceptance of the urgent need for change, the next must surely be to establish greater consensus and consistent standards on the attendant environmental metrics. And for such norms to be meaningful and command compliance they will require consistent and credible methods of evaluation. Of course, the challenge extends across a far wider field than 'simply' architecture and the built environment, but as this represents a major component of the problem, there is more than enough for the sector to address.

While there is definite progress in the promulgation of raised standards, it is considerably less certain how effectively these are being assimilated and applied within the construction industry. BS EN 15978 (2011), part of a suite of sustainability standards, provides a methodology for undertaking Life Cycle Assessments (LCA) of buildings, with a system of modules covering all stages from the preparation of materials, their supply chains and transportation, through the construction phase, then over the period of the building in use, to end-of-life aspects, including scope for reuse, recovery and recycling. The complementary standard BS EN 15804 (2012) gives guidance around core product category rules relating to Environmental Product

Declarations (EPDs) to ensure that construction products and services are derived, verified and presented in a harmonised way.

This appears to be going in the right direction, but given the default reference study period (RSP) of 60 years for new buildings, it is unlikely that any such accounting will be undertaken by the same personnel at each end of the whole Life Cycle Assessment. This is bound to raise doubts over the veracity of predictive computations, despite the requirement for transparency in citation of data sources. It must still be assumed that stringent and objective methodologies for assessing building physics and energy use will increasingly be embraced as comparative tools in the design development process, and eventually become a mandatory reporting protocol demanded not only by statutory authorities but also by progressive property clients. Similarly, the series of standards sponsored by the UK Government's Department for Business, Energy and Industrial Strategy (BEIS) sets out systematic procedures for assessing improved energy performance in retrofitting existing buildings. The specification issued by the British Standards Institution (BSI) PAS 2035 (2019) is presented as a key document in a framework of new and existing standards on how to conduct effective energy retrofits.[2] The standard addresses the assessment of dwellings for retrofit, identifying improvement options, design and specification of Energy Efficiency Measures (EEM) and the monitoring of retrofit projects. Meanwhile PAS 2030, which was redeveloped in conjunction with PAS 2035, covers the installation, commissioning and handover of retrofit projects. Organisations which trade using the Trustmark Government Endorsed Quality Scheme are required to comply with PAS 2035. The commercial and marketing advantages of measurable sustainability gains should add their own incentives. The question is, how universal and consistent will be their implementation?

As far as the heritage sector is concerned, more concerted efforts have been made to establish common guidelines for improving energy performance with specific reference to historic buildings. The EN 16883 Energy Standard, promulgated in 2017 by the Comité Européen de Normalisation CEN, based in Brussels (an association of national standardisation bodies – in 34 countries at the last count), is intended for application to buildings of any age, regardless of designation status, and seeks to reconcile sustainability goals with preservation of heritage values. This is inevitably a delicate balancing act in the most sensitive cases, where authentic architectural character is inherently inimical to normal techniques of envelope upgrade, yet worthwhile improvement may still be feasible through the combination of renewable energy and judicious intervention. The CEN initiative – reproduced in the UK by the British Standards Institution – in aiming for greater consistency in evaluation methods, documentation and analysis, enhanced Life Cycle Assessment tools, and better data sharing, surely adds momentum to linking heritage with the Green Agenda.

Wherever one looks, the picture is one of accelerating concern in seeking adequate responses to the environmental crisis. Yet the gap between rhetoric and reality is alarming. Setting targets is the easy part; meaningful proof of achievement is the real challenge. The common factor that emerges is the urgent need for more and better data, transparency in reporting and the introduction of mandatory requirements in terms of energy performance ratings, genuine product declarations, minimum energy efficiency standards and more consistent post-occupancy monitoring. Rather as the World Health Organization advised national governments to 'Test, test, test!' in the face of the Covid-19 pandemic, so the emerging mantra of the environmental conservation movement must surely be 'Measure, measure, measure!' if advances in the field are to become more scientific and systematic. Certain assessment systems – such as BREAM (Building Research Establishment Assessment Method), established in 1990, and the slightly younger LEED (Leadership in Energy and Environment Design, promulgated in 1993 by the US Green Building Council) – have become well established with a wide range of rating systems, though there is also an increasing number of rivals in the field. The GRESB (Global Real Estate Sustainability Benchmark), founded in 2009, is another system of environmental measurement and certification for listed property companies, funds and investors, offering third-party validation for members. The perceived value of formal certification in one or other of these systems has clearly helped to develop a culture of greater environmental responsibility across the construction and property sector.

What is less evident so far is a widening of criteria beyond the preoccupation with leaner or more innovative newbuilds and improved accounting for *operational* carbon. Important as these certainly are, they are still only a partial consideration of the much broader issue. The holistic valuation of *embodied* carbon in *existing* buildings as a vital contribution to changing conservation culture must surely also be brought more fully into the reckoning if a true sustainability audit of the built environment is to be achieved. This is where the metrics need to be meaningful. Advances in design technology software, such as Autodesk® BIM 360™, provide new and more systematic methods of coordinating design processes and measuring comparative outcomes in the quest for improving performance. Another such aid specifically directed towards energy analysis is cove.tool (founded in 2017), which exploits the power of the cloud and big data to compare parametrically thousands of energy models in a matter of minutes to help designers optimise evolving proposals from early concept stage to detailed schemes.

But there are also caveats. The increasingly eager promotion of new buildings for their green credentials can give misleading impressions of exactly how 'green' they really are.[3] It seems the sustainability debate has not yet reached the stage where real consensus exists among participants on what constitutes genuine progress and how it should be measured. In the absence of robust policing, the scope for 'greenwashing', 'carbon leakage' and other evasions, whether innocent or mischievous, will only increase. The current '*production*-based' system of carbon accounting, sanctioned by the Kyoto Protocol 1997, is another misleading metric in discounting the carbon *consumption* embedded in national imports from other countries.[4] As Dieter Helm argued in his compelling study *The Carbon Crunch*, in confronting the difficulties in adopting a workable regime of carbon pricing, 'The challenge is not to get the price exactly right, but to make progress away from a situation where carbon is not priced at all and therefore is exactly wrong.'[5] Some progress has indeed been made in the decade since, with carbon pricing schemes now deployed in 46 national and international jurisdictions, the EU being the largest, and the UK's Emissions Trading Scheme (ETS) having opened in May 2021. But, as has also been astutely noted, emission trading schemes alone are not a substitute for real, proactive measures that actually cut emissions.[6]

Figure 10.1
There is a vast amount of embodied energy in modern materials.

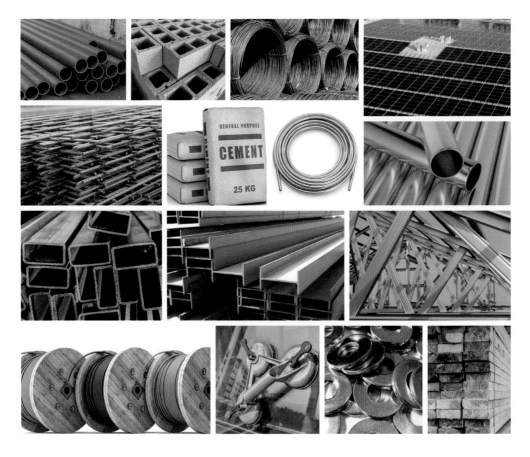

This is not, of course, to underestimate the importance of advances in the science of renewable energy, and specifically the vital work of organisations like IRENA (founded in 2009), the International Renewable Energy Agency, an intergovernmental organisation of over 160 states plus the EU, which promotes a sustainable energy future, and serves as the principal platform for international cooperation in the field. Yet while there has been significant progress in the science and calculation of energy consumption of buildings in use, the equivalent reckoning of embodied carbon in construction materials and *existing* development is still conspicuously underdeveloped, and there are still no mandatory national requirements to assess, report, control or tax *embodied* carbon emissions.[7] Yet many of the materials involved in modern construction – cement and concrete, steel, aluminium, glass, copper, oil-based products – have some of the highest embodied energy values of any materials (Figure 10.1), in addition to the sheer quantities being used. Concrete, for example, is reportedly the second most widely consumed substance on earth after water.[8]

The focus on reducing operational carbon through the expansion of renewable sources, lowering consumption and optimising recycling of materials in new building work ignores the estimated 75% of embodied carbon of a building's total emissions over its lifetime. Given that 80% of the built environment in 2050 already exists today, other gains in achieving net-zero carbon by that date must surely come from reducing, or preferably avoiding, disturbance of the embodied carbon in this existing inheritance through intelligent retrofit and reuse. By way of example, the recurrent refusal on heritage grounds to grant listed status for the Southbank Centre in London (see p 119) overlooks the other, more compelling, argument for retaining and refurbishing this mighty Modern asset which, it has been estimated, accounts for 22,000 cubic metres of concrete, with a carbon dioxide equivalent of 15,000 tonnes, quite apart from the quantities of steel reinforcement and rip-sawn Baltic pine shuttering timber also used in construction. We must begin to appreciate that the investment *already made* in all this energy and material constitutes another kind of heritage – less 'glamorous', perhaps, but still heritage nonetheless.[9]

MOBILISING PROFESSIONALS

Even the increasingly onerous requirements of Building Regulations across the UK in relation to energy use and building performance are already being criticised as inadequate by thought leaders in the architectural and allied professions. Launched in May 2019, the campaign 'Architects Declare', which has united over 1,000 UK architectural practices in calling attention to the industry's responsibilities in relation to the climate and biodiversity emergency, has broadened into the still greater movement 'Construction Declares', embracing structural, civil and building services engineering practices, landscape architects, contractors and project managers in the UK and internationally, amounting to over 6,000 practices across 25 countries. The network presents itself as both a worldwide declaration of our planet's environmental crises and also as a pledge to take action in response to climate breakdown and biodiversity collapse.[10] The declaration includes wide-ranging commitments, of which three in particular connect directly with the heritage conservation arguments being proposed here.

- Upgrade buildings for extended use, as a more carbon-efficient alternative to demolition and new build, whenever there is a viable choice.

- Include life-cycle costing, whole-life carbon modelling and post-occupancy evaluation as part of our basic scope of work, to reduce both embodied and operational resource use.

- Adopt more regenerative design principles in our studios, with the aim of designing architecture and urbanism that goes beyond the standard of net-zero carbon in use.

These objectives surely dovetail with those of Modern heritage in directing the agenda towards retention and retrofit as the default response at moments of uncertainty in the futures of existing buildings, but especially those unprotected by designation. Significantly, at the recent virtual conference of Architects Declare in April 2021, when more than 150 delegates were asked to name the single greatest imperative in preventing the current environmental damage of Business as Usual, the largest response by far in the resulting wordcloud was 'DEMOLITION'.

Meanwhile, the UK Government's recent consultation exercise on Parts L and F of the Building Regulations (Conservation of Fuel and Power, and Means of Ventilation) has provoked a strident response from the Architects Climate Action Network (ACAN), an alignment of several hundred professionals, urging more ambitious measures in respect of fabric performance targets, energy consumption reporting, local authority powers to set higher standards, and the inclusion of embodied carbon in the Future Homes Standard. On the homes front more recently, a group of leading housing associations has formed a 'Greener Futures Partnership' to improve the sustainability of their combined portfolio of 300,000 homes and develop greater collaboration in managing development methods.[11] How effective such initiatives prove to be in bringing about increased regulatory controls and improved practice in the areas noted remains unclear, but they surely cannot fail to promote a steady shift in consciousness across the social landlord sector in general. Ideally, the more progressive actors will incentivise the laggards to catch up. And such a dynamic can only accelerate the elision of 'conservation' in the generic sense of responsible environmental stewardship and 'conservation' as a specialist heritage discipline.

For sustainability methodologies to be effectively embraced as design tools by the construction professions, there will need to be significant upskilling. Meaningful Life Cycle Assessments (LCAs), especially if becoming a mandatory requirement at planning/listed building application and building control stages, will certainly entail additional professional resources if not also the emergence of a new species of professional consultant sufficiently versed in the evolving science of sustainability metrics. Aspiring young architects would be well advised to become literate in this burgeoning discipline before it is appropriated by another one of the building professions. In anticipation of these developments, the Architects Registration Board (ARB) has announced that new provisions for assessing the competence of registered architects in relation to sustainable architecture are soon to be introduced as a mandatory requirement of the Architects Code of Conduct and Practice, which it is obliged to issue under the Architects Act 1997 (Section 13) – the 'high-level wording' of the current code now being regarded as inadequate.[12] A 'strategic statement' issued in 2020 advises:

The Code now needs expansion in order to provide sufficient guidance to architects on how to approach the challenges of the Climate Emergency. Similarly, schools of architecture require further clarification and robust guidance on how we expect them to meet the Criteria in order to address the global crisis. All architects in practice have a responsibility to ensure that they are sufficiently competent in terms of the skills, knowledge, experience and behaviours in order to be able to address climate change through sustainable architecture. Given the long-term effects of design decisions, architects should also aspire to do more than just comply with current legislation and Codes. In order to do this all architects must have an understanding of the global context in which they practise and the implications their decisions and activities have for sustainability.

Alongside a commitment to strive for sustainable design solutions, architects need the technical knowledge and skills to apply the appropriate design principles and construction technologies and use resources efficiently in order to promote sustainability. To achieve this aim, architects need to be 'energy-literate' and take active steps to minimise the potential longer-term environmental impact of their work, by addressing where, how and with what materials constructions are designed.[13]

The statement makes no reference to any particular age of building or type of work, but these changing expectations must surely interlock with the concerns of modern conservation. Parallel moves to set an example include the RIBA 2030 Climate Challenge Targets, published in 2019, which seek to front-load the UK 2050 net-zero carbon timetable by setting architects more stringent benchmarks against five yearly milestones at 2020, 2025 and 2030 respectively, defining persistence of missed targets thereafter in the ensuing run-up to 2050 as 'unsustainable practice'.[14]

In the light of such moves, it seems inevitable that conservation of heritage can no longer remain in a silo of its own but must merge with conservation culture in the broadest sense. If, as the slogan has it, 'the greenest building is the one already built', then the question for modern conservationists is whether they are willing to venture into this territory and master the science and politics of sustainability, carbon accounting and embodied energy in the cause of keeping and upgrading worthy, if not exalted, Modern buildings? Of course, they can still be MoMo (Modern Movement) evangelists seeking to win heritage converts from a sceptical or indifferent audience. But they must also now engage with this larger challenge of *environmental* conservation and become fluent in its attendant metrics if owners of sub-iconic buildings and other stakeholders are to be persuaded of the benefits of retention and adaptive reuse. To this end, Docomomo's early ground-breaking work in researching the historiography and science of MoMo building physics needs to be consolidated and further developed in order to cover more recent practice.[15] The alternative, it seems to me, is that modern conservation will remain a niche specialism, increasingly divorced from the wide horizons and limitless aspirations that characterised the original Modernists.

GOVERNMENT REFORM

The single most significant achievement of Theresa May's administration may arguably be the Climate Change Act 2008 (2050 Target Amendment) Order 2019, a Statutory Instrument which revised the percentage reduction of UK carbon emissions against the 1990 baseline from 80% to 100%, or in other words imposed the legal deadline of 2050 for the UK to completely terminate all contributions to global warming and become net-zero carbon across the board. An explanatory note at the end of the brief text added somewhat ominously that 'a full impact assessment has not been produced for this instrument', but there is no doubt that it has now established the context for conservation and sustainability discourse for the next 30 years. This at least was a more positive move from a government that only a few years earlier had scrapped the zero-carbon homes programme introduced by Gordon Brown in 2006.

At national level, and possibly hastened by the responsibilities (and political opportunities) of hosting the UN Climate Change Conference, COP26, in Glasgow in November 2021, increasing scrutiny is turning to the environmental reforms incumbent on the government in its own practices. The Government Property Agency, established as an executive unit of the Cabinet Office in 2018, published its Government Estate Strategy, which includes some ambitious targets for improving the performance of its own portfolio in pursuance of the same Climate Change Act of 2008. The report acknowledges that buildings account for 40% of the UK's energy consumption and carbon emissions.[16] Dramatic reductions in total floor area (reportedly over 2 million square metres already), rationalisation of dispersed operations into a series of 'hub units', and smaller individual workspace allocations are all proposed in the drive for greater efficiency, with a commensurate reduction of carbon footprint and release of government property and land for housing use. The prospectus, naturally presented in the most positive possible language, implies large numbers of existing buildings will be vacated and potentially demolished for redevelopment – a scenario with potentially both pros and cons in terms of conservation and environmental impacts. Meanwhile, a new review of the Treasury Green Book, which governs public spending rules and investment decisions, and which was already revised in 2018, now proposes greater emphasis on establishing the 'benefits case' as distinct from merely the 'economic case' for development projects – albeit some commentators are not convinced of its sufficient ambition, and have argued for more holistic accounting criteria that take cognisance of unmonetisable factors as well as sustainability and resilience.[17]

In contrast to the plausible resolutions of government departments, the interventions of individual ministers seem particularly out of kilter with progressive trends, to judge from recent attempts to canvas populist support. See, for example, comments made in 2016 by John Hayes, Minister of State for Transport at the time, regarding 'Brutalist' architecture,[18] or the more recent declaration by the former Housing Secretary Robert Jenrick that the government's planning reforms create a 'big opportunity' to tear down unpopular buildings dating from the 1960s and 1970s. Speaking at the Conservative Party's 2020 virtual conference, Jenrick revealed that one of the reasons he had supported expanding Permitted Development (PD) rights as part of the proposed planning 'reforms' was to allow people to 'demolish some of the mistakes of the recent past'. The message has subsequently been further embellished.[19] Such views, while usually finding local cheerleaders, do not bode well for the fate of buildings like Derby Assembly Rooms (Figure 10.2), Swansea Civic Centre or Shirehall, Shropshire – among numerous others on C20's latest Buildings at Risk List. In the case of Derby, it is estimated that rebuilding something of equivalent size will cost just over 11,400 tonnes of CO_2, according to Prof Philip Oldfield of the University of New South Wales, Sydney.[20]

Figure 10.2
Derby Assembly Rooms, by Casson, Conder and Partners, 1977, set for demolition despite being less than 50 years old.

That these and similar comparatively recent buildings are routinely considered ripe for demolition without any account taken of the carbon cost implications is indicative of just how far we have yet to progress before any sort of responsible and consistent conservation culture among public authorities and central government is established. Although such dog-whistle outbursts are presumably intended as a populist smack at Modern architecture in general, one could hope that the views of those most directly implicated – the ministers of culture and/or the arts – would be more discriminating. Yet the volatility of listing decisions by recent UK Secretaries of State shows just how dependent is the support for Modern heritage on the uncertain tastes of the particular individual in post at the time. As for the Executive Order of outgoing President Trump requiring all new Federal buildings in the USA to be designed in the Classical style... one is reminded of Anatoly Lunacharsky's baleful observation at the foreclosure of the Constructivist period that 'the people too have a right to their colonnades'.[21] Hopefully with the ensuing change of administration, this particular inanity can be consigned to oblivion.

FORMING ALLIANCES

Such mixed messages in elevated political echelons provide disturbing evidence of the work still needed in achieving positive change in conservation culture. It is abundantly clear that over several decades of the Modern heritage lobby's existence, the promulgation of its message, while certainly effective in some quarters, has been extremely uneven in others. On the one hand, the professional, academic, student and – to an extent – even public audiences have become increasingly aware and engaged. Additionally, if the logos and lists published on Docomomo's various national websites and biennial collections of conference papers are anything to go by, there is an impressive range of institutional supporters and international partners. Quite how meaningfully engaged these various agencies actually are with the modern conservation mission may be another matter. Are they active in spreading the gospel or merely helpful in providing occasional financial support? Perhaps some just contribute the prestige of brand association, though the value of this kind of endorsement is not to be underestimated. This is an avenue to explore further, as these partners must surely be the next most accessible alliances upon which to build.

By contrast, the political and property investment sectors are conspicuously absent. 'The authorities' are named somewhat generically in Docomomo's original Eindhoven Statement, Article 1, as a constituency whose attention is to be drawn to the significance of the architecture of the Modern Movement, but apart from formal appearances in the ceremonial opening proceedings at biennial conferences, politicians and unelected officials seem noticeably absent from the modern conservation orbit. As for real estate investors and property owners, there is almost no sustained engagement except as opposition when contingent on a specific project. The reasons for this seem clear. As far as politicians are concerned, unless recruited to champion a particular local campaign, there may appear to be no obvious electoral mileage in promoting 'Modern architectural heritage' as a cause. Meanwhile, capital investors and building proprietors are typically ill-disposed towards any organised initiative that to them would suggest a curtailment of their freedom of action in matters of property development and real estate. To such interests the Modern heritage lobby is more probably associated with vigilante groups and local preservation societies – that is, just another irksome hurdle to be overcome in the process of gaining planning and/or listed building consent. Indeed, it is precisely the role of groups such as C20 and Docomomo to resist misconceived and detrimental MoMo-related projects. Yet the critical importance of both these constituencies – i.e. politicians and property developers (if one may describe them in such generic terms) – to the modern conservation cause can hardly be overestimated. They are responsible for, respectively, the policy context and the investment dynamic that together largely determine the whole built environment process. So how best might the Modern heritage movement be more effectively engaged with these, so far, indifferent or hostile audiences?

A natural instinct might be to double down on missionary evangelism – seeking to win converts by pure heritage advocacy. Enthusiasm for a cause can be influential if effectively communicated, but it is more likely to overcome ignorance than conquer prejudice – that is, arouse interest or curiosity in those who may have no prior knowledge of the inspirational Modern Movement story. In this endeavour, in February 2021 Docomomo-US initiated its *Modern Love + The Advocacy Fund* programme, following the much-lamented demolition of Paul Rudolph's Burroughs Wellcome Building (Figure 10.3) in North Carolina, and one must wish it well.[22] As we have seen, such crucial losses can become powerful generators of new commitment, though how effective this one will prove to be remains to be seen.

Figure 10.3
The Burroughs Wellcome Building, North Carolina, by Paul Rudolph, 1972. The building was demolished in 2021, less than 50 years after it was completed.

On the other hand, those already holding hostile opinions on Modern architecture, whose 'minds are already made up', are less likely to be susceptible. More promising in the context of such sceptical audiences might be to tailor the message to align with *their* primary interests. In the case of the politicians and their central or local government advisors, this – as already indicated – might be to underscore the environmental and social advantages of upgrade and adaptive reuse of the better elements of the Modern built legacy as against demolition and redevelopment, and demonstrate the alignment of these strategies with increasingly pressing environmental policy and legislation. This would then not be preaching about saving 'iconic heritage', which is unlikely to convince the tin-eared, but it might have considerable relevance in dealing with the 35% of EU building stock that is over 50 years old, to say nothing of the 75% that is still energy inefficient. The current rate of renovation, reportedly a mere 0.5–1.0%, is going to have to be improved dramatically to have any hope of meeting the Paris Climate Accords of 2015 or those that come after. While originally Modernism may have been identified with carbon-hungry demolition and new build, Modern *heritage* is concerned with transformative conservation and intelligent upgrade, yet it is estimated that some 50,000 buildings in the UK are still lost to demolition each year.[23] Against the broader canvas of progressive regulation, it is this picture of environmental inertia and avoidable waste that should eventually register with responsible politicians and attentive councillors. One immediate reform that could easily align policy with principle is revoking the 20% VAT rate that penalises refurbishment and renovation, as against the zero or 5% ratings that favour new build.

In the case of developers and building owners, there may be equivalent incentives for creative rehabilitation, thereby avoiding costly and time-consuming local resistance and more onerous consent procedures, as well as the social dislocation and economic disruption associated with demolition and redevelopment. The New London Architecture (NLA) agency has established useful traction with homeowners with its programme 'Don't move – improve!' but there is no reason why this principle may not be extended beyond the domestic property sector under such banners as 'Don't trash – transform!' or 'Don't destroy – redeploy!' In a similar vein, *The Architectural Review* is seeking to promote the drive for sustainable alternatives to building anew and in 2017 launched its programme of New into Old Awards to celebrate the creative ways buildings can be adapted and remodelled to accommodate new uses. The *Architects' Journal* campaign 'RetroFirst' points in the same direction, now running an awards scheme in nine categories of building type. Such initiatives surely align with the direction of travel in progressive environmental thinking. In many cases the otherwise uninitiated property owner may simply need more encouragement about the feasibility of achieving the necessary repurposing and upgrade of his or her asset, regardless of designation status. Often it is the impact of similar successful rehabilitation projects that may be the most persuasive agent in the process of changing minds – and perhaps eventually hearts. There is a growing back catalogue of exemplars and case studies, which if effectively mobilised, could provide compelling evidence of the benefits of pursuing adaptive reuse and upgrade strategies instead of demolition and disposal.

INTERNATIONAL PROGRESS

There have also been positive developments on the international stage over the last 20 years that surely augur well for the future. In 2001 the UNESCO World Heritage Centre, ICOMOS and Docomomo launched a joint programme for the identification, documentation and promotion of the built heritage of the 19th and 20th centuries – the Programme on Modern Heritage. This effectively harnessed the prestige and support of two 'world brands' to the key aims that Docomomo had identified at Eindhoven over a decade earlier. This potentially powerful alignment has been developed and promoted with financial support from the government of the Netherlands, raising awareness of the heritage of architecture, town planning and landscape design of the Modern era, which is considered to be particularly vulnerable because of weak legal protection and low appreciation among the general public. An important early achievement was the publication *Identification and Documentation of Modern Heritage*, featuring a series of substantial essays by an international cast of historians and scholars.[24] The Programme on Modern Heritage aims to establish a framework of conceptual thinking on the significance of this heritage, its preservation and some of the pivotal issues concerning identification and evaluation.

The framework has been further developed through a succession of Regional Meetings at widely ranging venues including Monterey, Chandigarh, Asmara, Miami and Alexandria. Projects are structured according to the Strategic Objectives adopted by the World Heritage Committee in pursuance of regional and thematic priorities, with support given for follow-up or spin-off initiatives. Support may also be considered for nominating Modern properties to UNESCO's List of World Heritage in Danger, as the representation of Modern heritage on this list is still extremely modest. There must surely be further mileage in pursuing this association with UNESCO, the organisation with pre-eminent name-recognition in the field of cultural heritage, and – by this link with Docomomo – now with *Modern* architectural heritage, even if the focus is still, for the time being, on what may be termed 'elite heritage'.

In another important initiative on the international stage, the World Monuments Fund (WMF) launched the biennial World Monuments Fund/Knoll Modernism Prize with founding sponsor Knoll in 2008 to recognise individuals and organisations that preserve Modern built heritage through pioneering architectural and design solutions. The prize honours contemporary architects and preservationists whose work ensures sustainable futures for at-risk Modern heritage and is part of the WMF's broader programming that addresses these challenges facing Modern sites through advocacy, education and conservation, including the World Monuments Watch. The prize stemmed from WMF's Modernism at Risk initiative, created in 2006 in response to the increasing threats to buildings representative of the Modern Movement. This prestigious award has already produced a worthy succession of winners.[25]

Broadening the scope of the modern conservation discourse beyond its typically Eurocentric confines is a vital part of developing international alliances, as well as reflecting the global reach and diverse regional variations of the original movement. Docomomo made early and important progress in 2003 in foregrounding underrepresented territories with its special study *Modern*

Heritage in Africa.[26] By 2020 national chapters had been established in Angola, Egypt, Ghana and Morocco, with many more in South America, Australia and Asia.[27] Meanwhile, Docomomo International itself has announced the relocation in 2022 of its headquarters from the Técnico, University of Lisbon, where it has flourished since 2014, to Delft University of Technology in the Netherlands – the place of its birth, where under the direction of new leadership its mission will surely be further progressed.

A more recent initiative in 2020 on the Modern heritage of Africa has been launched jointly by the University of Cape Town and the Bartlett School, UCL, and further progress on the international front has been made by the UCL Institute for Sustainable Heritage, which in March 2021 celebrated its first 20 years of operation with a wide-ranging four-day conference featuring international contributors covering many aspects of the developing field. The research focus of the Institute's work ranges widely across issues of resilience and heritage science, modern and future heritage, while being cross-disciplinary and collaborative and functioning as a powerful agent in the creation of new knowledge.

Likewise, the Getty Conservation Institute in Los Angeles, another organisation with significant international convening power, has progressed its Conserving Modern Architecture Initiative, originally launched in 2011, with a range of training programmes and publications. Alongside a developing series of monographs devoted to case studies on specific topics – concrete repair, energy and climate management, conservation plans – an ambitious collaboration with the ICOMOS International Scientific Committee on Twentieth-Century Heritage has recently produced a 'Historic Thematic Framework' described as a 'tool for assessing heritage places'. Based on 10 thematic categories, this offers a taxonomy for organising 20th-century history to identify and contextualise sites, people and events, which is hoped will assist users in the identification, conservation and promotion of their local heritage.[28] It remains to be seen whether and how widely this publication, which the authors frankly acknowledge has something of a Western bias, will establish a common *modus operandi* within the international heritage community. But with its Getty imprimatur and universal (*gratis*) availability it will surely help consolidate the growing awareness of modern conservation culture and stimulate the discourse among many engaged in the field.

SPREADING THE WORD

A proposal for compiling a new register of the most successful MoMo rehabilitation and adaptive reuse projects has already been suggested (see p 156), and such a compilation, effectively illustrated with 'before' and 'after' images and informed by authoritative critiques, could provide a powerful promotional and campaigning tool for dissemination to key figures and institutions in the constituencies mentioned above – in the case of the UK, such organisations as the British Property Federation, the Listed Property Owners Club and suchlike. On the international canvas, it could be represented at MIPIM, the largest property event of its kind, held annually in Cannes.

A potential vehicle for this has already been created by Docomomo International in the remarkable virtual exhibition launched in November 2015, which offers a selection of more than 3,000 buildings and sites of the Modern Movement across the globe. Part gazetteer, part inventory, this is a free database unique for its geographical reach and number of works. The virtual exhibition is a tool to promote study, interpretation and protection and generally increase public awareness of this often-devalued heritage.[29] Based on a world map, the user can search any building or architect, discover essential data, filter information by keywords, and find image galleries and videos. The buildings can be shared on major social networks or commented on directly. The MoMove tab also functions as a mobile app, making it easy to use while travelling or for compiling a tour itinerary. Contributions to the Docomomo virtual exhibition are made by individual national chapters so it will always be in transformation, but it provides an international infrastructure to which the register of exemplar retrofit projects could surely be harnessed. The next step in this direction has been taken in 2021 with the launch of the Docomomo International Rehabilitation Award, titled 'DRAW', which celebrates leading modern conservation projects in a range of different categories, on a biennial cycle that will hopefully attract wide media coverage, and help to project the movement's profile beyond its own parish.

HIGH-PROFILE CASES

Extending the discourse will also continue to entail taking a stand in contested contexts. The Eindhoven Statement enjoins all Docomomo chapters to 'oppose destruction and disfigurement of significant works' – or in other words, to join or mobilise campaigns to protect important MoMo buildings under threat. Most local chapters will have a range of such cases, and in many instances (as evidenced by the Heritage in Danger section of Docomomo International's website) these may be of such importance as to merit international intervention. Such coordinated action not only assists the particular campaign concerned, it also helps raise the profile of the network as an international voice when other national chapters intervene to lend support to local causes. The watchdog role is both part of its primary mission, and equally a means by which it may increase its public visibility. Of no less importance to flagging up cases in danger is the promotion of success stories involving projects that have been intelligently rescued and repurposed. By rewarding progressive authorities and responsible developers with encomia for 'doing the right thing', this becomes another means of cultivating the support of former adversaries.

WHOSE HERITAGE?

Finally, in this survey of the changing conservation culture, it is impossible to ignore the insistent pressure to rethink issues of heritage ownership. Even the most exemplary projects of rescue and retrieval can sometimes leave unanswered the question, 'To whom does this heritage belong?' Contrarily, the power of heritage to incite opposition can, *in extremis*, prompt devastating reprisals. One has only to consider the wilful destruction of the Buddhas of Bamiyan in Afghanistan in 2001, or the more recent succession of attacks on ancient sites of cultural significance in Syria, most notably Palmyra in 2015, to appreciate how the heritage of 'others' can mobilise vengeful instincts. More locally, and certainly more laudable, are such episodes as the upending of the Edward Colston statue in Bristol and his 'replacement' with Jen Reid (Figure 10.4) – evidence of the power of others' heritage when the tipping point (literally) arrives.[30]

Figure 10.4
'A Surge of Power', the temporary statue of Jen Reid, Bristol, 2020, replacing that of Edward Colston, local slave trader.

The ongoing debate over repatriation of artefacts gained through colonial expropriation has in recent years acquired an unprecedented intensity. The Elgin Marbles and Benin Bronzes are but two of the better-known cases where questions of ownership merge with larger concerns over the typically Eurocentric versions of history that such relics are used to present and the 'storehouse culture' of the museums in which they are held. Even the peerless Neil MacGregor's *History of the World in 100 Objects* draws criticism from some quarters for representing heritage through a privileged lens of Western precedence. Meanwhile, since its initiation in Cape Town in 2015, the Fallism movement has broadened from revolt against one university's association with Cecil Rhodes to become an international alliance challenging the whole legacy of white supremacism and its physical manifestations. These may seem extreme examples, yet they are contiguous with the same question as to whose heritage is being preserved in the future development of conservation culture and how it may be liberated from some of its elitist or exclusive connotations.

I have described elsewhere the effect of designation in instigating a sort of negotiation between two types of ownership – legal title and intergenerational equity, the latter often being promoted by a cadre of professional experts on behalf of a presumed community of beneficiaries. In the particular case of Modern heritage, the degree of proxy can become problematic when so much unloved architecture of the Welfare State is championed by enthusiasts in opposition to those for whom it was built. As we have seen, conservation agencies and amenity groups arguing for the retention or protection of unpopular Brutalist buildings may not always enjoy the support of proprietors or earn the gratitude of local communities. Yet, as also noted, it may often be due only to the actions of these agencies that many of the currently disputed assets are saved at all.

This is really the same phenomenon as that of overcoming the scepticism of the demoralised owner but on a larger scale. Given the intrinsically secular and inclusive aspirations of the original Modern Movement, it would seem particularly ironic if the quest for conservation of its most deserving achievements was not equally 'democratic'. Heritage of any period, especially when under threat, can function as a powerful social binder and its capacity to draw communities of mutual interest together and enrich individual experience cannot be overestimated. The very first article of Docomomo's founding statement enjoined members to 'bring the significance of the architecture of the Modern Movement to the attention of the public, the authorities, the professionals and the educational community'. Nothing wrong there, but pursuit of this objective, even if initially and necessarily the task of 'experts' or 'specialists' on the basis of nudge theory, will be self-defeating if it carries any hint of patronising the audience or imposing a received historical interpretation. Recent successes in London, such as the immaculate restoration of Peter Yates' mural (Figure 10.5) at Lubetkin's Bevin Court, in Islington, and the listing of the same architect's East End tower block Sivill House (see Figure 6.1),

Figure 10.5
Peter Yates' mural at Bevin Court, Islington, restored through local community support.

Figure 10.6
The Undercroft skatepark at the Southbank Centre, saved by its users.

in Tower Hamlets, were undoubtedly attributable not to the interventions of 'experts', but to the committed advocacy of their local communities. When people discover and assimilate heritage for themselves, it becomes a legacy they are prepared to defend.

Perhaps the most compelling spatial example of contested heritage ownership takes us back to London's South Bank and the recent struggle to overturn the proposed 'Festival Wing' development that would have entailed removing the famous skateboarders' venue (Figure 10.6) from its authentic centre in the Undercroft of the Queen Elizabeth Hall complex and relocating it to a purpose-built 'replacement space' below Hungerford Bridge. Here, surely, was the ultimate case of popular heritage in contradistinction to the supposedly benign intentions of formal authority. Early in 2014, after an already troubled history of local opposition to the proposals, Lambeth Council was confronted by 27,286 objections – apparently a record in UK planning history.[31] More than 130,000 people have since become members of the Long Live Southbank campaign, a telling counternarrative to compare with the repeated attempts by Modern heritage experts to have the architecture itself formally designated. Writings of the struggle surely express in its most lucid form the difference between formal and informal heritage, many of the original supporters of the Festival Wing project eventually coming round to recognising the strength of the skateboarders' case:

> True and honest expression is not something that can be contained by rules or structures, or that needs validation from any higher authority… The Undercroft is without question a mecca of free and uncontained creativity, and what has emerged from between the pillars of its Brutalist design has had a far bigger resonance than the original architects could ever have imagined. It is energizing to think of what the next 40 years of its evolution will bring.[32]

In the event, the campaigners did not need to wait so long. In 2019, after a conscientious repair and upgrade project, the Undercroft skatepark was reopened, retaining 'the original fabric and feel of the space', and looks set to become the definitive example of communal heritage as identified and appropriated by ongoing generations of creative users – an object lesson in inclusivity that professional conservationists would be wise to remember.[33]

HEARTS AND MINDS

To sum up, it has become clear after five decades of modern conservation that real progress is dependent not just on voluntary evangelism but also on the formation of strategic alliances and the steady assimilation of Modern heritage consciousness into official policy and practice. This necessarily entails not only the easier task of mobilising the open-minded, but also the more challenging process of encouraging governmental and non-governmental agencies, the development sector and the fourth estate to engage with the issues in their practice and public discourse. Reviewing the state of play in 2015, the historian Elain Harwood suggested that 'nearly 30 years after the listing of Bracken House, the battle for the hearts and minds of those with power – the conservationists as much as the politicians – has still to be won'.[34]

One could debate the applicability of Elain's military metaphor. To those of us immersed in the field, it seems less like a battle and more like a long siege punctuated with individual skirmishes of varying intensity, which, if 'won', may accumulate sufficient momentum as to reach a tipping point, after which a more enlightened culture will hopefully ensue. Perhaps the analogy then would be the car seatbelt campaign, or the prohibition of smoking in public places, both of which eventually brought about an irreversible conversion of social mores. My own take from reflecting on the changing conservation culture, and indeed the thrust of this book, is that as the question of how to deal with Modernism's vast legacy becomes increasingly enmeshed with the imperatives of environmental conservation, it will turn out to be easier to win minds than hearts. The irrefutable logic of adaptive reuse and upgrade in the quest for decarbonisation will steadily convince even the least enamoured of Modernism's aesthetic attractions that the greater part of its residues must be retained and revalued as a matter of social responsibility. Hearts can come later.

But come they surely will. If the modern conservation movement trains its gaze on the next half century the aim must surely be to move beyond the current Darwinian period, where

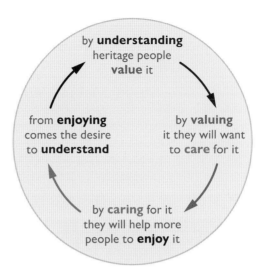

Figure 10.7
The virtuous heritage cycle.

by **understanding**
heritage people
value it

by **valuing**
it they will want
to **care** for it

by **caring** for it
they will help more
people to **enjoy** it

from **enjoying**
comes the desire
to **understand**

recognition and reuse of Modern heritage is still subject to the depredations of 'natural' selection, with its contested cases and uncertain outcomes. Then a time will come when popular acceptance of Modernism's legacy and ideals by a new audience (many as yet unborn) combines with a supportive regulatory culture, such that the benefits are not only expected, but also eventually even enjoyed. Then at last Modern architecture, revalued and revitalised, may enter the virtuous heritage cycle (Figure 10.7). This suggests that understanding the heritage of any age will lead to greater valuation of it, which in turn will encourage better care, then more enjoyment and thereafter greater understanding – a proposition that in the case of Modern heritage is perhaps most dependent on the first step – *understanding*.

This book has considered some of the ways this has begun to be cultivated over the last 50 years – whether through discourse, designation, documentation or demonstration in live projects. In the end, it may be the latter – the buildings themselves – that turn out to be the most compelling agents in initiating the desire to understand. Architecture – whether Modern or of any other age – is intrinsically rooted in location, time and direct personal experience, and ultimately it is surely its material presence that can provide the greatest stimulus. To visit, inhabit or experience a significant Modern building can trigger an emotional response that may not be gained through reading any number of illustrated books or scholarly essays. As one visitor to The Homewood (see Figures 1.19, 7.6, 10.9) later recounted, 'To enter this building and experience its space, its sense of ease and light, its vision of how modern life can be lived differently from the past, is like turning a switch in your mind.'[35] One could speculate that more prejudice has been erased, more minds opened, more interest in Modern architecture kindled through direct experience than by any number of learned papers and laboured polemic. The local tours that typically follow the final day of modern conservation conferences invariably leave the most vivid and lasting memories. The hundreds who queue patiently each year on Open House Day to visit the Isokon (Figure 10.8; see also p 32, p 52 and p 147) are living proof of people's appetite for such experience.

Thus the most persuasive advocacy for Modern heritage may lie in direct engagement with the works themselves, regenerated and re-presented as liberating and inspirational places to use and inhabit (Figure 10.9). And the more the best of such buildings are intelligently adapted, the

Figure 10.8
Queuing (in the rain) for
Modern heritage. Open House
Day at the Isokon, Camden,
north London, 2018.

more assimilated and sustainable our Modern heritage will become – regardless of whether it is listed or not. This is why I suggest that it is not more exhortation that will change reluctant hearts, it is more evidence.

Meanwhile, for old-fashioned Modernists (like myself), the enduring appeal of the Modern Movement, over and above its aesthetic attractions, was always its egalitarianism, its social commitment, its vast sense of possibility, and our motivation in defending and revaluing its legacy ultimately springs from continuing loyalty to such ideals, notwithstanding their oft-flawed implementation. Modern architecture at its finest was a potent carrier of these optimistic messages and it is upon their widening recognition and celebration that its survival – be it motivated by passion or pragmatism – will ultimately depend.

Figure 10.9
The Homewood, Surrey, in its setting – the ultimate Modern idyll, now open to the public.

Figure 10.10 (Following page)
The Isokon Apartments, Lawn Road, Camden London, restored with authentic colours by Avanti Architects 2004. Detail of gallery staircase.

REFERENCES

FOREWORD

1   See https://www.docomomo.com/rehabilitation-award (accessed 14 October 2021).
2   Ursula von der Leyen, President of the European Commission, State of the Union Address to the European Parliament, 16 September 2020. The Next Generation EU (NGEU) fund is a European Union economic recovery package to support member states adversely impacted by the Covid-19 pandemic. Agreed to by the European Council on 21 July 2020, the fund is worth €750 billion. The NGEU fund will operate from 2021 to 2023, and will be tied to the regular 2021–2027 budget of the EU's Multiannual Financial Framework.

INTRODUCTION

1   Professor Peter Blundell Jones, in conversation with the author, Sheffield, 25 July 2008.
2   See https://www.spab.org.uk (accessed 13 October 2021). The Manifesto of the SPAB was written by William Morris, Philip Webb and other founder members in 1877.
3   *The Burra Charter* 1979 et seq. The Australia ICOMOS Charter for Places of Cultural Significance, 2013, Article 3.1.
4   Ryle G, *The Concept of Mind*, Hutchinson, 1949/1962, p 16.

CHAPTER 1 · THE STORY SO FAR

1   Hughes R, *The Shock of the New*, 1980, Thames & Hudson, 2nd edition, 1991, p 376.
2   Jencks C, *Modern Movements in Architecture*, Penguin Books, 1973, pp 11–13.
3   Hughes, p 376.
4   Esher L, *A Broken Wave – The Rebuilding of England 1940–1980*, Allen Lane, 1981. Significantly, perhaps, one of the first attempts to write up Britain's experience of Modernism as history (Jackson A, *The Politics of Architecture – A History of Modern Architecture in Britain*, Architectural Press, 1970) concluded with sombre intimations of the disparity between 'stimulating projects' and their 'disagreeable reality' (p 205).
5   Cherry B, 'Pevsner's 50: Nikolaus Pevsner and the listing of Modern buildings', in *Transactions of the Ancient Monuments Society*, Vol 46, 2002. See also Harries S, *Nikolaus Pevsner – The Life*, Pimlico, 2013, pp 691ff. It is worth noting that the concept of 'conservation areas' (of which there are now nearly 9,800 in England) had been pioneered in the USA from as early as 1900 and was already well developed across the States, as well as in several countries in Europe, before reaching the UK. See Cantell T, 'The history of conservation areas', *Context*, No 148, Institute of Historic Building Conservation, March 2017.
6   The equivalent statutory provisions in Scotland and Northern Ireland are the Planning (Listed Buildings and Conservation Areas – Scotland) Act 1997, and the Planning (Northern Ireland) Order 1991.
7   See Harwood E, 'Keeping the Past in England: The history of post-war listing', in *The Journal of Architecture*, Vol 15, No 5, 2010, pp 671–82. Also 'Modernism joins the Classics', in *Architects' Journal*, 8 April 1987.
8   The conflation of age with respect was perhaps most succinctly expressed by John Huston's character in the film *Chinatown* (1974) who, when asked by Jack Nicholson if he is respectable, replies 'Of course I'm respectable – I'm old. Politician's, ugly buildings and whores all get respectable if they last long enough.'

9   Summerson J, *Heavenly Mansions*, The Cresset Press, 1949, pp 240–41.
10 The whole of the UK is served by government agencies dedicated to the protection and stewardship of the historic environment. English Heritage (officially the Historic Building and Monuments Commission for England) was formed in 1983 as the responsible government agency in England under the Department of Culture, Media and Sport (DCMS; renamed in 2017 the Department of Digital, Culture, Media and Sport). The equivalent organisations elsewhere in the UK are Cadw in Wales (since 1984), Historic Scotland (since 1991, now Historic Environment Scotland) and the Northern Ireland Environment Agency (formerly the Environment and Heritage Service). In the case of English Heritage, significant reorganisation was undertaken in 2015 whereby responsibility for the national heritage collection (and the name English Heritage) was vested in a separate charity endowed with a one-off government grant to address the backlog of maintenance and repair of the properties in public care. Meanwhile the advisory functions of the body and the processes of administering protection legislation and designation have, from 1 April 2015, been vested in the new entity Historic England. (This title is accordingly used in the rest of this essay unless referring to the body in its previous form.)
11 A recent review of the listing process has urged more systematic progress in both the geographic and thematic listing programmes, in addition to numerous other reforming measures, many of which Historic England reports are now underway or in hand. See Saunders M, *Towards a Strategy for the Future of the National Heritage List for England*, Historic England, November 2019, https://www.historicengland.org.uk/content/docs/listing/saunders-report-synopsis (accessed 13 October 2021).
12 See https://historicengland.org.uk/listing/selection-criteria/listing-selection (accessed 4 October 2021).
13 Published in 2010, updated in 2018; see https://www.gov.uk/government/publications/principles-of-selection-for-listing-buildings (accessed 6 October 2021).
14 See *Conservation Principles, Policies and Guidance*, English Heritage, 2008, with later revisions, https://historicengland.org.uk/advice/constructive-conservation/conservation-principles (accessed 6 October 2021).
15 See *Constructive Conservation in Practice*, English Heritage, 2008, https://historicengland.org.uk/images-books/publications/constructive-conservation-in-practice (accessed 6 October 2021).
16 See *Thirties – British Art and Design before the War*, Arts Council of Great Britain, 1979.
17 See Sharp D, 'The Greenside Case', in Macdonald S, Normandin K and Kindred B (eds), *Conservation of Modern Architecture*, Donhead, 2007, pp 116–30. See also https://c20society.org.uk/lost-modern/greenside-virginia-water-surrey (accessed 26 October 2021).
18 See Brown M, 'Goldfinger's Alexander Fleming House finally gets Grade II listing', *The Guardian*, 9 July 2013.
19 See *A Change of Heart – English Architecture since the War. A Policy for Protection*, Royal Commission on the Historical Monuments of England and English Heritage, 1992.
20 See Burman P (ed), *The Conservation of Twentieth Century Buildings*, Proceedings of Conference, 4–6 May 1993, Institute of Advanced Architectural Studies, The University of York, 1996.
21 Macdonald S (ed), *Modern Matters – Principles and*

Practice in Conserving Recent Architecture, Donhead, 1996. Macdonald S (ed), *Preserving Post-War Heritage – The Care and Conservation of Mid-Twentieth Century Architecture*, English Heritage, 2001.
22 Cunningham A (ed), *Modern Movement Heritage*, E & F Spon, 1998.
23 Macdonald S, Normandin K and Kindred B (eds), *Conservation of Modern Architecture*, Donhead, 2007.
24 See van Noord G (ed), *To Have and to Hold*, NVA Glasgow and Luath Press Ltd, Edinburgh, 2010, 2011. Also Watters D, *St Peter's, Cardross – Birth, Death and Renewal*, Historic Environment Scotland, 2016; Historic Environment Scotland (HES), St Peter's Seminary – Cardross: Advice Note to Scottish Ministers, HES, May 2019.
25 Barbican Listed Building Management Guidelines, 2005, https://www.cityoflondon.gov.uk/services/planning/historic-environment/barbican-estate-listed-building-management-guidelines (accessed 5 October 2021); Golden Lane Listed Building Management Guidelines, 2007, https://www.cityoflondon.gov.uk/services/planning/historic-environment/golden-lane-estate-listed-building-management-guidelines (accessed 5 October 2021).
26 See Powers A, *2 Willow Road Hampstead*, The National Trust, 1996; Mead A, 'The Importance of Being Ernö', *Architects' Journal*, 28 March 1996, pp 41–4. Also Bingham N, *The Homewood, Surrey*, The National Trust, 2004, 2011; Harwood E, 'Homewood Bound', *Architects' Journal*, 4 April, 2001, pp 32–9.
27 See *Isokon Gallery – The Story of a New Vision of Urban Living*, The Isokon Gallery Trust, 2016, 2021.
28 Allan J, 'Landmark of the Thirties Restored', *Concrete Quarterly*, No 157, pp 2–5, April–June 1988; 'Tectonic icon restored', *RIBA Journal*, February 1988, pp 30–32; 'Concrete and Clay – Restoration of the Penguin Pool', London Weekend Television, 7 October 1987.
29 See Fairley A, *De La Warr Pavilion – The Modernist Masterpiece*, Merrell, 2006.
30 See Daybelge L and Englund M, *Isokon and the Bauhaus in Britain*, Batsford, 2019. Also, Croft C, 'Isokon', *Architects' Journal*, 30 March 2006, pp 25–35.
31 See Field M, 'A pioneer partially restored to its former glory', *Architects' Journal*, 16 February 1995, pp 22–3. Glancey J, 'A vision still worth fighting for', *The Independent*, 29 March 1995.
32 See Glancey J, 'Pomp and circumstance', *The Guardian*, 30 May 2007.
33 See Dillon P and Douglas S, 'National Theatre, London', in Croft C and Macdonald S (eds) *Concrete – Case Studies in Preserving Modern Heritage*, The Getty Conservation Institute, 2018, pp 166–79.
34 *Understanding Conservation* – a freely available digital resource – is managed by the Council on Training in Architectural Conservation (COTAC), https://www.cotac.global (accessed 5 October 2021).
35 https://ihbc.org.uk (accessed 18 August 2021). An annual IHBC directory with editorial content and much useful information is published by Cathedral Communications, https://www.buildingconservation.com/cathcomm.htm (accessed 5 October 2021).
36 https://www.ucl.ac.uk/bartlett/heritage (accessed 24 August 2021).

CHAPTER 2 · AUTHENTICITY

1 David Fixler, FAIA, FAPT. Architecture Planning Preservation, AIA Taliesin Colloquium, 2017. (David has attributed this caution on the subject of authenticity to his discussions with the late Stanford Anderson, founder of MIT's History, Theory, Criticism programme.)

2 Riegl A, *Der Moderne Denkmalkultus: Sein Wesen und seine Entstehung*, Braumüller, 1903, translated as *The Modern Cult of Monuments: Its Character and Its Origin*, Forster KW and Ghirardo D, *Oppositions*, No 25, 1982, pp 21–51.

3 Benjamin W, *The Work of Art in the Age of Mechanical Re-production*, 1936, translated by Zohn H, Schocken/Random House, ed by Arendt H, transcribed by Blunden A, 1998, proofed and corrected 2005.

4 Berger J, *Ways of Seeing*, BBC/Penguin, 1972.

5 ICOMOS, *The Nara Document on Authenticity*, 1994, Para 11.

6 Pevsner N, *An Outline of European Architecture*, Penguin Books, 1943, 1958, p 23. Pevsner's famous opening sentence asserts, 'A bicycle shed is a building; Lincoln Cathedral is a piece of architecture,' going on to say, 'The term architecture applies only to buildings designed with a view to aesthetic appeal.' Inevitably this distinction has been an age-old irritation to Modernists of the Functionalist persuasion predisposed to claim that even a bicycle shed, if designed to be fit for purpose, may be regarded as 'a piece of architecture'. By a nice irony, one of the vanishingly few Grade I buildings in England is the bicycle store at St Catherine's College, Oxford, by Arne Jacobsen, listed in 1993.

7 'You know that it is life that is always right, and the architect who is wrong.' This was the reported comment by Le Corbusier when shown the 'vernacularisation' by the occupants of his housing estate at Pessac, Bordeaux, originally built in 1928 but progressively modified in the ensuing decades. In the later 1970s, however, the local culture began to change again and brought gradual and meticulous reinstatement of the original design, such that the Quartier Frugès is now designated a ZPPAUP (Zone for the Protection of Architectural, Urban and Landscape Patrimony). See Boudon P, *Lived-In Architecture: Le Corbusier's Pessac Revisited*, Lund Humphries, 1972; MIT Press, 1972.

8 Van Oers R, 'Introduction to the Programme on Modern Heritage', quoting from 'The Modern Movement and the World Heritage List, Advisory Report to ICOMOS', composed by Docomomo, in *Identification and Documentation of Modern Heritage*, World Heritage Papers No 5, pp 10–11, published in 2003 by the UNESCO World Heritage Centre, Paris.

9 See Kolganov A, 'Saving Narkomfin: The Modernist building at the heart of the Soviet Union's 1930 culture wars', *The Calvert Journal*, 14 Oct 2020. See also Ginzburg A, *The Narkomfin Building, Restoration, 2016–2020*, Department of Cultural Heritage of the City of Moscow, 2020.

10 The concept of the Ship of Theseus is one of the oldest in Western philosophy, having been discussed by Heraclitus and Plato in c. 500–400 BC.

11 DoE Circular 8/87 *Historic Buildings and Conservation Areas – Policy and Procedures*, 1987.

12 https://historicengland.org.uk/listing/what-is-designation/listed-buildings (accessed 29 April, 2021).

13 Ammer C, *The Dictionary of Clichés – A Word Lover's Guide to 4,000 Overused Phrases and Almost-Pleasing Platitudes*, Simon & Schuster, 2013.

14 *Conservation Principles, Policies and Guidance*, English Heritage, 2008, pp 71 and 45. The Glossary text, p 71, states that EH's definition of authenticity is 'based on the Nara Document'. Meanwhile the definition of 'integrity' is given simply as 'wholeness, honesty'.

15 Croft C and Macdonald S (eds), *Concrete – Case Studies in Conservation Practice*, The Getty Conservation Institute, 2018.

16 Macdonald S and Ana Paula Arato Gonçalves, *Conservation Principles for Concrete of Cultural Significance*, The Getty Conservation Institute, 2020.

17 Croft and Macdonald, p 177.

18 Ahmer C, 'Riegl's "Modern Cult of Monuments" as a theory underpinning practical conservation and restoration work', *Journal of Architectural Conservation*, Vol 26, 2020, issue 2, referencing Schädler-Saub U, 'Dealing with authenticity in the conservation-restoration of wall paintings and architectural surfaces', in Schädler-Saub U and Szmygin B (eds), *Conservation Ethics Today: Are our Conservation, Restoration and Practice Ready for the 21st Century?* Florence, 1–3 March, 2018 (ICOMOS, 2019), p 116.

19 Drexler A, 'Engineer's Architecture: Truth and its Consequences', in *Architecture of the Ecole des Beaux Arts*, Secker & Warburg, 1977, p 43.

CHAPTER 3 · CHARTERS

1 Conrads U, *Programmes and Manifestos on 20th Century Architecture*, Verlag Ullstein, 1964; Lund Humphries, 1970.

2 *The Athens Charter for the Restoration of Historic Monuments*, a seven-point manifesto adopted at the First International Congress of Architects and Technicians of Historic Monuments, in Athens in 1931.

3 There were two Xi'an Declarations, in 2005 and 2013: the Xi'an Declaration on the Conservation of the Setting of Heritage Structures, Sites and Areas, adopted in Xi'an, China, by the 15th General Assembly of ICOMOS on 21 October 2005; the Xi'an Declaration on the Conservation of Modern Heritage in Different Contexts, adopted in Xi'an by the 1st Council Assembly of Docomomo China and delegates of the 2013 Xi'an International Conference on Modern Architectural Heritage, 'Other MoMo, Other Heritage', on 10 October 2013.

4 *The APT Principles for Renewing Modernism* 2016 was published in draft form in the *Association for Preservation Technology (APT) Bulletin*, Vol XLVIII, No 2–3, 2017, pp 4–7: 'Toward APT Consensus Principles for Practice in Renewing Modernism'.

5 *The Eindhoven–Seoul Statement*, Docomomo International, 2014.

6 *Approaches for the Conservation of Twentieth-Century Architectural Heritage*, Madrid Document, International Scientific Committee on Twentieth-Century Heritage, ICOMOS, 2011, quoted from 2nd edition, 2014.

7 The concept of 'plan-led development', often regarded as the norm, is arguably more honoured in the breach than in the observance. For concern over its uneven application, see, for example, Mason L, Public Policy Officer, National Trust, 'A revised planning system: An erosion of plan-led development?', ntcomms, 11 April 2018, https://ntplanning.wordpress.com/2018/04/11/a-revised-planning-system-an-erosion-of-plan-led-development (accessed 26 October 2021). Also Buitelaar E, Galle M and Niels Sorel N, 'Plan-led planning systems in development-led practices: An empirical analysis into the (lack of) institutionalisation of planning law', *Environment and Planning A*, 2011, Vol 43, pp 928–41.

8 *Conservation Principles, Policies and Guidance*, English Heritage, 2008, with later revisions, https://historicengland.org.uk/advice/constructive-conservation/conservation-principles (accessed 6 October 2021).

9 John Vanbrugh, Letter to the Duchess of Marlborough, 11 June 1709, quoted in Summerson J, *Heavenly Mansions*, The Cresset Press, 1949, p 220.

10 *Conservation Principles, Policies and Guidance*.

11 For a model example of such a document, see *The Eames House Conservation Management Plan*, The Getty Conservation Institute, 2018.

12 Barbican Listed Building Management Guidelines, 2005, https://www.cityoflondon.gov.uk/services/planning/historic-environment/barbican-estate-listed-building-management-guidelines (accessed 5 October 2021); Golden Lane Listed Building Management Guidelines, 2007, https://www.cityoflondon.gov.uk/services/planning/historic-environment/golden-lane-estate-listed-building-management-guidelines (accessed 5 October 2021).

13 The equivalent statutory provisions in Scotland and Northern Ireland are the Planning (Listed Buildings and Conservation Areas – Scotland) Act 1997, and the Planning (Northern Ireland) Order 1991.

14 See the Paul Drury Partnership with the Environmental Project Consulting Group, *Streamlining Listed Building Consent: Lessons from the Use of Management Agreements: A Research Report*, commissioned by English Heritage and the Department for the Environment, Transport and the Regions (later ODPM), 2006.

15 An important collection of conservation management plan case studies is due to be published by the Getty Conservation Institute, LA, in c. 2022/23. See also Allan J, 'Conservation by consensus: Heritage management in large housing estates', in *Docomomo International Journal*, No 65, 2021, pp 42–9.

CHAPTER 4 · LISTING

1 *A Change of Heart – English Architecture since the War – A Policy for Protection*, Royal Commission on the Historical Monuments of England and English Heritage, 1992.

2 Ibid, p 13.

3 Harwood E, *England – A Guide to Post-War Listed Buildings in England*, Ellipsis, 2000, Batsford 2003 and 2015.

4 Planning (Listed Buildings and Conservation Areas) Act 1990, paragraphs 1(1), 1(3a) and 1(3b).

5 See https://www.bbc.co.uk/sport/football/52468544 (accessed 13 October 2021).

6 Cooke C, 'What is the point of saving old buildings?', *Architectural Research Quarterly*, Vol 4, No 2, 2000, pp 137–48.

7 *Principles of Selection for Listed Buildings*, Department of Culture, Media and Sport (DCMS), March 2010, revised November 2018.

8 Ibid., paragraph 18.

9 Ibid.

10 Ibid., paragraph 19.

11 Brand S, *How Buildings Learn*, Viking Press, 1994.

12 *Listing Selection Guides*, Historic England, 4 December 2017. The series comprises: *Agricultural Buildings; Commemorative Structures; Commerce and Exchange Buildings; Culture and Entertainment Buildings; Domestic 1: Vernacular House; Domestic 2: Town Houses; Domestic 3: Suburban and Country Houses; Domestic 4: The Modern House and Housing; Education Buildings; Garden and Park Structures; Health and Welfare Buildings; Industrial Buildings; Law and Government Buildings; Maritime and Naval Buildings; Military Structures; Places of Worship; Sports and Recreation Buildings; Street Furniture; Infrastructure: Transport; Infrastructure: Utilities and Communication*.

13 *Listing Selection Guides: Domestic 4: The Modern House and Housing*, Historic England, April 2011, reissued December 2017, pp 19–20.

14 *Listing Selection Guides: Education Buildings*, Historic England, April 2011, reissued December 2017, p 18.

15 *Principles of Selection for Listed Buildings*, 2018, p 8, note 1.

16 Ibid., paragraph 23.

17 Baillieu A, 'EH fails to support Robin Hood Gardens' and 'Erased from our memories', *Building Design*, 9 May 2008, pp 1 and 2.

18 See *Robin Hood Gardens Re-Visions*, Twentieth Century Society, 2010, and its Bibliography.

19 Brown M, 'V&A acquires segment of Robin Hood Gardens council estate', *The Guardian*, 9 November 2017.

20 Smithson A and Smithson P, *The Charged Void – Architecture*, The Monacelli Press, 2001, p 19.

21 Denys Lasdun's critical admiration of Le Corbusier, for example, is precisely captured in the series of 12 articles 'Thoughts in progress', published in *Architectural Design* (AD) 1956–57. For example: 'It will take a long time and a lot of work to create a new image as moving and as productive as the one expressed in the Pavillon Suisse; but the whole urban idea which was put into its final, most eloquent and most memorable form in the Unite d'habitation, Marseilles, seems now to have run its course.' AD, July 1957. Quoted from Curtis W, *Denys Lasdun – Architecture, City, Landscape*, Phaidon, 1994, p 212.

22 Team X, formed in the early 1950s, was a group of architects and others who challenged the urban theories of CIAM.

23 For example, see Frampton K, *Modern Architecture – A Critical History*, Thames & Hudson, 1980. Widely regarded as a standard definitive account of 20th-century Modern architecture, this book devotes almost an entire chapter to the Smithsons' Hunstanton School and subsequent unbuilt works, without any mention of the competition-winning schemes that were realised by others.

24 The Justus van Effen housing complex, located in the Spangen neighbourhood of Rotterdam, a residential area for the city's port workers, was designed by Dutch architect Michiel Brinkman in 1922 and pioneered the 'street in the air' concept, with wide access walkways at second-floor level. This estate has recently been comprehensively refurbished (see note 32, below).

25 Smithson and Smithson, 2001, p 296.

26 Ibid., p 11.

27 See Hibbert M, 'The City of London Walkway Experiment', *APA Journal*, Autumn 1993, pp 433–50.

28 Jacobs J, *The Death and Life of Great American Cities*, Random House, 1961.

29 See Amery C and Wright L, 'Lifting the witch's curse', in *An Interim Report on the Work of Darbourne and Darke*, RIBA Publications, 1977, p 7.

30 Hill J, 'Robin Hood Gardens not to be listed', *Wharf*, 15 May 2009.

31 The same argument might be made in the more recent case of Central Hill housing estate, Gypsy Hill, Lambeth, designed by architect Rosemary Stjernstedt, which was rejected for listing by Historic England in 2016, and accordingly slated for demolition when – irrespective of heritage claims – there must be compelling sustainability reasons for retention and upgrade. See Jessel E, 'Kate Mackintosh joins last ditch bid to save 60s estate from bulldozers', *Building Design*, 11 May 2021.

32 The Justus van Effen estate restoration project won the 2016 World Monuments Fund/Knoll Modernism Prize. See also Syed S, 'Invisible 11 year retrofit of huge Geneva housing estate nears completion', *Architect's Journal Building Study*, 16 June 2021.

33 See Moore R, 'We're not too late to save this school', *London Evening Standard*, 12 February 2008.

34 Bancroft v Secretary of State (SoS), Westminster City Council [CO/874/2004] A judicial review of the SoS's decision to issue a COI in respect of Pimlico School in Westminster.

35 Banham R, *Theory and Design in the First Machine Age*, Architectural Press, 1960, 1982 edition, p 321.

36 Smithson A and Smithson P, *The Heroic Period of Modern Architecture*, Thames & Hudson, 1981, p 70.

37 For a good example of the calibre of investigation that should be expected, see Schneider T, *This Building Should Have Some Sort of Distinctive Shape – The Story of the Arts Tower in Sheffield*, PAR – Praxis for Architectural Research, 2008.

38 See Berman A (ed), *Jim Stirling and the Red Trilogy – Three Radical Buildings*, Frances Lincoln, 2010.

39 For the official guidance, see HM Treasury, *The Green Book – Supplementary Guidance on Optimism Bias*, 21 April 2013.

40 *Principles of Selection for Listed Buildings*, 2018, p 6, paragraph 17.

41 *The Survey of London* (Vol 45, pp 71–6) recounts the contemporaneous disagreement over the tower between the Royal Fine Arts Commission (Godfrey Samuel) and the Secretary of State for War (John Profumo). Having met both these gentlemen personally in the 1970s (Samuel as Berthold Lubetkin's first partner in Tecton; Profumo as Chairman of Toynbee Housing Association, with whom I was involved in a local project at the time), I am inclined to conclude that such diverging views in such cultured observers ultimately cancel each other out. Meanwhile the variety of other tall, and certainly less distinguished, buildings that have since appeared around

the edges of the Royal Parks – the London Hilton, the Lancaster Hotel, the Royal Garden Hotel, Kensington, etc. – suggests that this issue is not ultimately material to the consideration of the case of listing Hyde Park Barracks. 'Knightsbridge Barracks: The New Barracks, 1967–70', in Greenacombe J (ed) *Survey of London: Volume 45, Knightsbridge*, 2000, pp 71–6, British History Online, http://www.british-history.ac.uk/survey-london/vol45/pp71-76 (accessed 12 October 2021).

42 *Principles of Selection for Listed Buildings*, 2010, p 5, paragraph 11.

43 DCMS letter on behalf of the minister to Listing Group, Historic England, 30 September 2015.

44 See also Anthony Blee's request for review, dated 28 October 2015, citing many errors in the minister's decision resulting from advice to the minister.

45 Application for Certificate of Immunity from Listing (COI). Dunelm House, New Elvet Riverside, City of Durham, DH1 3AN. Historic England Application Reference Number: 1434598, by Montagu Evans, 24 March 2016.

46 Historic England Advice Report, dated 6 December 2016. The HE report included the following observation, 'In June 1966 Robert Donat [sic], who photographed the building for *Architectural Review*, commented "It was tragic to have to take pictures before the students have moved in and turned it into their own. The building cries out to be used – even abused; it can stand it – and longs for its complement of life and people."' (The photographs are, in fact, by John Donat, son of Robert – the actor.)

47 Historic England letter to C20, 6 December 2016, reporting that the minister was minded to issue a COI.

48 DCMS letter to Historic England, 26 October 2017.

49 See Morreau P (ed), *Ove Arup 1895–1988*, Institution of Civil Engineers, 1995.

50 DCMS letter dated 8 July 2021. Planning (Listed Buildings and Conservation Areas) Act 1990. Buildings of special architectural interest – Dunelm House, Dunelm Student Union, New Elvet, Durham, DH1 3AN.

51 This may be an optimistic hope, however. The flurry of correspondence that followed the minister's decision shows just how confused and controversial the matter of modern listing remains. See especially, Morrison R, 'The public should have a say in whether ugly buildings are preserved', *The Times*, 16 July, 2021: 'After a five-year battle that swung this way and that, the champions of brutalism – the post-war movement that gave us all those harshly angular tower blocks, shopping centres and public buildings fashioned in raw concrete – won a great victory. And it's a victory that could lead to dozens of widely disliked and run-down postwar buildings across Britain being preserved in perpetuity.' Also follow-up correspondence on 17, 19 and 21 July 2021.

CHAPTER 5 · PROTECTION

1 See Sharp D, 'The Greenside case – Another one bites the dust', in Macdonald S (ed), *Conservation of Modern Architecture*, Donhead, 2007, pp 117–30.

2 Planning (Listed Buildings and Conservation Areas) Act 1990, Section 7.

3 Ibid., Part I, Chapter III, paragraph 33 ff.

4 https://historicengland.org.uk/listing/the-list/understanding-list-entries (accessed 7 October 2021).

5 https://historicengland.org.uk/listing/what-is-designation/listed-buildings/listing-and-the-erra (accessed 14 October 2021).

6 See Saunders M, *Towards a Strategy for the Future of the National Heritage List for England*, Historic England, November 2019, https://www.historicengland.org.uk/content/docs/listing/saunders-report-synopsis (accessed 13 October 2021).

7 *National Planning Policy Framework*, 2021, paragraphs 11 and 199–202.

8 Ibid. Considering potential impacts, paragraph 199 ff.

9 *R. (ooo James Hall and Company Limited) v City of Bradford Metropolitan District Council and Co-Operative Group Limited [2019]* EWHC 2899 (Case No 1863/2019). See especially paragraph 34. The judgement clarified that even

'negligible' harm must be included within the category of 'less than substantial harm' since, though 'negligible', it must be more than no harm at all. The definition of harm included in NPPF 2021, paragraph 199, is referenced as three types – substantial harm, total loss, or less than substantial harm to [the asset's] significance. A more recent example of the controversy arising from this definition is the UK Holocaust Memorial at Victoria Tower Gardens in Westminster, London (case reference APP/XF990/V/19/3240661).

10 SRG Baird BA (Hons) MRTPI. Appeal Ref: APP/P0119/W/17/3189592. Appeal Decision 14 May 2019.

11 *Constructive Conservation – Sustainable Growth for Historic Places*, English Heritage, 2013.

12 See, for example, 'Park Hill in *The Guardian*', The Twentieth Century Society, 2013, https://c20society.org.uk/2013/01/11/park-hill-in-the-guardian (accessed 7 October 2021). See also Hatherley O, 'Regeneration? – What's happening in Sheffield's Park Hill is class cleansing', *The Guardian*, 28 September 2011. Moore R, 'Park Hill estate, Sheffield – review', *The Observer*, 21 August 2011.

13 *Conservation Principles, Policies and Guidance*, English Heritage, 2008, with later revisions, https://historicengland.org.uk/advice/constructive-conservation/conservation-principles (accessed 6 October 2021).

14 https://en.wikipedia.org/wiki/Commonwealth_Education_Trust (accessed 7 October 2021).

15 'Enabling development' is a technical term in planning law; for an official definition, see *Historic Environment Good Practice Advice in Planning Note 4, Enabling Development and Heritage Assets*, Historic England, 2020.

16 In the event, a statement was prepared by English Heritage itself, though only as retrospective due diligence. *The Commonwealth Institute, A Statement of Significance*, prepared by English Heritage, August 2009.

17 *Conservation Management Plan – The Brownfield Estate*, Avanti Architects, December 2007.

18 See *Principles of Selection for Listed Buildings*, Department of Culture, Media and Sport (DCMS), March 2010, revised November 2018, paragraph 16, which states, 'Special interest may also apply to… significant plan forms.'

19 See, for example, Harnack M and Stollmann J, 'Which Second Life? Adaptive Reuse as a Contested Paradigm', paper in Docomomo 14th International Conference Proceedings, *Adaptive Reuse: The Modern Movement Towards the Future*, Docomomo International, Lisbon 2016, pp 796–804, which cites Denys Lasdun's Keeling House and Ernö Goldfinger's Trellick Tower as earlier examples of such gentrification.

20 See Hatherley O, 'We couldn't stop Balfron Tower from being privatised. In fact we probably helped it along', *Dezeen*, 3 May 2019, and the comments that followed. Also, Williams F, 'Studio Egret West's Balfron Tower overhaul slammed as "tragic" missed opportunity', *Architects' Journal*, 13 March 2019. Goldfinger's other major London housing work, the Edenham Estate in the Royal Borough of Kensington and Chelsea, is facing equivalent pressures for substantial intervention at the time of writing. Whether these can be reconciled with a conservation sensibility worthy of its Grade II* listed status, and whether the 'lessons of Balfron' are brought to bear, remains to be seen.

21 See *Barbican Renewal: Design Brief*, https://sites.barbican.org.uk/renewal (accessed 12 Sep 2021). Also, Fulcher M, 'Barbican Centre launches international contest for major revamp', *Architects' Journal*, 8 September 2021.

22 Harwood E, *England – A Guide to Post-War Listed Buildings*, Batsford, English Heritage, 2003, p 684. Also, Fulcher M, 'Demo tonight: 55,000 oppose Elliott School demolition', *Architects' Journal*, 12 August 2012.

23 The Xi'an Declaration on the Conservation of the Setting of Heritage Structures, Sites and Areas was adopted by the 15th General Assembly of ICOMOS, Xi'an, China, 17–21 October 2005.

24 *National Planning Policy Framework*, 2019, Annex 2, Glossary.

25 *Historic Environment Good Practice Advice in Planning*

Note 3: *The Setting of Heritage Assets* (2nd edition), Historic England, 22 December 2017, paragraph 19. In the attempt to be specific, the French (as early as 1943) introduced the *zone protegé* – defined as an area within 0.5km radius of a listed building, where any new building must be approved by central government. To this provision was added the law introduced by Minister of Cultural Affairs André Malraux in 1962 designating *secteurs sauvegardés*, colloquially referred to as 'Malraux'. See Loew S, *Modern Architecture in Historic Cities – Policy, Planning and Building in Contemporary France*, Routledge, 1998.

26 Golden Lane Estate Listed Building Management Guidelines, 2007, https://www.cityoflondon.gov.uk/services/planning/historic-environment/golden-lane-estate-listed-building-management-guidelines (accessed 5 October 2021).

27 For the COLPAI (City of London Primary Academy Islington) development, a joint venture between the City of London and the London Borough of Islington, see https://www.colpai-project.co.uk (accessed 7 October 2021); also https://democracy.islington.gov.uk/documents/s14560/COLPAI.pdf (accessed 7 October 2021).

28 See Jessel E, 'Barbican Estate: Outcry over "major threat" from Nicholas Hare's school expansion plans', *Architects' Journal*, 28 May 2019.

CHAPTER 6 · WEAKNESSES

1 Planning (Listed Buildings and Conservation Areas) Act 1990, Chapter 1, (1), (4)(b).

2 See *Arrangements for Handling Heritage Applications*, Ministry of Housing, Communities and Local Government (MHCLG) Direction, 2015.

3 Cooke C, 'What is the point of saving old buildings?' *Architectural Research Quarterly*, Vol 4, No 2, 2000, pp 137–48.

4 Thurley S, 'Saving the 20th century', Gresham College Lecture, London, 2 November 2016.

5 See Hopkirk E, 'Lubetkin's Sivill House listed after residents' campaign', *Building Design*, 5 June 2020.

CHAPTER 7 · FROM RELICS TO RESOURCES – THE NEW PARADIGM

1 Hanks P (ed), *Collins Dictionary of the English Language*, William Collins, 1979, p 1233, 1242.

2 See Meurs P and van Thoor M-T (eds), *Sanatorium Zonnestraal*, NAi Publishers, 2010.

3 Allan J, 'Restoration of the Penguin Pool at London Zoo', *Docomomo Newsletter 3*, June 1990, pp 25–7.

4 See Henket H-J, 'The icon and the ordinary', in Cunningham A (ed), *Modern Movement Heritage*, E & FN Spon, 1998, pp 13–17. The distinction there, now nearly 25 years ago, precedes the sense intended in my use of the phrase whereby the conservation cause has necessarily progressed *from* the former *towards* the latter. Some of the examples used here are nonetheless still well above the level of 'ordinary'.

5 The report of the Intergovernmental Panel on Climate Change (IPCC), published on 7 August 2021 as the final edit of this book was being concluded, is the most comprehensive study ever undertaken to confirm that the warming of the earth's atmosphere, ocean and land has been caused by human influence. This will (or should) effectively define the agenda not only for the UN climate change conference COP26, which will have taken place by the time this book is published, but for generations to come.

6 Allan J, 'Points of balance', in *Conservation of Modern Architecture*, Donhead, 2007, pp 13–46.

7 See Meurs and van Thoor. See also Hammer-Tugendhat D, Hammer I and Tegethoff W, *Tugendhat House*, Birkhauser, 2015.

8 See Mead A, 'The Importance of being Ernö', *Architects' Journal*, 28 March 1996; Harwood E, 'Homewood bound', *Architects' Journal*, 4 April 2001.

9 See Mead A, 'Modern Movement classic on a Highgate

hilltop', *Architects' Journal*, 12 September 1996.

10 For detailed commentary on this series of projects, see the following. For Miramonte: Powers A, *Modern – The Modern Movement in Britain*, Merrell, 2005, pp 114–15; for 66 Frognal: Mead A, 'In the modern world', *Architects' Journal*, 24 March 2005; for The Hill House: Powers A, 'High commission', *Architects' Journal*, 9 May 2002. (The projects undertaken at Harbour Meadow and Cherry Hill remain unpublished.)

11 See Croft C, 'Isokon', *Architects' Journal*, 30 March 2006.

12 See Allan J, 'Hackney courage', *Building Design Refurbishment*, May 2009, pp 25–31. See also Ike Ijeh, "Shouldn't you be revising ?", *Building Magazine*, 16 November 2012 in which it is suggested that the Haggerston example (completed ahead of schedule for £14m) provided a cogent counter case to that of Elliott School in Putney (also listed), where, having been cut from the BSF Programme a substantial part of the site was to be sold to raise funds for its refurbishment.

13 https://www.iconichouses.org (accessed 8 October 2021).

14 Pawley M, *Terminal Architecture*, Reaktion Books, 1998, p 98.

15 Jury Citation, The Pritzker Prize for Architecture, Hyatt Foundation, 16 March 2021. See also Oliver Wainwright, '"Sometimes the answer is to do nothing": Unflashy French duo take architecture's top prize', *The Guardian*, 16 March 2021.

16 See 'Carbon dioxide in construction', *Designing Buildings*, 3 November 2020. The Technology Strategy Board was originally set up within the Department of Trade and Industry in 2004 by the Labour Government, becoming an independent body in 2007, and from 2014 known as Innovate UK. Its stated purpose is to accelerate UK economic growth by stimulating and supporting business-led innovation.

17 See *Historic Environment Good Practice Advice in Planning Note 4, Enabling Development and Heritage Assets*, Historic England, 2020, Section 6, Glossary, p 23, for a technical definition of 'conservation deficit'.

18 See Sharp D and Cooke C (eds), *The Modern Movement in Architecture: Selections from the Docomomo Registers*, 010 Publishers, 2000.

19 See https://www.docomomo.com/rehabilitation-award (accessed 14 October 2021).

CHAPTER 8 · QUICKFIRE Q & A

1 See Zunz J, 'My life and times with Ove', in *Ove Arup 1895–1988*, Institution of Civil Engineers, 1988, pp 54–62.

2 Allan J, 'Conservation of modern buildings – A practitioner's view', in Macdonald S (ed), *Modern Matters – Principles and Practice in Conserving Recent Architecture*, Donhead, 1996, p 125.

3 For a concise study (among the vast literature) of the role of Classical architecture and theory in Modernism, see Colquhoun A, *Modernity and the Classical Tradition, Architectural Essays 1980–1987*, MIT Press, 1989. A definitive view from the other end of the telescope is Rykwert J's remarkable *The First Moderns – The Architects of the Eighteenth Century*, MIT Press, 1980. Also such seminal texts as Rowe C's 'The mathematics of the ideal Villa: Palladio and Le Corbusier compared', originally published in *The Architectural Review*, 31 March 1947. Republished as *The Mathematics of the Ideal Villa and Other Essays*, MIT Press, 1976.

4 Breuer M, 'Architecture and material', in Martin L, Nicholson B and Gabo N (eds), *Circle – International Survey of Constructive Art*, Faber and Faber, 1937 (1971 edition), p 194.

5 See Desilvey C, *Curated Decay – Heritage beyond Saving*, University of Minnesota, 2017, for a variety of examples.

6 *Conservation Principles, Policies and Guidance*, English Heritage, 2008, with later revisions, https://historicengland.org.uk/advice/constructive-conservation/conservation-principles (accessed 6 October 2021).

7 See ICOMOS, 'Venice Charter under review by ICOMOS', *ICOMOS Newsletter*, No 8, Paris, 1976. Also Erder C, 'The Venice Charter under review', Scribd, 1977, as one of many critical evaluations of the Charter. See Australia

ICOMOS, *Burra Charter*, editions 1979, 1981, 1988, 1999, 2013, et seq. Also Hanna B, 'Innovation in conservation: A timeline history of Australia ICOMOS and the Burra Charter', report commissioned by Australia ICOMOS, Sydney, 2015 (amended 2017).

8 This topic is explored in more detail in the author's paper, 'Joining the past with the future: The rescue and adaptive reuse of St Peter's Seminary, Scotland', Docomomo 14th International Conference Proceedings, *Adaptive Reuse: The Modern Movement Towards the Future*, Docomomo International, Lisbon, 2016, pp 356–63.

9 There are various registers and trade associations based around specific Modern heritage materials and products, such as the Concrete Repair Association (formed in 1989), which includes specialist contractors, product manufacturers and product distributors in the field of concrete repair, as well as associated organisations, such as test laboratories and consulting engineers. Similarly, the Steel Window Association represents the majority of UK steel window manufacturers.

10 Paul Drury Partnership with the Environmental Project Consulting Group, *Streamlining Listed Building Consent: Lessons from the Use of Management Agreements: A Research Report*, commissioned by English Heritage and the Department for the Environment, Transport and the Regions (later ODPM), 2006.

11 See Semple Kerr J, *The Conservation Plan*, National Trust of Australia, 1982 and ICOMOS later editions to 2013; Clark K, *Informed Conservation*, English Heritage, 2001, p 62ff; Historic England Advice Note 5, *Setting up a Listed Building Heritage Partnership Agreement*, 2015; forthcoming – *Planning and Management Tools: Case Studies in Conservation Practice*, The Getty Conservation Institute, due 2022.

12 Saunders M, *Towards a Strategy for the Future of the National Heritage List for England*, Historic England, November 2019, https://www.historicengland.org.uk/content/docs/listing/saunders-report-synopsis (accessed 13 October 2021).

13 See Historic England Advice Note 1, *Conservation Area Appraisal, Designation and Management*, 2nd edition, 2018. First published by English Heritage, March 2011. (Published as: *Understanding Place: Conservation Area Designation, Appraisal and Management*, then republished as Historic England Advice Note 1, *Conservation Area Appraisal, Designation and Management*, 2016.)

CHAPTER 9 · LESSONS LEARNED

1 The pool has experienced mixed fortunes since the major restoration project discussed here. The project completion in 1987 was accompanied by a ceremonial reopening, which reunited its creators Lubetkin and Ove Arup (the original engineer, assisted by Felix Samuely), and attracted much media coverage – 'Concrete and clay – restoration of the Penguin Pool', London Weekend Television, 7 October 1987; see also Allan J, 'Tectonic icon restored', *RIBA Journal*, February 1988, pp 30–32; Allan J, 'Landmark of the thirties restored', *Concrete Quarterly* No 157, April/June 1988. For the first few years afterwards, a maintenance regime ensured the building (which must withstand severe conditions) remained in good order, with an annual 'deep clean' for which the birds were temporarily removed to a nearby pond within the zoo gardens. At our last revisit, we were instructed to apply a layer of quartz granules to the surfaces of the ramps to enhance their slip resistance for the benefit of the keepers. This, however, did not make them more agreeable for the penguins. The concrete paving surfaces of the pool (and, by implication, also the original architect) have subsequently been blamed for the design being injurious to the birds – causing a condition known as 'bumblefoot' – and are now cited as the reason for their removal from the enclosure altogether. However, it should be noted that the original walkways of 1934 were not concrete, but were finished with alternating areas of slate paviors and rubber compound, with the specific intention of providing varied and considerate surfaces for the birds, initially an Antarctic species, who have some practice in

walking on slippery surfaces, as well as different nesting habits to the later inhabitants, South American Humboldts. At some point after the war these surfaces were removed and replaced throughout with concrete screed by the zoo, such that, with its limited budget, the restoration project could only reinstate the original colours of grey and red (as seen in Figure 1.21), not the materials themselves. See Allan J, *Berthold Lubetkin – Architecture and the Tradition of Progress*, Artifice Books on Architecture, 2012, pp 208–12 and p 594. While the 'bumblefoot story' has now become part of the Penguin Pool's folklore and a useful alibi for the enclosure lying empty (the penguins were moved from the pool in 2004), the blame may not, after all, be laid at the original architect's door. See Dex R, '"Pool that gave the penguins sore feet may have had its day", says architect's daughter', *London Evening Standard*, 6 January 2019; and Allan J, 'Penguin Pool surely has not had its day', *London Evening Standard*, 7 January 2019. See also Block I, 'Berthold Lubetkin's empty Penguin Pool should be blown "to smithereens" says daughter', *Dezeen*, 8 January 2019. Meanwhile, while attitudes to the display of captive animals in zoos have, of course, changed utterly since Lubetkin's day, it may be worth noting that the life expectancy of the occupants of his pool was reportedly double that of birds in the wild, while the clean lines and surfaces of the enclosure substantially reduced the incidence of avian malaria in comparison with 'naturalistic' zoo habitats elsewhere.

2   For a definitive account of the work of the practice, see Sharp D and Rendel S, *Connell, Ward and Lucas – Modern Movement Architects in England 1929–1939*, Frances Lincoln, 2008. See also Mead A, 'Balancing conservation with improved performance', *Architects' Journal*, 16 February 1994, pp 18–20.

3   Interestingly, an original Crittall Windows promotional advert of 1932 describes the window colour as 'dark-maroon-red', though in the Sharp–Rendel account the colour is given as 'leaf green' (Sharp and Rendel, p 70). It was certainly not white.

4   For the background history of Finsbury Health Centre, see Allan, 2012, pp 330–48. Also, Allan J, 'Finsbury at 50 – Caring and causality', *The Architectural Review*, June 1988, pp 46–50; and Carolin P, 'Modern theory of repair' in *Renovation*, *Architects' Journal Supplement*, March 1989.

5   The hope has eventually been fulfilled, albeit after a further interval of 27 years (at time of writing), as Avanti Architects have again (spring 2021) been appointed to undertake further restoration work to the building exterior.

6   See Field M, 'A pioneer partially restored to its former glory', *Architects' Journal*, 16 February, 1995, pp 22–3.

7   See Allan, 2012, pp 80, 277 and 603.

8   See Blundell Jones P, 'A careful reading', *Building Design*, April 2010, pp 14–20.

9   For the background history of Priory Green, see Allan, 2012, pp 348–51 and 405–14.

10 See Bateson K, 'True to form', *Building Design*, 17 November 2000, pp 16–19. Also Powell K, *New London Architecture*, Merrell, 2001, pp 180–81.

CHAPTER 10 · CHANGING CONSERVATION CULTURE

1   IPCC Working Group I report, *Climate Change 2021: The Physical Science Basis*, IPCC, Geneva, 9 August 2021. The Working Group I report is the first instalment of the IPCC's *Sixth Assessment Report* (AR6), to be completed in 2022. The Intergovernmental Panel on Climate Change (IPCC) is the international body for assessing the science related to climate change. The IPCC was set up in 1988 by the World Meteorological Organization (WMO) and United Nations Environment Programme (UNEP) to provide policymakers with regular assessments of the scientific basis of climate change, its impacts and future risks, and options for adaptation and mitigation. (Quoted from the IPCC website: https://ipcc.ch/about, accessed 12 August, 2021). However, even aspects of the latest IPCC report are being questioned for being too optimistic. See Fairs M, 'Cement and concrete

"are not carbon sinks" says Cambridge materials scientist', *Dezeen*, 31 August 2021, where it is suggested by materials scientist Darshil Shah that the claimed ability of concrete to absorb atmospheric carbon equivalent to around half the quantity of carbon emitted in cement production is greatly overestimated after accounting for the fossil fuels that are burnt to power the cement production plants themselves.

2   PAS (Publicly Available Specification) 2035: 2019: Retrofitting Dwellings for Improved Energy Efficiency – Specification and Guidance. The most recent (2019) version of PAS 2030 has been embedded in PAS 2035.

3   See Wainwright O, 'The dirty secret of so-called fossil-fuel free buildings', *The Guardian*, 3 April 2021.

4   See Rees E, 'UK's greenhouse gas emissions reductions an "illusion"', *The Ecologist*, 2 February 2011.

5   Helm D, *The Carbon Crunch – How We're Getting Climate Change Wrong – And How to Fix It*, Yale University Press, 2012, p 71.

6   See EDIE (Environmental Data Interactive Exchange) newsroom, 'UK ETS post-Brexit carbon market opens for first time with carbon price topping £50 per tonne', 19 May 2021.

7   There is, however, some encouragement to be drawn from the reported acceptance of carbon taxing in principle. See Harvey F, 'Carbon tax would be popular with UK voters, poll suggests', *The Guardian*, 24 February 2021.

8   Cohen J-L and Moeller GM, Jr (eds), *Liquid Stone – New Architecture in Concrete*, Princeton Architectural Press, 2006. There are, of course, now many novel and varied concrete products available, several with highly specialised properties, though there are also doubts as to whether some of the industrial waste materials used in so-called 'low carbon concretes' are themselves residues of carbon-intensive processes.

9   Estimated figures kindly provided by Peter Clegg and Richard Battye of FCB Studios, in emails to the author, 31 August 2021. For more examples of pioneering work in this field, see Hammond GP and Jones CI, *Inventory of Carbon and Energy* (ICE), Beta Version V1.5, Department of Mechanical Engineering, University of Bath, 2006; also, the RICS *Whole Life Carbon Assessment for the Built Environment Professional Statement,* 2017; RIBA *Embodied and Whole Life Carbon Assessment for Architects,* 2018; and more recently the London Energy Transformation Initiative (LETI), *Climate Emergency Design Guide*, 2020.

10 See https://www.architectsdeclare.com (accessed 15 October 2021) and builtenvironmentdeclares.com (accessed 15 October 2021).

11 Heath L, 'Major housing associations form partnership to improve energy efficiency of 300,000 homes', *Inside Housing*, 9 April 2021, https://www.insidehousing.co.uk/news/news/major-housing-associations-form-partnership-to-improve-energy-efficiency-of-300000-homes-70348 (accessed 12 October 2021).

12 ARB Code, 2017, Standards 2 and 5.

13 Architects Registration Board, *Strategic Statement – Climate Change and Sustainability*, 2020.

14 https://www.architecture.com/about/policy/climate-action/2030-climate-challenge (accessed 12 October 2021).

15 Docomomo Preservation Technology Dossier 9, *Climate and Building Physics in the Modern Movement*, September 2006. More recently there have been calls for the wholesale revision of orthodox architectural history and its reappraisal through the lens of energy consumption. See Calder B and Bremner GA, 'Buildings and energy: Architectural history in the climate emergency', *The Journal of Architecture*, Vol 26, No 2, March 2021, pp 79–115.

16 The Cabinet Office, *Government Estate Strategy*, July 2018, p 36.

17 Turner R, 'Plan to "rip up" Treasury Green Book is an opportunity', Grant Thornton, 5 February 2020.

18 See Stone J, 'Government declares war on Brutalist architecture', *The Independent*, 2 November 2016. Ironically, this article was illustrated with three listed buildings – Balfron Tower, Alexandra Road Estate and Preston Bus Station

– plus the Euston Arch, which the minister vowed to rebuild. See also https://www.gov.uk/government/speeches/the-journey-to-beauty (accessed 12 October 2021).

19 See Ing W, 'Jenrick vows to stop architects "imposing" their visions on communities', *Building Design*, 7 May 2021. Also Crook L, 'Brutalist building in Derby set to be demolished without plans for replacement', *Dezeen* 14 April, 2021.

20 See Hurst W, 'Derby Assembly Rooms' carbon cost of demolition laid bare', *Architects' Journal*, 22 June 2021, where it was computed that the carbon cost of demolishing and replacing the Derby Assembly Rooms was equivalent to more than a third of the City Council's entire annual greenhouse gas footprint.

21 See Small Z, 'Trump makes Classical style the default for Federal buildings', *The New York Times,* 21 December 2020.

22 See https://www.docomomo-us.org/news/surprise-demo-permit-for-paul-rudolph-s-burroughs-wellcome-causes-outcry (accessed 24 August 2021). The destruction was described by the Paul Rudolph Foundation as inflicting a 'deep wound to the cultural heritage of this country'. Being constructed entirely of reinforced concrete, one can only speculate on the vast loss of embodied energy resulting from the demolition of this enormous complex.

23 Hurst W, 'Demolishing 50,000 buildings a year is a national disgrace', *The Times*, 28 June 2021. Specifically in the case of public sector housing, as has been astutely pointed out by Paul Finch, former Chair of CABE (Commission for Architecture and the Built Environment), premature demolition of property typically funded originally by 60-year loans means continuing to pay for something you no longer have, whilst then also funding costs of temporary and/or permanent replacement accommodation. Finch P, *Architect's Journal*, 10 September 2009, p19.

24 *Identification and Documentation of Modern Heritage*, World Heritage Papers No. 5, published in 2003 by the UNESCO World Heritage Centre, Paris, with financial contribution from the Netherlands Funds-in-Trust.

25 https://www.wmf.org/world-monuments-fund-knoll-modernism-prize (accessed 24 August 2021). The 2021 Knoll prize has been awarded to the Preston Bus Station conservation project, an unthinkable result only a few years ago. See Fig. 1.13.)

26 Le Roux H (ed), *Modern Heritage in Africa, Docomomo International Journal*, No 28, March 2003.

27 Further issues of the *Docomomo International Journal* have consolidated these broader horizons. See particularly No 29, *Modernism in Asia Pacific*, September 2003; No 33, *The Modern Movement in the Caribbean Islands*, September 2005; No 38, *Canada Modern*, March 2008; No 40, *Tel Aviv 100 Years*, March 2009; No 43, *Brasilia*, 2010/2; No 48, *Modern Africa*, 2013/1; No 57, *Modern Southeast Asia*, 2017/2; No 59, *An Eastern European Vision*, 2018/02; No 60, *Architectures of the Sun*, 2019/02; and No 63, *Tropical Architecture in the Modern Diaspora*, 2020/02.

28 Marsden S and Spearritt P, *The Twentieth-Century Historic Thematic Framework*, J. Paul Getty Trust, 2021.

29 http://exhibition.docomomo.com/MoMove (accessed 16 August, 2021). The docomomo virtual exhibition, Docomomo International, launched 2015.

30 See Wall T, Interview with Jen Reid, *The Observer*, 6 December 2020.

31 See Blayney S et al., *Long Live Southbank*, Heni Publishing, 2014. See Simon Ricketts, p 391.

32 Ibid. Ironically, in the absence of designation, the attempt was made to have the skatepark formally registered as a village green – a classification for which it apparently fitted the criteria perfectly.

33 See Ravenscroft T, 'Refurbished Undercroft skatepark reopens beneath London's Southbank Centre', *Dezeen*, 8 August 2019.

34 Harwood E, *Space, Hope and Brutalism – English Architecture 1945–1975*, Historic England, 2015, p 569.

35 Alan Powers, in conversation with the author, 2003.

FURTHER READING

The extent of literature on modern architectural conservation is now very considerable – indeed so much so that any comprehensive bibliography could easily occupy a book in itself. The endnotes for the foregoing chapters provide an outline of some of the material consulted for this book, and the following suggestions for further reading, though not a bibliography as such, will hopefully offer useful pointers for those interested in exploring the field and its evolving history more widely.

The material available on the various UK government agency websites is a major source of information and advice, and is strongly recommended for anyone wanting an overview of official policy and guidance in the UK. These include Historic England (https://historicengland.org.uk); Historic Environment Scotland (https://www.historicenvironment.scot); Cadw (https://cadw.gov.wales) and the Northern Ireland Environment Agency (https://www.daera-ni.gov.uk) (all websites accessed 12 October 2021).

The publications of Docomomo International, including collected conference papers, technical dossiers and the regular *International Journal* (currently numbering 65 issues), also now offer a vast range of historical, theoretical and practical material, produced over the 30-plus years of the network's activity. Details of national Docomomo chapters are given on the international website (https://www.docomomo.com, accessed 12 October 2021). These also publish regular newsletters.

The Association for Preservation Technology International (APT) (https://www.apti.org, accessed 12 October 2021), founded in 1968, includes membership from over 30 countries and maintains a wide-ranging programme of publications, conferences and training. The *APT Bulletin*, published three times per annum, promulgates peer-reviewed content on all aspects of preservation practice and technology.

Other organisations in the field include ICOMOS (https://www.icomos.org); the Getty Conservation Institute's Conserving Modern Architecture Initiative (CMAI; http://www.getty.edu); the Institute of Historic Building Conservation (IHBC; https://www.ihbc.org.uk) and the Twentieth Century Society (C20; https://c20society.org.uk), all of which maintain a considerable publications output (all websites accessed 12 October 2021).

SELECTED FURTHER TITLES

Arrhenius T, *The Fragile Monument – On Conservation and Modernity*, Artifice Books on Architecture, 2012

Baker-Brown D, *The Re-Use Atlas: A Designer's Guide Towards a Circular Economy*, RIBA Publishing, 2017

Calder B, *Architecture – From Prehistory to Climate Emergency*, Pelican, 2021

Carughi U and Visione M (eds), *Time Frames – Conservation Policies for Twentieth-Century Architectural Heritage*, Routledge, 2017, 2018

Croft C and Macdonald S (eds), *Concrete – Case Studies in Conservation Practice*, Paul Getty Trust, 2018

Delafons J, *Politics and Preservation – A Policy History of the Built Heritage 1882–1996*, E & FN Spon, 1997, Spon Press, 2004

Dorling D, *Slowdown – The End of the Great Acceleration – And Why It's a Good Thing*, Yale University Press, 2020, 2021

Flaman B and McCoy C (eds), *Managing Energy Use in Modern Buildings – Case Studies in Modern Conservation*, Getty Publications, 2021

Forsyth, M (ed), *Understanding Historic Building Conservation*, John Wiley 2007

Glendinning M, *The Conservation Movement: A History of Architectural Preservation: Antiquity to Modernity*, Routledge, 2013

Helm D, *Net Zero – How We Stop Causing Climate Change*, William Collins, 2020

Henket H-J and Heynen H (eds), *Back from Utopia – The Challenge of the Modern Movement*, 010 Publishers, Rotterdam, 2002

Kuipers M and de Jonge W, *Designing from Heritage – Strategies for Conservation and Conversion*, TU Delft – Heritage and Architecture (Fac. Architecture) on behalf of the Rondeltappe Bernoster Kemmers Foundation, 2017

Prizeman O (ed), *Sustainable Building Conservation – Theory and Practice of Responsive Design in the Heritage Environment*, RIBA Publishing, 2015

Prudon T, *Preservation of Modern Architecture*, John Wiley & Sons, 2008

Scott F, *On Altering Architecture*, Routledge, 2008

Tostões A and Ferreira Z (eds), *Adaptive Reuse – The Modern Movement Towards the Future*, Docomomo International Casa Arquitectura, Lisbon, 2016

Tostões A (ed), *Modern Heritage: Reuse, Renovation, Restoration*, Docomomo International/Birkhäuser, 2022

INDEX

IMAGE CREDITS

Author Image: Catherine Shakespeare Lane

CHAPTER 1
Figure 1.1 and 1.14: RIBA Collections
Figure 1.2: F. S. Bond
Figure 1.3: Aerofilms
Figure 1.4: Berthold Lubetkin / Felton
Figure 1.6: Alan Williams
Figure 1.7: Alastair Hunter / RIBA Collections
Figure 1.9 and 1.25: Christopher Hope-Fitch / RIBA
   Collections
Figure 1.10 and 1.13: Architectural Press Archive / RIBA
   Collections
Figure 1.11: John Donat / RIBA Collections
Figure 1.12: Commission Air / Alamy Stock Photo
Figure 1.16: Dennis Gilbert - VIEW / Alamy Stock Photo
Figure 1.17: Reigart / Edward Z Smith
Figure 1.18: Avanti Architects
Figure 1.19: Morley von Sternberg
Figure 1.20: Tom de Gay
Figure 1.21: Panabode Ltd
Figure 1.22: Martin Charles / RIBA Collections
Figure 1.23: Nicholas Kane
Figure 1.24: Docomomo International
Figure 1.26: Glyn Thomas Photography / Alamy Stock
   Photo

CHAPTER 2
Figure 2.1: Hemis / Alamy Stock Photo
Figure 2.2: Raphael Salzedo / Alamy Stock Photo
Figure 2.3a: Roland Halbe / RIBA Collections
Figure 2.3b: Anna Dziubinska / RIBA Collections
Figure 2.4a-b: © Ginzburg Architects
Figure 2.4c: Roman Vyshnikov / Alamy Stock Photo
Figure 2.5: © Ginzburg Architects / Photographer:
   J.Palmin, 2020
Figure 2.7: Tom de Gay

CHAPTER 3
Figure 3.1: SPAB
Figure 3.2a: ISC20C ICOMOS David Barker
   (Kaleidoscope Graphics)
Figure 3.2b: ISC20C ICOMOS (Images Sheridan Burke)
Figure 3.3 and 3.4: Avanti Architects / City of London

CHAPTER 4
Figure 4.1: Bernard Cox / RIBA Collections
Figure 4.2: Tom de Gay
Figure 4.3, 4.13 and 4.15: RIBA Collections
Figure 4.4: John Maltby / RIBA Collections
Figure 4.5: Anthony Palmer / RIBA Collections
Figure 4.6: Ioana Marinescu
Figure 4.9: Christopher Hope-Fitch / RIBA Collections
Figure 4.7, 4.12, 4.14 and 4.21: Architectural Press
   Archive / RIBA Collections
Figure 4.10: Molenaar & Co Architecten and Hebly
   Theunissen Architecten / Photographer: BK Visuals
   Bas Kooij
Figure 4.11: Paola Corsini
Figure 4.17, 4.18 and 4.19: John Donat / RIBA Collections
Figure 4.20a-b: ACP

CHAPTER 5
Figure 5.1: English Heritage / Historic England
Figure 5.2a: Henk Snoek / RIBA Collections
Figure 5.2b, 5.4 and 5.10a: Architectural Press Archive /
   RIBA Collections
Figure 5.7: I-Wei Huang / Alamy Stock Photo
Figure 5.8: Nathaniel Noir / Alamy Stock Photo
Figure 5.9: John Maltby / RIBA Collections

CHAPTER 6
Figure 6.1: Tom de Gay
Figure 6.2: Grant Smith-VIEW / Alamy Stock Photo

CHAPTER 7
Figure 7.2: Martin Charles
Figure 7.5: Morley von Sternberg / RIBA Collections
Figure 7.6: Ray Main/Mainstreamimages / Architect:
   Patrick Gwynne
Figure 7.7 and 7.9: Morley von Sternberg
Figure 7.8, 7.10, 7.12, 7.15a, 7.19b and 7.20: Nicholas
   Kane
Figure 7.11, 7.15b, 7.23 and 7.25: Tom de Gay
Figure 7.13, 7.14, 7.17a, 7.17b, 7.18, 7.19a, 7.22a-b and
   7.24: Avanti Architects
Figure 7.16: RIBA Collections
Figure 7.21: John Donat / RIBA Collections
Figure 7.26: 010 Publishers, Rotterdam
Figure 7.27: Arcaid Images / Alamy Stock Photo and
   FreePNGImg

CHAPTER 9
Figure 9.1: Snowdon, 1985
Figure 9.2: Berthold Lubetkin
Figure 9.6a-e: McAlpine
Figure 9.5: Martin Charles
Figure 9.8: James Connell / Book Art Picture Library
Figure 9.11 and 9.23: Morley von Sternberg
Figure 9.12: RIBA Collections
Figure 9.13, 9.14a and 9.19: Architectural Press Archive /
   RIBA Collections
Figure 9.14b: Dell & Wainwright / RIBA Collections
Figure 9.16, 9.25, 9.28a-b, 9.33a-c and 9.36: Avanti
   Architects
Figure 9.18: Peter Cook
Figure 9.24: Henk Snoek / RIBA Collections
Figure 9.26, 9.27, 9.29, 9.30, 9.38 and 9.39: Tom de Gay
Figure 9.31: Wainwright
Figure 9.34 and 9.35: Nicholas Kane
Figure 9.37: Morley von Sternberg / RIBA Collections

CHAPTER 10
Figure 10.1: All images sourced from Pixabay.
Figure 10.2: Architectural Press Archive / RIBA
   Collections
Figure 10.3: Burroughs-Wellcome Company Building
   (Raleigh, North Carolina), Job #4812. Joseph W.
   Molitor architectural photographs, 1935-1985.
   Drawings and Archives, Avery Architectural & Fine
   Arts Library, © Columbia University in the City of
   New York.
Figure 10.9: © National Trust Images / Dennis Gilbert
Figure 10.10: Avanti Architects

All other images are provided by the author.